Essential I
for Risk Assessments

DOWNLOAD ZONE FOR BOOKS

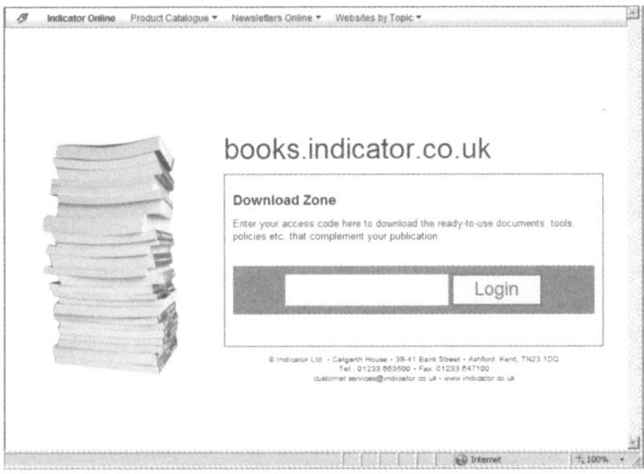

Go to

http://books.indicator.co.uk

and enter your access code

DCZ327

for instant access to all the ready-to-use documents, tools, policies, etc. that complement this publication.

indicator

ISBN 978-1-906892-16-6

Second Edition - Third Print - E02P3

Introduction

What's the first thing you'll be asked for when an inspector walks through the door? It's unlikely to be a cup of tea - more probably he'll ask to see your risk assessment documents. Are they what an inspector - or insurance assessor - will want to see? Until now, there haven't been many sources of reference (at least not without paying a consultant) to benchmark yours against - so maybe you've just taken your best shot and hoped everything will be OK? To remove the mystery, and to show what we think a risk assessment should look like, we've created this book: **Essential Documents for Risk Assessments**. It's full of forms that simplify the risk assessment process by providing example hazards, risks and control measures in numerous workplace scenarios.

This fully updated edition is divided into two sections. Section One includes over 80 task-based risk assessments. These are pretty standard tasks that are completed every day across UK workplaces. We've analysed them and highlighted the generic risks that we feel might be found. So rather than starting from scratch, you can add/delete content to suit your own workplace. You might even find that our documents cover all of the risks found in your business, complete with suitable control measures, meaning there won't be much to amend, if anything.

Section Two contains location-based risk assessment documents. As with the task-based assessments, we've highlighted some of the generic risks found in parts of buildings. For example, the risks that might be found if you're working in a plant and equipment room. Again, these documents can be amended to suit your own premises.

All of the documents are available in Microsoft Word format on the complementary Download Zone website which accompanies this book.

This book should become a useful companion and help ensure that your risk assessment documents satisfy all the legal requirements. If you would like to see additional documents added, please contact us and we will endeavour to include them in future editions.

Simon Wakeham CMIOSH
Editor-in-Chief

March 2010

Table of contents

Section 1 - Task-based risk assessments

Construction

Chemicals

General

Machinery

Office

Section 2 - Location-based risk assessments

Section 1

Task-based risk assessments

Construction

Avoidance of buried services

When digging holes and trenches, whether on a construction site, the highway or a pavement, the chances are that you may come across buried utility services such as gas, water, communications or electricity.

Managing the risks

To help you identify the hazards associated with the avoidance of buried services and the appropriate ways of controlling them, use our example **Risk Assessment - Avoidance of Buried Services**. It covers the generic hazards associated with this type of activity and suggests control measures to reduce risks to an acceptable level.

You should ensure that your document only addresses "significant" hazards, i.e. any that could, and more importantly are likely to, cause an accident or injury.

Make your instructions clear

Don't include activities in your document that simply don't need to be there. Work to the principle that if there is any chance of your staff being unaware of the safe way of doing something, then you will need to make it clear in your document. Finally, always ensure that any control measures you identify and follow only go so far "as is reasonably practicable".

Note. The list of potential hazards is not exhaustive. However, for your risk assessment to be considered suitable and sufficient in the eyes of the law it must accurately reflect the "significant" hazards found when working in the vicinity of buried services.

RISK ASSESSMENT - AVOIDANCE OF BURIED SERVICES

ACTIVITY	PERSON AT RISK	SIGNIFICANT HAZARDS	RISK*			RISK CONTROL MEASURES	RESIDUAL RISK**		
			L	S	DR		L	S	DR
Preparing to dig holes or trenches	Staff	Failure to obtain plans and maps from utility service providers may lead to contact with buried services	4	4	16	• Plans and maps to be obtained before any work commences. • Where any doubt exists regarding the location of any services the utility company to be contacted and asked to visit site.	3	2	6
As above	As above	Failure to use a locating device may lead to contact with buried services	4	4	16	• A locating device (such as a CAT - cable avoidance tool) to be used to locate the route of buried services before excavation starts and throughout excavation work. • Routes of services to be marked on the ground surface with either waterproof crayon, chalk or paint.	3	2	6
Digging holes and trenches by hand	As above	Use of power tools in areas where services are suspected may cause damage to buried services and injuries to user	4	4	16	• Where a locator indicates the presence of buried services all digging to be undertaken carefully by hand. • Additional care to be taken when using picks or insulated crowbars. • Staff to wear the relevant PPE, e.g. gloves and protective footwear.	3	2	6
Digging holes and trenches using excavating machinery	As above	Failure to detect buried services may lead to excavator coming into contact with them	4	4	16	• Before an excavator is used, trial holes to be dug by hand. • Excavators not to be allowed to work within a 300mm radial distance of electricity cables. • All staff to be kept clear of the bucket and excavator whilst it is working in the vicinity of electric cables.	3	2	6

RISK ASSESSMENT - AVOIDANCE OF BURIED SERVICES

ACTIVITY	PERSON AT RISK	SIGNIFICANT HAZARDS	RISK*			RISK CONTROL MEASURES	RESIDUAL RISK**		
			L	S	DR		L	S	DR
Digging holes or trenches (general)	Staff	Breaking up concrete that is surrounding an electricity cable may lead to damage and electric shock	4	4	16	• Where concrete surrounding an electricity cable is to be broken up then the utility company to be asked to turn off the power before work commences.	3	2	6
As above	As above	Damage to services during digging operations may lead to a serious risk of injury	3	5	15	• If accidental damage occurs to a buried service, then the area to be left clear and the utility company contacted immediately to carry out any necessary repairs. • When damage is suspected the utility company to be asked to verify the safety of the excavation before any further work takes place.	3	2	6

LIKELIHOOD (L) = Frequent (5) - Probable (4) - Occasional (3) - Improbable (2) - Remote (1)
SEVERITY (S) = Catastrophic (5) - Major (4) - Reportable (3) - Serious (2) - Minor (1)
Degree of Risk (DR) = LIKELIHOOD x SEVERITY
* Numbers used are for illustrative purposes only.
** Residual risk is the level of risk that remains after suitable and sufficient control measures are introduced.

Signed originator.. Job title...

Date completed.. Date for revision..

Cutting holes in concrete and brickwork

Cutting holes in concrete and brickwork is a high-risk activity if not managed properly. Not only does the equipment used have the potential to cause injury, the dusts produced can cause ill-health.

To reduce the likelihood of a problem, you should complete a risk assessment for cutting such holes which identifies all "significant" hazards and appropriate "reasonable" ways of reducing risks to an acceptable level.

Managing the risks

To help you identify the hazards associated with cutting such holes and the appropriate ways of controlling them, use our example **Risk Assessment - Cutting Holes in Concrete and Brickwork**. It covers the generic hazards associated with this type of activity and suggests control measures to reduce risks to an acceptable level. You should ensure that your document only addresses "significant" hazards, i.e. any that could, and more importantly are likely to, cause an accident or injury.

Make your instructions clear

Don't include activities in your document that simply don't need to be there. Work to the principle that if there is any chance of your staff being unaware of the safe way of doing something, then you will need to make it clear in your document. Finally, always ensure that any control measures you identify and follow are decided upon the principle of "so far as is reasonably practicable".

Note. The list of potential hazards is not exhaustive. However, for your risk assessment to be considered suitable and sufficient in the eyes of the law it must accurately reflect the "significant" hazards found when carrying out these operations at each particular worksite.

RISK ASSESSMENT - CUTTING HOLES IN CONCRETE AND BRICKWORK

ACTIVITY	PERSON AT RISK	SIGNIFICANT HAZARDS	RISK*			RISK CONTROL MEASURES	RESIDUAL RISK**		
			L	S	DR		L	S	DR
Use of power tools – saws/ chisels etc. into concrete/ brick	Operator	Use of incorrect cutting blade/disc may lead to blade/ disc shattering and causing physical injuries	3	4	12	• All staff to be trained in the correct operation of the power tools. • All staff to be trained in cutting blade/disc selection and fitting. • All staff to be issued with relevant personal protective equipment.	3	2	6
Use of hand tools including hammers, picks etc.	Staff	Incorrect application of hammers and picks may cause masonry/ concrete to fall, causing injuries	3	4	12	• All staff to be trained in the correct operation of the tools to be used. • Staff to be given a safe system of work detailing the safe removal of brickwork/concrete. • All staff to be issued with relevant personal protective equipment.	3	2	6
Cutting holes etc. and removing debris	Operator, other people	Injuries may be caused by falling masonry/concrete etc.	3	4	12	• Work area to be cordoned off to prevent access by other people not involved in the work. • Staff to be given a safe system of work detailing the safe removal of brickwork/concrete.	3	2	6
Dealing with dust caused by the work activity	As above	Failure to control dust may lead to ill-health and equipment damage	3	3	9	• Work area to be sealed off using high-density polythene sheeting to contain dust. • All remaining equipment to be sheeted off as above. • Respiratory protection to be worn by staff involved in the work.	2	1	2

RISK ASSESSMENT - CUTTING HOLES IN CONCRETE AND BRICKWORK

ACTIVITY	PERSON AT RISK	SIGNIFICANT HAZARDS	RISK*			RISK CONTROL MEASURES	RESIDUAL RISK**		
			L	S	DR		L	S	DR
Dealing with dust caused by the work activity	Operator, other people	Failure to control dust may lead to ill-health and equipment damage	3	3	9	• Where possible, work area to be dampened down before work begins to control dust emissions. • All debris to be dampened down on completion of the work and before clean-up commences.	2	1	2
Use of tools to break through brickwork/ concrete etc.	Operator	Incorrect tool selection may lead to noise being emitted which is above the noise control limit	3	3	9	• Hand tool noise emissions to be checked against manufacturer's data and the noise limits assessed accordingly. • Staff to be issued with hearing protection.	3	1	3
Cleaning the worksite	Operator, others	Failure to clean the site on completion of the work may lead to hazards causing slips and trips etc.	3	3	9	• Staff to be instructed to clean up all debris on completion of the work. • All debris to be removed from site.	2	1	2

LIKELIHOOD (L) = Frequent (5) - Probable (4) - Occasional (3) - Improbable (2) - Remote (1)
SEVERITY (S) = Catastrophic (5) - Major (4) - Reportable (3) - Serious (2) - Minor (1)
Degree of Risk (DR) = LIKELIHOOD x SEVERITY
* Numbers used are for illustrative purposes only.
** Residual risk is the level of risk that remains after suitable and sufficient control measures are introduced.

Signed originator.. Job title...

Date completed.. Date for revision...

Ground works - excavations

Ground works involving excavation present risks to staff and members of the public which, left unmanaged, could cause accidents and potentially put you on the wrong side of the law.

Safe digging

To ensure that this doesn't happen, you should complete a risk assessment of the work to be carried out, which identifies all "significant" hazards and appropriate "reasonable" ways of reducing risks to an acceptable level.

Note. Some excavation work will come under the **Construction (Design and Management) Regulations 2007** and, as such, the management of many of the associated risks will be the responsibility of the work "designer" as well as the "principal contractor" or other contractors.

Managing the risks

To help you identify the hazards and appropriate ways of controlling them, use our example **Risk Assessment - Ground Works - Excavations** document. It covers the generic hazards associated with excavation work and suggests control measures to reduce risks to an acceptable level.

You should ensure that your document only addresses "significant" hazards, i.e. any that could and more importantly are likely to cause an accident or injury.

Make your instructions clear

There is no point in putting activities on the document that simply don't need to be there. Work to the principle that if there is any chance of your staff being unaware of the safe way of working on or near excavations and the effect such work can have on them or members of the public, then you will need to make it clear on your document. Finally, always ensure any control measures you identify and follow only go so far "as is reasonably practicable".

Note. The list of potential hazards is not exhaustive. For your risk assessment to be considered suitable and sufficient in the eyes of the law it must accurately reflect the "significant" hazards associated with the work you are carrying out.

RISK ASSESSMENT - GROUND WORKS - EXCAVATIONS

ACTIVITY	PERSON AT RISK	SIGNIFICANT HAZARDS	RISK*			RISK CONTROL MEASURES	RESIDUAL RISK**		
			L	S	DR		L	S	DR
Carrying out excavation work by hand	Staff	Excavation may collapse injuring staff if not adequately shored up	4	5	20	• Where possible, excavations to be carried out using machinery. • If being dug by hand, then sides of excavations to be adequately shored up using timber, trench boxes or hydraulic walling. Alternatively, the sides should be battered to a safe angle.	3	2	6
Staff working in excavations	As above	Material falling into excavations may cause injury to staff	3	3	9	• Protect edges of excavations with toe boards. • Spoil and materials to be kept away from excavation edges. • Staff to wear safety helmets when working in excavations.	3	1	3
Other staff and vehicles working in the vicinity of excavations	As above	Vehicles falling into excavations may cause serious injury to staff	3	5	15	• If the excavation is 2m or deeper, substantial barriers to be provided, e.g. guard rails and toe boards. • Vehicles to be kept away from excavations wherever possible. Use brightly painted baulks or barriers where necessary. • Where vehicles have to tip materials into excavations, stop blocks to be used to prevent them from over-running. Remember that the sides of the excavation may need extra support.	2	2	4
Staff working in and around excavations	As above	Staff may be injured by being hit by moving plant	3	4	12	• Staff to be kept separate from moving plant such as excavators. Where this is not possible, safe systems of work to be used to prevent people being struck.	2	2	4
Carrying out excavation work	As above	Staff coming into contact with buried electrical services may be seriously injured or killed	3	5	15	• No excavation work to commence until plans of buried services are made available. • Locating equipment to be used before any excavation work commences. • Staff to be trained in safe digging practices.	2	2	4

RISK ASSESSMENT - GROUND WORKS - EXCAVATIONS

ACTIVITY	PERSON AT RISK	SIGNIFICANT HAZARDS	RISK*			RISK CONTROL MEASURES	RESIDUAL RISK**		
			L	S	DR		L	S	DR
Carrying out work in excavations	Staff	Staff working in excavations may be overcome by fumes from vehicle or plant exhausts	3	3	9	• Diesel engined equipment such as generators or compressors not to be sited at, or near, the edge of an excavation unless fumes can be ducted away or the area can be ventilated. • Staff to evacuate excavations at the first sign of the presence of fumes and report to their supervisor.	2	2	4
Preparing to start work in an excavation	Staff	Excavation may collapse if in poor condition, injuring staff	4	5	20	• A competent person to inspect all excavations before work commences or after any event likely to affect the strength or stability of the excavation.	3	2	6
Walking in the vicinity of excavations in public areas	Pedestrians	Pedestrians falling into excavations causing personal injury	3	4	12	• All excavations in public places to be fenced off to prevent pedestrians and vehicles falling into them. • Where children might get onto a site out of hours, precautions to be taken (e.g. backfilling or securely covering excavations) to reduce the chance of them being injured.	2	2	4

LIKELIHOOD (L) = Frequent (5) - Probable (4) - Occasional (3) - Improbable (2) - Remote (1)
SEVERITY (S) = Catastrophic (5) - Major (4) - Reportable (3) - Serious (2) - Minor (1)
Degree of Risk (DR) = LIKELIHOOD x SEVERITY
* Numbers used are for illustrative purposes only. ** Residual risk is the level of risk that remains after suitable and sufficient control measures are introduced.

SSigned originator.. Job title..

Date completed... Date for revision...

Land survey work

Carrying out land surveys can present risks to surveyors which, left unmanaged, could cause accidents and potentially put you on the wrong side of the law.

Managing the risks

To help you identify the hazards associated with land survey work and the appropriate ways of controlling them, use our example **Risk Assessment - Land Survey Work**. It covers the generic hazards associated with this type of activity and suggests control measures to reduce risks to an acceptable level.

You should ensure that your document only addresses "significant" hazards, i.e. any that could, and more importantly are likely to, cause an accident or injury.

Make your instructions clear

Don't include activities in your document that simply don't need to be there. Work to the principle that if there is any chance of your staff being unaware of the safe way of doing something, then you will need to make it clear in your document. Finally, always ensure that any control measures you identify and follow only go so far "as is reasonably practicable".

Note. The list of potential hazards is not exhaustive. However, for your risk assessment to be considered suitable and sufficient in the eyes of the law it must accurately reflect the "significant" hazards found with your land surveying activities.

RISK ASSESSMENT - LAND SURVEY WORK

ACTIVITY	PERSON AT RISK	SIGNIFICANT HAZARDS	RISK*			RISK CONTROL MEASURES	RESIDUAL RISK**		
			L	S	DR		L	S	DR
Accessing uneven ground on greenfield sites	Surveying staff	Walking on uneven ground may lead to slips, trips and falls causing personal injuries	3	3	9	• All surveying staff to wear appropriate safety footwear with ankle support. • Surveying staff to access greenfield sites using any defined pathways. • Surveying staff to constantly check for tripping hazards in any undergrowth.	3	1	3
Access on sites where work may be in progress	As above	Hazards created by excavations, trenches, test holes etc. may lead to falls causing personal injuries	3	4	12	• Surveying staff to contact the person in control of the site before work commences to obtain information on existing work in the area they need to access.	3	2	6
As above	As above	Hazards may be created if working in close proximity to moving machinery (excavators, dumper trucks etc.) leading to accidents causing personal injuries	3	5	15	• Surveying staff to inform the person in control of the site where they will be working and ask for all machinery etc. to be kept clear for the duration of the work. • All surveying staff to wear high visibility garments and safety helmets.	3	2	6
Work in excavations and trenches	As above	Unsupported trench and excavation walls may collapse causing crushing injuries	3	5	15	• Surveying staff to not enter trenches or excavations unless the side walls have been adequately supported or the sides ramped up.	3	2	6

RISK ASSESSMENT - LAND SURVEY WORK

ACTIVITY	PERSON AT RISK	SIGNIFICANT HAZARDS	RISK*			RISK CONTROL MEASURES	RESIDUAL RISK**		
			L	S	DR		L	S	DR
Carrying tools and equipment on to site	Surveying staff	Hazards created by carrying heavy loads over uneven ground may cause sprains and strains	3	3	9	• Surveying staff to carry the minimum tools and equipment necessary for their work. • Where necessary, loads to be divided between the staff involved. • Where possible, tools and equipment to be carried using mechanical aids, e.g. trolleys.	3	1	3
Lone working	As above	Injuries on site when working alone may lead to delays in getting first aid treatment etc.	3	4	12	• Surveying staff working alone should carry a mobile telephone or other device to allow them to summon assistance.	3	2	6
Use of handtools when setting out	As above	Hazards caused by incorrect use of handtools may cause injuries to hands etc.	3	2	6	• Surveying staff to use all handtools correctly when driving in pegs etc. whilst setting out. • Surveying staff to wear industrial gloves to prevent splinters from wooden pegs etc.	3	1	3

LIKELIHOOD (L) = Frequent (5) - Probable (4) - Occasional (3) - Improbable (2) - Remote (1)
SEVERITY (S) = Catastrophic (5) - Major (4) - Reportable (3) - Serious (2) - Minor (1)
Degree of Risk (DR) = LIKELIHOOD x SEVERITY
* Numbers used are for illustrative purposes only.
** Residual risk is the level of risk that remains after suitable and sufficient control measures are introduced.

Signed originator.. Job title...

Date completed.. Date for revision..

Laying paving slabs and kerbs

Laying paving slabs and kerbs may present risks to staff, especially through manual handling. Left unmanaged, these could cause accidents, injuries and potentially put you on the wrong side of the law.

Managing the risks

To help you identify the hazards associated with laying slabs and kerbs and the appropriate ways of controlling them, use our example **Risk Assessment - Laying Paving Slabs and Kerbs**. It covers the generic hazards associated with this type of activity and suggests control measures to reduce risks to an acceptable level.

You should ensure that your document only addresses "significant" hazards, i.e. any that could, and more importantly are likely to, cause an accident or injury.

Make your instructions clear

Don't include activities in your document that simply don't need to be there. Work to the principle that if there is any chance of your staff being unaware of the safe way of doing something, then you will need to make it clear in your document. Finally, always ensure that any control measures you identify and follow only go so far "as is reasonably practicable".

Note. The list of potential hazards is not exhaustive. However, for your risk assessment to be considered suitable and sufficient in the eyes of the law it must accurately reflect the "significant" hazards found when your staff handle and lay paving slabs and kerbs.

RISK ASSESSMENT - LAYING PAVING SLABS AND KERBS

ACTIVITY	PERSON AT RISK	SIGNIFICANT HAZARDS	RISK*			RISK CONTROL MEASURES	RESIDUAL RISK**		
			L	S	DR		L	S	DR
Taking delivery of slabs and kerbs to worksite	Staff	Unloading of heavy packs may lead to manual handling accidents/injuries	4	3	12	• Mechanical aids to be used to lift slabs and kerbs from vehicle, e.g. lorry mounted crane, forklift truck etc. • Slabs and kerbs to be unloaded close to point of work. • Unloading areas to be kept clear of obstructions.	3	2	6
Unpacking of slabs and kerbs	As above	Failure to clear away packing materials and strapping may lead to trips and falls causing injuries	4	3	12	• All packing to be removed immediately prior to use. • All packaging materials including strapping to be removed from worksite immediately after unpacking.	3	2	6
Preparing sub base for slabs and kerbs	As above	Using shovels, picks, wheelbarrows etc. for long periods or using them incorrectly may lead to strains and sprains	4	3	12	• All staff to be trained in the use of hand tools. • Wheelbarrows not to be overloaded when handling sand, concrete etc. and staff to only handle loads within their capability. • Where possible concrete to be poured direct from the mixer to prevent manual handling.	3	1	3
Handling slabs and kerbs	As above	Incorrect manual handling techniques may lead to back injuries etc.	4	4	16	• Mechanical aids, such as vacuum lifters etc. to be used so far as is possible to prevent manual handling injuries. • Where scissor lifts are used then the operation to require two members of staff to complete the lift. • All staff to be trained in manual handling operations. • All staff to wear protective footwear.	3	2	6

RISK ASSESSMENT - LAYING PAVING SLABS AND KERBS

ACTIVITY	PERSON AT RISK	SIGNIFICANT HAZARDS	RISK*			RISK CONTROL MEASURES	RESIDUAL RISK**		
			L	S	DR		L	S	DR
Use of mechanical aids	Staff	Failure of mechanical aids may lead to slabs/ kerbs falling causing injuries to feet and legs	4	3	12	• All mechanical aids to be maintained in good working order. • Staff to report the failure of lifting equipment to their supervisor who will arrange the necessary repairs. • All staff to be trained in the use of all relevant mechanical aids.	3	1	3
Cutting concrete slabs and kerbs	As above	Dust generated using cutting tools may cause respiratory health problems or eye injuries	4	3	12	• Only concrete cutters fitted with diamond blades to be used to cut slabs and kerbs. • Water flow lubrication to be used to minimise dust. • Dust suppression equipment to be fitted to all mechanical cutters. • All staff to wear the appropriate PPE, e.g. eye protection, dust masks, etc.	3	1	3

LIKELIHOOD (L) = Frequent (5) - Probable (4) - Occasional (3) - Improbable (2) - Remote (1)
SEVERITY (S) = Catastrophic (5) - Major (4) - Reportable (3) - Serious (2) - Minor (1)
Degree of Risk (DR) = LIKELIHOOD x SEVERITY
* Numbers used are for illustrative purposes only.
** Residual risk is the level of risk that remains after suitable and sufficient control measures are introduced.

Signed originator.. Job title..

Date completed.. Date for revision..

Safe demolition of external walls

The demolition of brick, block or stone external walls - those walls which separate property and land - could, if carried out incorrectly lead to accidents resulting in personal injury to both staff and members of the public who may be in the vicinity.

Managing the risks

To help you to identify the hazards associated with the demolition of external walls and the appropriate ways of controlling them, use our example **Risk Assessment - Safe Demolition of External Walls**. It covers the generic hazards associated with this type of activity and suggests control measures to reduce risks to an acceptable level. You should ensure that your document only addresses "significant" hazards, i.e. any that could, and more importantly are likely to, cause an accident or injury.

Make your instructions clear

Don't include activities in your document that simply don't need to be there. Work to the principle that if there is any chance of your staff being unaware of the safe way of doing something, then you will need to make it clear in your document. Finally, always ensure that any control measures you identify and follow are decided upon the principle of "so far as is reasonably practicable".

Note. The list of potential hazards is not exhaustive. However, for your risk assessment to be considered suitable and sufficient in the eyes of the law it must accurately reflect the "significant" hazards in your workplace when demolishing external brick or stone walls.

Note. This risk assessment deals with the generic risks associated with the demolition of external brick, block or stone walls. It does NOT cover walls that are part of premises such as dividing walls or other load bearing walls etc. The demolition of property will require separate risk assessments.

RISK ASSESSMENT - SAFE DEMOLITION OF EXTERNAL WALLS

ACTIVITY	PERSON AT RISK	SIGNIFICANT HAZARDS	RISK*			RISK CONTROL MEASURES	RESIDUAL RISK**		
			L	S	DR		L	S	DR
Pre-work planning	Staff, others	Failure to prepare a demolition plan before work starts may lead to walls collapsing, injuring staff and others	3	5	15	• All wall demolition work to be properly planned before work starts. • Demolition plans to be prepared by a competent person. • Demolition plans to include a safe system of work which is to be briefed to all staff involved in the work. • Where walls are in a hazardous condition consideration to the provision of bracing or support to take place prior to work starting.	3	2	6
As above	Staff, members of the public	Failure to secure the site so that people are kept away during the demolition process may lead to accidents resulting in physical injuries	3	4	12	• Before work commences, work areas to be fenced off to prevent access to those not involved. • Work area to be signposted to indicate that demolition work is in progress before work commences.	3	2	6
Demolition of walls (general)	Staff	Incorrect demolition methods may lead to the collapse of a wall resulting in physical injuries	3	5	15	• Walls to be demolished from the top down. • Walls to be demolished a course at a time. • Walls that are in danger of collapse must be suitably braced during the demolition process.	3	2	6
Working at height	As above	Failure to carry out work at height correctly may lead to falls resulting in serious injuries	3	5	15	• All work at height to be subject to a separate risk assessment. • All work at height to be carried out from a substantial work platform.	3	2	6
Getting around in general	As above	Failure to clear rubble etc. may lead to slips, trips and falls resulting in physical injuries	3	4	12	• Demolition materials to be regularly removed from the work area as demolition progresses. • Rubble not to be allowed to accumulate against a wall under demolition so that it will affect the stability of the wall.	3	2	6

RISK ASSESSMENT - SAFE DEMOLITION OF EXTERNAL WALLS

ACTIVITY	PERSON AT RISK	SIGNIFICANT HAZARDS	RISK*			RISK CONTROL MEASURES	RESIDUAL RISK**		
			L	S	DR		L	S	DR
Use of machinery to demolish walls	Staff	Incorrect use of machinery to demolish walls may lead to accidents resulting in physical injuries	3	5	15	• Only trained operators to be allowed to use machinery during the demolition process. • Machinery to be used on stable ground only. • Machinery to be left in a safe position overnight with keys removed etc. • All staff to be kept away from the demolition area when machinery is operating.	3	2	6
Manual handling	As above	Incorrect manual handling techniques may lead to back injuries etc.	3	4	12	• All staff to be trained in the correct manual handling procedures. • Where possible, manual handling to be avoided.	3	2	6
Dust during demolition process	As above	Inhalation of dust may lead to respiratory conditions	3	4	12	• Work areas to be dampened down with water to minimise dust. • Staff to wear respiratory protection. • Respirators to be maintained in a good condition and changed when dirty.	3	2	6
Access to the workplace	As above	Failure to designate and keep a proper access to the demolition site may lead to staff being injured during work progress	3	4	12	• All access and egress routes to be clearly designated. • All access routes to be protected from falling materials and debris.	3	1	3
Deliberate collapse of walls	As above	Collapse of walls may lead to serious physical injuries	3	5	15	• All walls to be assessed for accidental collapse. • Deliberate collapse of walls to be carried out only under defined conditions. • Deliberate collapse of walls to be planned and supervised at all times.	3	3	9

RISK ASSESSMENT - SAFE DEMOLITION OF EXTERNAL WALLS

ACTIVITY	PERSON AT RISK	SIGNIFICANT HAZARDS	RISK*			RISK CONTROL MEASURES	RESIDUAL RISK**		
			L	S	DR		L	S	DR
Noise during the demolition process	As above	The use of mechanical equipment for demolition may create excessive noise leading to hearing impairment in staff.	3	4	12	• All mechanical equipment such as jack-hammers etc. to be fitted with silencers to reduce noise. • Staff to wear hearing protection at all times that mechanical equipment is in use.	3	2	6

LIKELIHOOD (L) = Frequent (5) - Probable (4) - Occasional (3) - Improbable (2) - Remote (1)
SEVERITY (S) = Catastrophic (5) - Major (4) - Reportable (3) - Serious (2) - Minor (1)
Degree of Risk (DR) = LIKELIHOOD x SEVERITY
* Numbers used are for illustrative purposes only.
** Residual risk is the level of risk that remains after suitable and sufficient control measures are introduced.

Signed originator.. Job title..

Date completed.. Date for revision...

Safe erection and dismantling of tubular scaffolding

Tubular scaffolding erected or dismantled incorrectly could lead to accidents involving serious personal injuries. The Work at Height Regulations 2005 require employers to assess all work at height - you can use our risk assessment as a basis when preparing a job-specific assessment for work with tubular scaffolding.

Managing the risks

To help you to identify the hazards associated with the erection and dismantling of tubular scaffolding and the appropriate ways of controlling them, use our example **Risk Assessment - Safe Erection and Dismantling of Tubular Scaffolding**. It covers the generic hazards associated with this type of activity and suggests control measures to reduce risks to an acceptable level. You should ensure that your document only addresses "significant" hazards, i.e. any that could, and more importantly are likely to, cause an accident or injury.

Make your instructions clear

Don't include activities in your document that simply don't need to be there. Work to the principle that if there is any chance of your staff being unaware of the safe way of doing something, then you will need to make it clear in your document. Finally, always ensure that any control measures you identify and follow are decided upon the principle of "so far as is reasonably practicable".

Note. The list of potential hazards is not exhaustive. However, for your risk assessment to be considered suitable and sufficient in the eyes of the law it must accurately reflect the "significant" hazards found when erecting or dismantling tubular scaffolding at the relevant place of work.

Note. This risk assessment only deals with the generic risks associated with tubular scaffolding. As such equipment differs in size, type and function, you should ensure that your assessment reflects the site conditions where the scaffolding is to be erected and eventually dismantled.

RISK ASSESSMENT - SAFE ERECTION AND DISMANTLING OF TUBULAR SCAFFOLDING

ACTIVITY	PERSON AT RISK	SIGNIFICANT HAZARDS	RISK*			RISK CONTROL MEASURES	RESIDUAL RISK**		
			L	S	DR		L	S	DR
Erecting and dismantling tubular scaffolding	Scaffolders	Incorrect assembly or dismantling of tubular scaffolds may lead to scaffolding failure resulting in serious accidents to scaffolders and others	3	5	15	• All tubular scaffolding to be erected and dismantled in accordance with the National Access and Scaffolding Confederation (NASC) Technical Guidance Note TG20:08 *"Guide to good practice for scaffolding with tubes and fittings"*. • Only trained scaffolders to erect and dismantle tubular scaffolds. • All tube and fitting scaffolds to be designed, and have strength and stability calculations provided by a competent person, unless it is a "Basic Scaffold" designed in accordance with NASC Technical Guidance TG20:08.	3	2	6
As above	As above	Falls from height may lead to serious injuries/ death	3	5	15	• Fall arrest equipment to be used during tubular scaffold erection and dismantling. • All staff to be trained in the use of the fall arrest equipment. • Scaffolds to be erected and dismantled in accordance with a safe system of work.	3	2	6
As above	As above	Failure to manage the passing up of scaffolding components may lead to head injuries etc.	3	4	12	• Scaffolding components to be raised and lowered by either "handballing (or chaining)", use of a "light line (hand line)" or by a gin wheel and rope. • All loose scaffolding fittings to be raised and lowered in a fitting bag which will be marked with the appropriate safe working load. • All scaffolders to wear the relevant protective clothing, e.g. head protection.	3	2	6

RISK ASSESSMENT - SAFE ERECTION AND DISMANTLING OF TUBULAR SCAFFOLDING

ACTIVITY	PERSON AT RISK	SIGNIFICANT HAZARDS	RISK*			RISK CONTROL MEASURES	RESIDUAL RISK**		
			L	S	DR		L	S	DR
Erecting and dismantling tubular scaffolding	Members of the public, other trades people	Failure to keep others away from the work area may lead to injuries from scaffolding components during erection and dismantling operations	3	4	12	• During the erection, altering and dismantling of scaffolding measures to be taken to exclude the public and other trades people from the work area and, where possible, a safe distance around it. • Where possible, the work area to be segregated using guards, barriers etc.	3	2	6
Modifications to existing tubular scaffolds	Scaffolders and other trades people	Carrying out incorrect modifications to scaffolds may render them unsafe and lead to falls from height	3	4	12	• Modifications to tubular scaffolds must only be carried out by trained scaffolders.	3	2	6
Inspection of a completed scaffold	Scaffolder	Failure to inspect a completed scaffold may lead to it being left in an unsafe condition	3	3	9	• All completed scaffolds to be inspected by a competent person and a handover certificate to be issued to the user. • A scaffolding register to be provided after this inspection has been completed.	3	2	6

RISK ASSESSMENT - SAFE ERECTION AND DISMANTLING OF TUBULAR SCAFFOLDING

ACTIVITY	PERSON AT RISK	SIGNIFICANT HAZARDS	RISK*			RISK CONTROL MEASURES	RESIDUAL RISK**		
			L	S	DR		L	S	DR
Regular inspection of scaffolds	User	Failure to regularly inspect the condition of a scaffold may lead to it becoming unsafe during use	3	4	12	• Users to be instructed to inspect each scaffold on a daily basis before use. • A weekly inspection by a competent person to be undertaken and an entry made in the scaffold register. • All defects and corrective actions to be entered into the scaffold register. • Only authorised staff to carry out modifications to scaffolds.	3	2	6
Unauthorised use of incomplete scaffolds	Other trades people	Use of incomplete scaffolds may lead to scaffold collapse or falls from height	3	4	12	• All incomplete scaffolds to display warning signs identifying the areas where access is restricted and be suitably protected by physical means to prevent unauthorised access.	3	3	9
Erection of scaffolding in areas accessible to the public	Scaffolders	Failure to protect members of the public may lead to personal injuries	3	4	12	• A permit to be obtained from local councils etc. where scaffolding is to be erected in areas where members of the public have access, e.g. adjacent to the public highway.	3	2	6

LIKELIHOOD (L) = Frequent (5) - Probable (4) - Occasional (3) - Improbable (2) - Remote (1)
SEVERITY (S) = Catastrophic (5) - Major (4) - Reportable (3) - Serious (2) - Minor (1) Degree of Risk (DR) = LIKELIHOOD x SEVERITY
* Numbers used are for illustrative purposes only. ** Residual risk is the level of risk that remains after suitable and sufficient control measures are introduced.

Signed originator.. Job title..

Date completed.. Date for revision..

Safe erection of post and board fencing

If the erection of post and board fencing is carried out incorrectly, it could lead to accidents resulting in serious personal injuries.

Managing the risks

To help you to identify the hazards associated with the safe erection of post and board fencing and the appropriate ways of controlling them, use our example **Risk Assessment - Safe Erection of Post and Board Fencing**. It covers the generic hazards associated with this type of activity and suggests control measures to reduce risks to an acceptable level. You should ensure that your document only addresses "significant" hazards, i.e. any that could, and more importantly are likely to, cause an accident or injury.

Make your instructions clear

Don't include activities in your document that simply don't need to be there. Work to the principle that if there is any chance of your staff being unaware of the safe way of doing something, then you will need to make it clear in your document. Finally, always ensure that any control measures you identify and follow are decided upon the principle of "so far as is reasonably practicable".

Note. The list of potential hazards is not exhaustive. However, for your risk assessment to be considered suitable and sufficient in the eyes of the law it must accurately reflect the "significant" hazards found when erecting post and board fencing.

Note. This risk assessment only deals with the generic risks associated with the erection of this type of fencing. As such fencing varies in size and weight and that each location differs, your assessment should address the hazards with each particular operation.

RISK ASSESSMENT - SAFE ERECTION OF POST AND BOARD FENCING

ACTIVITY	PERSON AT RISK	SIGNIFICANT HAZARDS	RISK*			RISK CONTROL MEASURES	RESIDUAL RISK**		
			L	S	DR		L	S	DR
Delivery and unloading of materials	Staff, others	Failure to carry out manual handling of loads properly may lead to strains and sprains to backs, legs and arms	3	4	12	• All delivery vehicles to be unloaded as close as possible to the worksite. • Only staff trained in manual handling to unload materials by hand and personal protective equipment (PPE) is to be worn. • Mechanical aids such as forklift trucks etc. to be used to unload heavy materials. Only trained drivers to operate forklift trucks. • All unloading by mechanical means to be under the control of a banksman.	3	2	6
Excavation of holes for fence posts	Staff	Failure to identify buried electrical services may lead to electric shock	3	5	15	• Service plans for buried electrical services to be obtained before any digging commences. • If any doubts exist as to the presence of electrical services, then the area is to be swept using a cable detecting device (CAT and Genny etc.) and holes are to be dug by hand.	3	3	9
As above	As above	Failure to carry out digging operations properly may lead to back and leg strains	3	4	12	• All hand digging to be carried out using long-handled shovels. • Good posture to be adopted when using picks or shovels.	3	2	6
As above	As above	Failure to guard excavations may lead to slips and falls resulting in physical injuries	3	4	12	• All excavations to be covered until fence posts are installed. • All excavations to be filled in as soon as possible after fence posts are installed.	3	1	3

RISK ASSESSMENT - SAFE ERECTION OF POST AND BOARD FENCING

ACTIVITY	PERSON AT RISK	SIGNIFICANT HAZARDS	RISK*			RISK CONTROL MEASURES	RESIDUAL RISK**		
			L	S	DR		L	S	DR
Erection of fence panels and posts	Staff	Failure to carry out manual handling of loads properly may lead to strains and sprains to backs, legs and arms	3	4	12	• All staff who handle fence panels and posts to have received training in manual handling techniques. • Fence panels and posts to be erected using two staff members. • Staff to wear relevant PPE.	3	2	6
Erection of fence panels and posts	Staff	The incorrect use of power tools during fence erection may lead to electric shock	3	5	15	• All tools to be 110v and have a valid PAT test sticker displayed. • All tools to be inspected before use. • If any tools show signs of damage, they are to be quarantined until they have been repaired and certified fit for use.	3	2	6
As above	As above	Regular contact with concrete may lead to skin conditions	3	4	12	• All staff handling concrete to be provided with suitable PPE. • Staff to be informed of good hygiene practices, i.e. regular washing of hands and forearms.	3	1	3
Re-instatement of grounds	As above, others	Failure to backfill excavations may lead to tripping hazards being left	3	3	9	• All excavations to be backfilled to leave the ground at its previous level. • All residual spoil to be removed when work is complete.	3	1	3

RISK ASSESSMENT - SAFE ERECTION OF POST AND BOARD FENCING

ACTIVITY	PERSON AT RISK	SIGNIFICANT HAZARDS	RISK*			RISK CONTROL MEASURES	RESIDUAL RISK**		
			L	S	DR		L	S	DR
Working in public areas	Staff, others	Failure to segregate work area from members of the public may lead to accidents resulting in physical injuries	3	4	12	• Work area to be segregated from the public by the use of barriers or barrier tape. • Warning signs to be erected to warn members of the public of work in progress.	3	2	6
Working in the vicinity of other contractors	Staff, others	Failure to segregate work area from other contractors and their machinery may lead to accidents resulting in physical injuries	3	5	15	• Site supervisors to be kept informed of areas where work is taking place. • Warning signs to be erected to warn other contractors of work in progress.	3	2	6

LIKELIHOOD (L) = Frequent (5) - Probable (4) - Occasional (3) - Improbable (2) - Remote (1)
SEVERITY (S) = Catastrophic (5) - Major (4) - Reportable (3) - Serious (2) - Minor (1)
Degree of Risk (DR) = LIKELIHOOD x SEVERITY
* Numbers used are for illustrative purposes only.
** Residual risk is the level of risk that remains after suitable and sufficient control measures are introduced.

Signed originator.. Job title...

Date completed.. Date for revision..

Safe handling of scaffolding equipment

If scaffolding equipment is handled incorrectly, then this could lead to accidents involving personal injuries.

Managing the risks

To help you to identify the hazards associated with handling scaffolding equipment and the appropriate ways of controlling them, use our example **Risk Assessment - Safe Handling of Scaffolding Equipment**. It covers the generic hazards associated with this type of activity and suggests control measures to reduce risks to an acceptable level. You should ensure that your document only addresses "significant" hazards, i.e. any that could, and more importantly are likely to, cause an accident or injury.

Make your instructions clear

Don't include activities in your document that simply don't need to be there. Work to the principle that if there is any chance of your staff being unaware of the safe way of doing something, then you will need to make it clear in your document. Finally, always ensure that any control measures you identify and follow are decided upon the principle of "so far as is reasonably practicable".

Note. The list of potential hazards is not exhaustive. However, for your risk assessment to be considered suitable and sufficient in the eyes of the law it must accurately reflect the "significant" hazards found when handling scaffolding equipment at each specific location.

Note. This risk assessment only deals with the generic risks associated with handling scaffolding equipment during the erection or dismantling of scaffolds. You should amend this assessment to include items that are specific to the scaffold that is being worked upon.

RISK ASSESSMENT - SAFE HANDLING OF SCAFFOLDING EQUIPMENT

ACTIVITY	PERSON AT RISK	SIGNIFICANT HAZARDS	RISK*			RISK CONTROL MEASURES	RESIDUAL RISK**		
			L	S	DR		L	S	DR
Erecting and dismantling scaffolding	Scaffolders	Handling scaffolding equipment such as tubes, fittings and boards etc. may lead to cuts or skin abrasions	4	3	12	• All scaffolders to wear suitable gloves when handling scaffolding tubes, fittings, boards etc. • Damaged boards that could give rise to splinters etc. to be discarded and placed out of use.	3	1	3
As above	As above	Incorrect lifting and handling of scaffold tubes and boards may lead to back or arm injuries	3	3	9	• All scaffolders to have received basic manual handling training. • Supervisors to ensure that the correct manual handling techniques are observed.	3	1	3
As above	As above	Failure to adopt a safe method of working when passing tubes, fittings and boards up or down to others may lead to equipment falling causing personal injuries	3	4	12	• A safe system of work to be adopted when passing fittings or boards up or down to others during scaffold erection and dismantling. • Small items to be passed up in bags and, where necessary, using a line or rope. • Boards and tubes etc. to be handled so that the person receiving them has a good grip of them before the other person sets them free. • PPE to be worn to protect staff members. • The work area to be kept free from other people not involved in the work.	3	2	6

RISK ASSESSMENT - SAFE HANDLING OF SCAFFOLDING EQUIPMENT

ACTIVITY	PERSON AT RISK	SIGNIFICANT HAZARDS	RISK*			RISK CONTROL MEASURES	RESIDUAL RISK**		
			L	S	DR		L	S	DR
Erecting and dismantling scaffolding	Scaffolders	Failure to work from a properly constructed platform when working at height may lead to falls resulting in serious injury or death	3	5	15	• Scaffolders to erect suitable work platforms on incomplete scaffolds when handling scaffolding equipment at height. • Scaffolders to employ the use of a harness securely clipped on to a substantial fixing when handling scaffolding equipment at height.	3	3	9
As above	As above	Incorrect use of equipment hoists may lead to items falling and causing injuries to people below	3	5	15	• A safe system of work to be established and in place prior to the commencement of any hoist operation. • All loads to be contained within the confines of the platform/cage and to be evenly distributed. • Hoists to be operated by those scaffolding operative(s) who are competent and authorised to operate it. • All loads to be held in place securely, e.g. using purpose built racks for scaffold materials.	3	3	9

LIKELIHOOD (L) = Frequent (5) - Probable (4) - Occasional (3) - Improbable (2) - Remote (1)
SEVERITY (S) = Catastrophic (5) - Major (4) - Reportable (3) - Serious (2) - Minor (1) Degree of Risk (DR) = LIKELIHOOD x SEVERITY
* Numbers used are for illustrative purposes only.** Residual risk is the level of risk that remains after suitable and sufficient control measures are introduced.

Signed originator.. Job title...

Date completed.. Date for revision...

Safe tree felling

The risks associated with the use of chainsaws and felling trees are significant. Failure to manage them is likely to result in a serious, even fatal, accident and could well lead to enforcement action being taken.

To ensure that this doesn't happen, you should complete a risk assessment prior to using the chainsaw, which identifies all "significant" hazards and appropriate "reasonable" ways of reducing risks to an acceptable level.

Managing the risks

To help you identify the hazards associated with chainsaw use and the appropriate ways of controlling them, use our example **Risk Assessment - Safe Tree Felling.** It covers the generic hazards associated with this type of activity and suggests control measures to reduce risks to an acceptable level. You should ensure that your document only addresses "significant" hazards, i.e. any that could, and more importantly are likely to, cause an accident or injury.

Note. This example risk assessment only deals with the general use of petrol-driven rear-handled chainsaws and is in two parts: Part 1 General risks and Part 2 Tree work at ground level. By "ground level" we mean operations such as tree felling and cross-cutting (sawing up timber at ground level after felling.) This example risk assessment does NOT cover working aloft in trees with a chainsaw. This is a specialist area where the work is normally completed using a top-handled chainsaw and is usually carried out by highly trained arborculturalist. Neither does it cover the use of chainsaws from MEWPS etc.

Make your instructions clear

Don't include activities in your document that simply don't need to be there. Work to the principle that if there is any chance of your staff being unaware of the safe way of doing something, then you will need to make it clear in your document. Finally, always ensure that any control measures you identify and follow are decided upon the principle of "so far as is reasonably practicable".

Note. The list of potential hazards is not exhaustive. However, for your risk assessment to be considered suitable and sufficient in the eyes of the law it must accurately reflect the "significant" hazards found when using chainsaws for tree felling.

RISK ASSESSMENT - SAFE TREE FELLING

ACTIVITY	PERSON AT RISK	SIGNIFICANT HAZARDS	RISK*			RISK CONTROL MEASURES	RESIDUAL RISK**		
			L	S	DR		L	S	DR
Use of chainsaws	Chainsaw operators	Untrained staff using chainsaws may lead to serious accidents/ injuries	4	4	16	• Only staff with a recognised certificate of competence to be allowed to use chainsaws. • Operators to receive regular refresher training. • All staff using chainsaws to be over the age of 16. • All staff to be physically fit to use a chainsaw.	2	3	6
Re-fuelling a chainsaw	As above	Contact with petrol could cause skin conditions Risk of fire or explosion with fatal results	3	5	15	• Only trained operators with the correct PPE to re-fuel chainsaws. • A COSHH assessment to be available for petrol. • All fuel to be stored in approved containers. • A designated re-fuelling area away from ignition sources to be allocated. • A no smoking ban to be in operation. • Fuel spill kits to be provided and all spillages to be dealt with immediately. • Suitable fire extinguishers to be provided.	2	2	4
Use of chainsaw (general)	As above	Failure to observe a safe system of work may lead to accidents/injuries	3	3	9	• A documented safe system of work to be prepared before work on site commences and all staff to sign it. • The site works supervisor to monitor to ensure that the system is being followed and oversee any changes as work progresses.	2	3	6
As above	As above	Failure to ensure chainsaw maintenance may lead to serious accidents/injuries	3	4	12	• All chainsaws to be kept in a fully maintained condition. • All chainsaws to be inspected by the operator before use. • All operators to be trained in maintenance procedures.	3	3	9

RISK ASSESSMENT - SAFE TREE FELLING

ACTIVITY	PERSON AT RISK	SIGNIFICANT HAZARDS	RISK*			RISK CONTROL MEASURES	RESIDUAL RISK**		
			L	S	DR		L	S	DR
Use of chainsaw (general)	Chainsaw operators	Failure to wear the correct PPE may lead to injuries	4	4	16	• All operators to be issued with relevant PPE as specified for chain saw use. • All operators to wear their PPE at all times during chainsaw use.	2	3	6
Maintaining chainsaws	Chainsaw operator	Contact with lubricating oils may lead to skin conditions; contact with saw blade may lead to cuts and abrasions	3	2	6	• Only trained operators to maintain chainsaws. • A COSHH assessment to be available for lubricating oils. • Relevant protective clothing to be worn when handling saw blades.	2	1	2
Lone working when using a chainsaw	As above	Lone workers may be unable to raise the alarm in the event of an emergency	3	4	12	• Lone working to be avoided as far as possible. • Where it is unavoidable, a means of communication to be available for the summoning of assistance in the event of an emergency.	3	2	6
Use of chainsaw (general)	As above	Inability to render first aid may lead to serious injuries/death	2	5	10	• All chainsaw operatives to have training in basic first aid treatment. • All chainsaw operatives to have access to a first aid kit. • Emergency procedures to exist detailing the action to be taken after an accident on site.	2	2	4
As above	As above	Excessive noise from chainsaws may lead to hearing impairment	3	3	9	• All operators to wear hearing protection. • All other staff working in the close vicinity to wear hearing protection. • Chainsaws to be purchased that demonstrate the lowest feasible noise emissions.	3	1	3

RISK ASSESSMENT - SAFE TREE FELLING

ACTIVITY	PERSON AT RISK	SIGNIFICANT HAZARDS	RISK*			RISK CONTROL MEASURES	RESIDUAL RISK**		
			L	S	DR		L	S	DR
Use of chainsaw (general)	Chainsaw operator	Excessive vibration from prolonged use of chainsaws may lead to hand/arm vibration conditions	3	3	9	• All chainsaws to be assessed for vibration and where necessary their use to be restricted on a time basis. • Operators to wear gloves when using a chainsaw. • All chainsaws to be properly maintained to reduce vibration.	3	1	3
Getting about in general when using chainsaws	Chainsaw operator, other work team members	Slips, trips and falls due to uneven terrain etc. may lead to physical injuries	3	3	9	• Brush and vegetation to be cleared as the work progresses. • Protective footwear to be worn at all times.	3	1	3
Assessing worksite conditions	As above, other work team members and the general public	Failure to assess worksite conditions may lead to injuries caused by tree felling etc.	3	4	12	• All worksites to be surveyed before work commences. • Where necessary, barriers to be installed to prevent unauthorised access. • Work near roadways to be assessed for traffic control. • Work area to be evaluated to take into account weather conditions, e.g. wind, rain, snow ice etc. • Work to stop if weather conditions dictate.	3	2	6
Use of chainsaw (general)	Chainsaw operator	Contact with moving parts/ kickback may cause physical injuries	3	4	12	• All chainsaw operators to be trained and have a certificate of competence. Regular refresher training to be undertaken. • All chainsaw operators to be adequately supervised. • All chainsaws to be fitted with a chain brake. • All chainsaw operators to wear suitable protective equipment.	3	2	6

RISK ASSESSMENT - SAFE TREE FELLING

ACTIVITY	PERSON AT RISK	SIGNIFICANT HAZARDS	RISK*			RISK CONTROL MEASURES	RESIDUAL RISK**		
			L	S	DR		L	S	DR
Cutting using chainsaws	Chainsaw operator, other people in the vicinity	Dust, flying wood chips etc. may cause eye injuries and respiratory conditions	4	3	12	• Chainsaw operator to wear a helmet fitted with a face visor. • Other people in the vicinity to wear eye protection. • Disposable dust masks to be worn during cutting operations.	3	2	6
Felling trees	Chainsaw operator, other people in the vicinity	Throwback as tree falls through other trees, lands on objects or uneven terrain may cause injuries	3	3	9	• Area to be surveyed prior to felling for objects that might cause hazards. • Where possible felling through other trees/objects to be avoided. • A clear escape path to be established prior to felling. • All other persons to be kept out of the work area.	3	2	6
Felling trees	As above	Lodged or windblown trees, hung branches that have not completely fallen etc. may present a hazard if not removed correctly	3	3	9	• An individual assessment to be carried out by experienced staff that are trained and competent in dealing with problem trees and hung branches. • Only trained staff to carry out any subsequent removal. • If considered necessary, specialist staff to be brought in to clear hung branches etc.	3	2	6
As above	As above	Entanglement with vines or branches from other trees may prevent tree from falling properly	3	3	9	• A survey to be carried out before progressing to tree felling. • Any entanglements to be cleared using tools from ground level, e.g. pole saw. • If considered necessary, specialist staff to be brought in to clear entanglement.	3	2	6

RISK ASSESSMENT - SAFE TREE FELLING

ACTIVITY	PERSON AT RISK	SIGNIFICANT HAZARDS	RISK*			RISK CONTROL MEASURES	RESIDUAL RISK**		
			L	S	DR		L	S	DR
Felling trees	Chainsaw operator	Dead or rotten trees present in work area may fall, causing injuries	3	2		• An individual assessment to be carried out by experienced staff to identify any dead or rotten trees in the work area. • If considered necessary, a specialist contractor to be used to remove them.	3	1	3
As above	As above	Tree or branch under stress due to pressure or tension may lead to breaking, falling and injuries	3	3	9	• An individual assessment to be carried out and staff trained to progressively release the energy using the chainsaw. • All other persons to be excluded from the immediate vicinity.	3	2	6
As above	As above, other people in the vicinity	Failure to assess the fall zone for the tree may lead to injuries	3	3	9	• The chainsaw operator to determine the fall zone of trees before commencing felling. • Other staff members to be made aware of the fall zone and instructed to keep clear. • Where necessary, guards to be posted to prevent public access.	3	2	6
As above	Chainsaw operator	Contact may be made with overhead power lines resulting in fatal electric shock	3	5	15	• Assessment to be made by competent chainsaw operator to ensure trees are outside a minimum distance of twice the height away from power lines. • Contact to be made to the power company owner to request a work permit or request that they carry out the necessary tree felling.	3	3	9

RISK ASSESSMENT - SAFE TREE FELLING

ACTIVITY	PERSON AT RISK	SIGNIFICANT HAZARDS	RISK*			RISK CONTROL MEASURES	RESIDUAL RISK**		
			L	S	DR		L	S	DR
Felling trees	Chainsaw operator, other people in the vicinity	Failure to assess the fall zone for the tree may lead to injuries	3	3	9	• The chainsaw operator to determine the fall zone of trees before commencing felling. • Other staff members to be made aware of the fall zone and instructed to keep clear. • Where necessary, guards to be posted to prevent public access.	3	2	6
As above	Chainsaw operator	Contact may be made with overhead power lines resulting in fatal electric shock	3	5	15	• Assessment to be made by competent chainsaw operator to ensure trees are outside a minimum distance of twice the height away from power lines. • Contact to be made to the power company owner to request a work permit or request that they carry out the necessary tree felling.	3	3	9
Cutting felled trees	As above	Failure to keep a clear work area may leas to slips, trips and falls	3	2	6	• A work area to be cleared to allow crosscutting of felled trees. Branches to be removed and cleared away before cutting up of the tree trunk.	3	1	3

RISK ASSESSMENT - SAFE TREE FELLING

ACTIVITY	PERSON AT RISK	SIGNIFICANT HAZARDS	RISK*			RISK CONTROL MEASURES	RESIDUAL RISK**		
			L	S	DR		L	S	DR
Stacking felled trees	Chainsaw operator	Incorrect manual handling may lead to muscular injuries and strains	3	3	9	• All staff to be trained in manual handling techniques. • A risk assessment for manual handling to be carried out before work commences. • Timber to be cut to manageable sizes to reduce weight. • Where access is possible, a vehicle-mounted crane to be used to load timber onto vehicles.	3	1	3

LIKELIHOOD (L) = Frequent (5) - Probable (4) - Occasional (3) - Improbable (2) - Remote (1)
SEVERITY (S) = Catastrophic (5) - Major (4) - Reportable (3) - Serious (2) - Minor (1)
Degree of Risk (DR) = LIKELIHOOD x SEVERITY
* Numbers used are for illustrative purposes only.
** Residual risk is the level of risk that remains after suitable and sufficient control measures are introduced.

Signed originator.. Job title...

Date completed.. Date for revision..

Safety in bricklaying

Bricklaying involves inherent risks. Therefore, if this type of work is not carried out correctly, it can result in injuries and ill-health to staff. This applies whether it is bricks or blocks etc. being laid.

Managing the risks

To help you to identify the hazards associated with bricklaying and the appropriate ways of controlling them, use our example **Risk Assessment - Safety in Bricklaying**. It covers the generic hazards associated with this type of activity and suggests control measures to reduce risks to an acceptable level. You should ensure that your document only addresses "significant" hazards, i.e. any that could, and more importantly are likely to, cause an accident, injury or ill-health.

Make your instructions clear

Don't include activities in your document that simply don't need to be there. Work to the principle that if there is any chance of your staff being unaware of the safe way of doing something, then you will need to make it clear in your document. Finally, always ensure that any control measures you identify and follow are decided upon the principle of "so far as is reasonably practicable".

Note. The list of potential hazards is not exhaustive. However, for your risk assessment to be considered suitable and sufficient in the eyes of the law it must accurately reflect the "significant" hazards found during bricklaying operations on each particular site on which you work.

Note. This risk assessment only deals with the generic risks associated with bricklaying. As such, tasks differ depending upon site conditions so you should ensure that relevant awareness and induction training is undertaken before the work starts. Your own risk assessment should accurately reflect the conditions on your work site.

RISK ASSESSMENT - SAFETY IN BRICKLAYING

ACTIVITY	PERSON AT RISK	SIGNIFICANT HAZARDS	RISK*			RISK CONTROL MEASURES	RESIDUAL RISK**		
			L	S	DR		L	S	DR
Mixing and using mortar	Staff	Regular skin contact with mortar may cause serious skin conditions and/or burns	4	4	16	• Direct skin contact with mortar to be avoided by the use of suitable PVC gloves. • Staff to be given a toolbox talk on the dangers of skin contact with mortar. • Adequate washing facilities to be provided for staff. • First aid equipment to include eyewash bottles of sterile water.	3	2	6
Cutting bricks (1)	As above	Staff may be subject to eye injuries when cutting bricks	3	3	9	• Eye protection to be provided for use when cutting bricks. • Supervisors to regularly check that eye protection is being worn.	3	1	3
Cutting bricks (2)	As above	Staff may be exposed to silica dusts when cutting or sawing bricks leading to respiratory conditions	4	3	12	• Angle grinders not to be used for cutting bricks. • Brick splitters to be used to cut bricks to reduce dust. • Respiratory protection to be worn if chasing using electrical equipment. • Dust to be wetted before sweeping up.	3	2	6
Operating a cement mixer	As above	Staff may be injured if mixer topples because of unstable ground. Damage to electrical parts of the mixer may lead to electric shock resulting in burns/death	3	4	12	• Cement mixer to be located on firm level ground. • Mixer to be fitted with all relevant guarding. • Mixer to operate at 110Volts and be PAT tested every three months. • Mixer to be inspected for damage each day prior to work commencing.	3	2	6

RISK ASSESSMENT - SAFETY IN BRICKLAYING

ACTIVITY	PERSON AT RISK	SIGNIFICANT HAZARDS	RISK*			RISK CONTROL MEASURES	RESIDUAL RISK**		
			L	S	DR		L	S	DR
Getting around on site	Staff	Stepping on nails or other sharp objects may cause shoe penetration leading to foot injuries	3	3	9	• All site staff to be provided with safety footwear with steel toecaps and mid-sole protection. • Supervisors to ensure that protective footwear is worn at all times on site. • Construction waste to be cleared up regularly to minimise this risk.	3	1	3
Working at height	As above	Falls from height may lead to serious physical injuries or death	3	5	15	• All work at height to be minimised as far as possible. • Where this is not feasible, agreement must be made at the contract stage for the erection of tubular scaffolding etc. • Supervisors to check that scaffolds are erected correctly, are at the correct height and of the proper load rating. • Bricklayers to be instructed that only scaffolders should modify scaffolds. • Scaffolds to be inspected each time before work commences and at least weekly by a competent person; a scaffolding diary will indicate records of such inspections. • Where ladders are to be used, they are to be erected on solid ground and tied in accordingly. • Bandstands with handrails to be used for work on internal walls and erected by trained personnel.	3	2	6
General site work	Staff, others	Falling objects may cause serious head injuries	3	5	15	• Safety helmets to be provided and worn at all times when working on site. • Brick guards to be kept in position on scaffolding. • All waste materials to be regularly removed from scaffolding as work progresses.	3	2	6

RISK ASSESSMENT - SAFETY IN BRICKLAYING

ACTIVITY	PERSON AT RISK	SIGNIFICANT HAZARDS	RISK*			RISK CONTROL MEASURES	RESIDUAL RISK**		
			L	S	DR		L	S	DR
Working in areas with other tradespeople	Staff	Excessive noise from other trades equipment, such as angle grinders etc., may cause hearing loss	3	4	12	• The construction phase plan will identify other tradespeople who may use machinery with an excessive noise level. Bricklayers to be kept a sufficient distance away from such activities. Where this is not possible, hearing protection to be supplied and worn at all times.	3	2	6
The provision of welfare facilities and first aid	As above	Failure to provide washing facilities or first aid may lead to skin conditions and inability to provide emergency first aid treatment	3	4	12	• The principal contractor on site to prove adequate welfare facilities prior to work commencing. No work to start unless these facilities have been provided. Facilities must include: flushing WC; hot and cold running water with a wash basin and soap and towels; facilities to eat meals; first aid equipment and a place to dry wet clothing. • Supervisor to brief bricklayers as to the facilities available and the arrangements to keep them clean.	3	1	3
Manual handling on site	As above	Failure to carry out manual handling operations safely may lead to back injuries	4	3	12	• Bricks, mortar etc. to be transported and lifted onto scaffolding using a telehandler. • Bricks and blocks to be covered in storage to prevent them taking up water and increasing their weight. • Spot boards to be lifted to a convenient working height. • Trolleys to be used for moving loads of bricks/blocks around the scaffold lift. • Arrangements to be identified at the tender stage for the movement of bricks and lintels over 20kg.	3	2	6

RISK ASSESSMENT - SAFETY IN BRICKLAYING

ACTIVITY	PERSON AT RISK	SIGNIFICANT HAZARDS	RISK*			RISK CONTROL MEASURES	RESIDUAL RISK**		
			L	S	DR		L	S	DR
Working near site machinery	Staff	Staff coming into contact with moving machinery may suffer serious or fatal injuries	3	5	15	• Supervisor to agree a transport plan with the principal contractor and highlight pedestrian walkways as per the construction phase health and safety plan. • Bricklayers to receive information relating to site access as part of their site induction process.	3	2	6
Working in the vicinity of other trades, waste materials etc.	As above	Slips, trips and falls leading to physical injuries may occur as a result of waste materials such as brick bands, pallet debris etc.	3	3	9	• Good housekeeping to be maintained at all times as work progresses. • All waste to be placed in waste skips on site on a regular basis. • Protective footwear to be provided to all bricklayers. • Supervisors to report failings of other trades to the principal contractor.	3	1	3

LIKELIHOOD (L) = Frequent (5) - Probable (4) - Occasional (3) - Improbable (2) - Remote (1)
SEVERITY (S) = Catastrophic (5) - Major (4) - Reportable (3) - Serious (2) - Minor (1)
Degree of Risk (DR) = LIKELIHOOD x SEVERITY
* Numbers used are for illustrative purposes only.
** Residual risk is the level of risk that remains after suitable and sufficient control measures are introduced.

Signed originator.. Job title...

Date completed.. Date for revision..

Safety in plastering work

If plastering work is carried out incorrectly, then this could lead to accidents involving serious personal injuries and ill-health.

Managing the risks

To help you to identify the hazards associated with plastering work and the appropriate ways of controlling them, use our example **Risk Assessment - Safety in Plastering Work**. It covers the generic hazards associated with this type of activity and suggests control measures to reduce risks to an acceptable level. You should ensure that your document only addresses "significant" hazards, i.e. any that could, and more importantly are likely to, cause an accident or injury.

Make your instructions clear

Don't include activities in your document that simply don't need to be there. Work to the principle that if there is any chance of your staff being unaware of the safe way of doing something, then you will need to make it clear in your document. Finally, always ensure that any control measures you identify and follow are decided upon the principle of "so far as is reasonably practicable".

Note. The list of potential hazards is not exhaustive. However, for your risk assessment to be considered suitable and sufficient in the eyes of the law it must accurately reflect the "significant" hazards found when your staff carry out plastering work at each work site.

Note. This risk assessment only deals with the generic risks associated with plastering work. Your risk assessment should consider any additional hazards that exist at the actual place of work. These hazards and their control measures can be added to this assessment.

RISK ASSESSMENT - SAFETY IN PLASTERING WORK

ACTIVITY	PERSON AT RISK	SIGNIFICANT HAZARDS	RISK*			RISK CONTROL MEASURES	RESIDUAL RISK**		
			L	S	DR		L	S	DR
Working with dry plaster mix	Plasterer, others	Contact with dry plaster may lead to skin irritation or respiratory problems	4	4	16	• Only trained staff to handle and mix dry plaster powder. • Respiratory protection to be worn when mixing dry plaster powder. • Suitable gloves to be provided to protect hands. • A water supply to be made available for the washing of hands, face and forearms. • Work area to be regularly cleaned and any damaged bags of plaster to be disposed of in the appropriate waste skip. • Plasterers to wear eye protection when plastering ceilings. • Supervisors to hold regular toolbox talks to remind staff of the hazards and the control measures.	3	2	6
Working at height	Plasterer	Falls from height may lead to serious or fatal injuries	3	5	15	• Work at height to be avoided as far as is possible. • Step-ups to be provided. • Platform trellis, with guardrails to be used for stairwells. • Staff to be trained in the erection, use and dismantling of platform trellis. • No work to be carried out on stairs and landings unless they are fitted with handrails.	3	2	6
Getting around in general	As above, others	Coming into contact with obstacles may lead to slipping, tripping and falls resulting in physical injuries	3	3	9	• All staff to be issued with suitable protective footwear. • Staff to maintain an effective good housekeeping regime and clean the work area at regular intervals. • All trailing cables to be tied up and kept away from walkways etc. • Walkways on sites subject to the CDM regulations to be agreed with the principal contractor and be based upon the health and safety plan.	3	1	3

RISK ASSESSMENT - SAFETY IN PLASTERING WORK

ACTIVITY	PERSON AT RISK	SIGNIFICANT HAZARDS	RISK*			RISK CONTROL MEASURES	RESIDUAL RISK**		
			L	S	DR		L	S	DR
Manual handling of work equipment	Plasterer, others	Failure to manage handling and lifting operations may lead to serious back injuries	4	4	16	• All manual handling tasks to be minimised. • All staff to receive advice on the correct methods of handling and lifting on site. • Where bags of plaster are delivered to site unloading to be carried out by mechanical means. • Dry plaster mix to be supplied in bags weighing less than 25kg. • Plasterboards to be delivered in the smallest practical sizes. • Only trained staff to fix plasterboards to ceilings.	3	2	6
Plastering	Plasterer	Regular use of the plaster trowel may lead to repetitive strain problems	4	4	16	• Job rotation between plastering walls and ceilings to be put in place. • Supervisors to provide regular toolbox talks on the dangers of repetitive strain injuries.	3	2	6
As above	As above	Danger of electric shock from contact with live electrical services whilst plastering	3	5	15	• Supervisors to ensure arrangements are made to isolate electrical supplies before plastering work commences. • 110 Volt supply to be provided for lighting. • All staff to receive a toolbox talk on the dangers of electricity on site.	3	2	6

LIKELIHOOD (L) = Frequent (5) - Probable (4) - Occasional (3) - Improbable (2) - Remote (1)
SEVERITY (S) = Catastrophic (5) - Major (4) - Reportable (3) - Serious (2) - Minor (1) Degree of Risk (DR) = LIKELIHOOD x SEVERITY
* Numbers used are for illustrative purposes only. ** Residual risk is the level of risk that remains after suitable and sufficient control measures are introduced.

Signed originator.. Job title..

Date completed... Date for revision..

Unloading vechicles on a construction site

If the unloading of vehicles on a construction site is not carried out correctly, it could lead to accidents involving serious personal injuries as well as goods/property damage.

Managing the risks

To help you identify the hazards associated with the safe unloading of vehicles and the appropriate ways of controlling them, use our example **Risk Assessment - Unloading of Vehicles on a Construction Site**. It covers the generic hazards associated with this type of activity and suggests control measures to reduce risks to an acceptable level. You should ensure that your document only addresses "significant" hazards, i.e. any that could, and more importantly are likely to, cause an accident or injury.

Make your instructions clear

Don't include activities in your document that simply don't need to be there. Work to the principle that if there is any chance of your staff being unaware of the safe way of doing something, then you will need to make it clear in your document. Finally, always ensure that any control measures you identify and follow are decided upon the principle of "so far as is reasonably practicable".

Note. The list of potential hazards is not exhaustive. However, for your risk assessment to be considered suitable and sufficient in the eyes of the law it must accurately reflect the "significant" hazards found when unloading vehicles on sites your staff work on.

Note. This risk assessment only deals with the generic risks associated with vehicle unloading. As vehicles and their loads differ in size, type and function, you should ensure that your assessment reflects the situation in your workplace.

RISK ASSESSMENT - UNLOADING VEHICLES ON A CONSTRUCTION SITE

ACTIVITY	PERSON AT RISK	SIGNIFICANT HAZARDS	RISK*			RISK CONTROL MEASURES	RESIDUAL RISK**		
			L	S	DR		L	S	DR
Delivery vehicle arriving at site	Driver, others	Failure of the driver to report to the site manager before entering the site may lead to conflict between the vehicle and other workers on site resulting in accidents	3	4	12	• Drivers to report to the site manager/supervisor before entering the site. • Drivers to remain with their vehicle at all times until directed to parking/unloading areas.	3	2	6
Driving on site	As above	Failure to observe the site traffic management plan may lead to conflict between vehicle and other workers resulting in accidents	3	4	12	• Drivers to await instruction for on-site traffic routes before entering the site. • Drivers to follow on-site traffic routes at all times unless directed by the site supervisor/manager.	3	2	6
As above	As above	Failure to observe site traffic speed limits may lead to accidents to the driver and others	3	4	12	• Drivers to ask what the site speed limits are. • Drivers to observe site traffic speed limits at all times.	3	2	6
Parking in unloading areas	As above	Failure to park the vehicles in designated areas may lead to conflict with other site traffic etc. resulting in accidents	3	4	12	• Drivers to park their vehicles in designated unloading areas only. • Drivers to remain with their vehicles at all times prior to unloading.	3	2	6

RISK ASSESSMENT - UNLOADING VEHICLES ON A CONSTRUCTION SITE

ACTIVITY	PERSON AT RISK	SIGNIFICANT HAZARDS	RISK*			RISK CONTROL MEASURES	RESIDUAL RISK**		
			L	S	DR		L	S	DR
Unloading vehicles	Driver, others	Failure to keep unloading area free from other staff may lead to accidents resulting in personal injuries	3	4	12	• Drivers to liaise with the site supervisor/manager to ensure that the unloading area is kept free from other staff not involved in unloading operations.	3	2	6
As above	As above	Where tipper trucks are being used to unload loose materials such as sand etc., then failure to keep staff away from the rear of the vehicle may lead to accidents	3	4	12	• Drivers to ensure that the rear of tipper vehicles are kept free of other staff during the unloading operation.	3	2	6
As above	As above	Where other vehicles such as forklift trucks etc. are to be used to assist in unloading, failure to keep clear of the unloading operation may lead to accidents	3	4	12	• Drivers to ensure that unloading areas used by other vehicles are kept free of other staff not involved in the unloading operation.	3	2	6
As above	As above	Failure to ensure that the unloading of cement or concrete-carrying vehicles is carried out on stable ground may lead to vehicle overturning	3	5	15	• Cement/concrete-carrying vehicles to be kept away from the edges of trenches etc. • Where necessary, chutes are to be used to direct concrete into trenches, foundations etc. • Cement/concrete-carrying vehicles to be parked on stable ground before unloading.	3	3	9

RISK ASSESSMENT - UNLOADING VEHICLES ON A CONSTRUCTION SITE

ACTIVITY	PERSON AT RISK	SIGNIFICANT HAZARDS	RISK*			RISK CONTROL MEASURES	RESIDUAL RISK**		
			L	S	DR		L	S	DR
Unloading vehicles	Driver, others	Failure to keep the boom of crane-mounted delivery vehicles away from overhead cables may lead to electrocution	3	5	15	• Only trained drivers to drive crane-mounted delivery vehicles. • Drivers of crane-mounted delivery vehicles to ensure that the boom is kept clear from overhead electric cables during unloading operations. • Where necessary, a banksman to be used during the unloading operation.	3	3	9

LIKELIHOOD (L) = Frequent (5) - Probable (4) - Occasional (3) - Improbable (2) - Remote (1)
SEVERITY (S) = Catastrophic (5) - Major (4) - Reportable (3) - Serious (2) - Minor (1)
Degree of Risk (DR) = LIKELIHOOD x SEVERITY
* Numbers used are for illustrative purposes only.
** Residual risk is the level of risk that remains after suitable and sufficient control measures are introduced.

Signed originator.. Job title..

Date completed... Date for revision...

Use of mechanical excavators on construction sites

Use of mechanical excavators on construction sites may present risks to drivers and others working in the vicinity, which left unmanaged could cause accidents, injuries and potentially put you on the wrong side of the law.

Managing the risks

To help you identify the hazards associated with the use of such vehicles and the appropriate ways of controlling them, use our example **Risk Assessment - Use of Mechanical Excavators on Construction Sites**. It covers the generic hazards associated with this type of activity and suggests control measures to reduce risks to an acceptable level.

You should ensure that your document only addresses "significant" hazards, i.e. any that could, and more importantly are likely to, cause an accident or injury.

Make your instructions clear

Don't include activities in your document that simply don't need to be there. Work to the principle that if there is any chance of your staff being unaware of the safe way of doing something, then you will need to make it clear in your document. Finally, always ensure that any control measures you identify and follow only go so far "as is reasonably practicable".

Note. The list of potential hazards is not exhaustive. However, for your risk assessment to be considered suitable and sufficient in the eyes of the law it must accurately reflect the "significant" hazards found when using mechanical excavators on your particular site.

RISK ASSESSMENT - USE OF MECHANICAL EXCAVATORS ON CONSTRUCTION SITES

ACTIVITY	PERSON AT RISK	SIGNIFICANT HAZARDS	RISK*			RISK CONTROL MEASURES	RESIDUAL RISK**		
			L	S	DR		L	S	DR
Driving mechanical excavators	Staff	Inexperienced or untrained staff operating excavators may lead to accidents on site resulting in personal injury and machine damage	4	4	16	• Only trained staff to be allowed to operate excavators. • All work using excavators to be planned to reduce accidents. • All work using excavators to be carried out in accordance with the site-specific risk assessment.	3	3	9
As above	As above	Driving excavators at speed over unstable ground surfaces may lead to them overturning and serious injuries to the operator	4	5	20	• All site speed limits to be observed by drivers. • Where ground conditions are uneven or unstable, excavators to only be driven at low speeds. • Seat belts, where provided, to be worn at all times by drivers. • Appropriate PPE to be worn at all times by drivers.	3	3	9
As above	As above	Using an excavator for purposes other than for digging excavations may lead to it overturning or mechanical failure resulting in personal injuries to the operator	4	4	16	• Excavators only to be used for their intended purpose. • Only planned work to be undertaken by operators. • Excavators to be used in accordance with site rules.	3	2	6
Use of attachments on excavators	Operator	Use of incorrect attachments or failure to secure attachments may lead to mechanical failure and personal injury	4	3	12	• Only specified attachments to be fitted to excavators. • All attachments to be properly secured in accordance with the manufacturer's instructions. • Operators' training to include the methods for fitting attachments.	3	2	6
Use of excavators close to trenches	As above plus others in the vicinity	Using excavators too close to trenches may cause them to collapse and excavator to overturn	4	5	20	• Excavator operators to be trained so that they only operate the machine at a safe distance from any un-shored trenches. • Operators to ensure that the ground adjacent to trenches is capable of withstanding the machine weight. • No excavation work using the machine to take place whilst others are working in trenches.	3	3	9

RISK ASSESSMENT - USE OF MECHANICAL EXCAVATORS ON CONSTRUCTION SITES

ACTIVITY	PERSON AT RISK	SIGNIFICANT HAZARDS	RISK*			RISK CONTROL MEASURES	RESIDUAL RISK**		
			L	S	DR		L	S	DR
Use of excavators	Operator	Digging without plans for buried services may cause damage to gas and water mains and electric cables	4	4	16	• No excavation work to take place until service plans from the utility companies have been obtained and service routes have been marked out. • Where the presence of electricity cables is likely, then the area to be checked with cable location equipment.	3	2	6
Parking of excavators	Other people	Failure to park with the jib arm lowered and keys removed may lead to others attempting to drive the excavator resulting in equipment damage or injury	3	3	9	• All operators to park excavators in the designated parking area. • Operators to remove keys from their machine and keep them secure. • Machines to be parked with their jib arm lowered to the ground.	2	1	2

LIKELIHOOD (L) = Frequent (5) - Probable (4) - Occasional (3) - Improbable (2) - Remote (1)
SEVERITY (S) = Catastrophic (5) - Major (4) - Reportable (3) - Serious (2) - Minor (1)
Degree of Risk (DR) = LIKELIHOOD x SEVERITY
* Numbers used are for illustrative purposes only.
** Residual risk is the level of risk that remains after suitable and sufficient control measures are introduced.

SSigned originator.. Job title..

Date completed.. Date for revision...

Chemicals

Control of substances hazardous to health (COSHH)

To ensure that any substance you use in the workplace doesn't, or won't, put staff or others at risk, you need to assess all of the potential risks.

Risk assessment

Risk assessments for substances that may be injurious to health are a requirement of the **Control of Substances Hazardous to Health Regulations 2002 (as amended 2004)** (COSHH). The type of assessment required here differs from the assessment for normal work activities so we have produced a template that reflects this - our **Risk Assessment - Control of Substances Hazardous to Health** (COSHH).

Before any assessment is undertaken you should obtain a copy of the Material Safety Data Sheet (MSDS) for the particular substance from the manufacturer/supplier. This sheet will list the significant hazards associated with the product as well as most of the information required for your COSHH assessment. You will then need to examine how you use the substance and from this you can determine the control measures you need.

An MSDS is not a COSHH risk assessment

The purpose of a COSHH risk assessment is to describe how the chemicals will be used in your workplace and under what circumstances. An MSDS doesn't do this as it merely gives information on how a chemical will perform or react under certain conditions.

Additional information

Supplementary to the COSHH Regulations, the HSE sets workplace exposure limits (WELs) for hazardous substances at work and publishes these limits in EH40, a publication which is updated annually.

This publication can be purchased from the HSE bookshop and the weblink is: http://www.hsebooks.com.

These WELs are concentrations of the hazardous substances in the air, averaged over a specified period of time referred to as a time weighted average (TWA). Two time periods are used: long-term (eight hours) and short-term (15 minutes). Short-term exposure limits (STELs) are set to prevent effects, such as eye irritation, which may occur following exposure for a few minutes.

Exposure should be reduced as far below the WEL as is reasonably practicable and should not exceed the WEL when averaged over the specified reference period. For substances given a short-term WEL (15-minute reference period) this level of exposure, averaged over the period, should never be exceeded.

In many instances the control limit or WEL will be included on the MSDS and should allow you to make a decision as to what action you must take if the exposure in your workplace exceeds the requirement.

Because COSHH is a reasonably specialised subject you may find that you will need professional help in completing such an assessment. For many hazardous substances the assessment will be relatively straightforward but for others it may require the actual measurement of exposure such as air monitoring etc. and you will need specialised equipment to do this.

RISK ASSESSMENT - CONTROL OF SUBSTANCES HAZARDOUS TO HEALTH

Form No:

Substance/material: **Trade name:**

What is the substance used for?
(e.g. cleaning floors, protective coating, etc.)

What are the hazardous ingredients/chemicals in the substance? (list below)

Do any of the chemicals have a workplace exposure limit (WEL)? (From HSE EH40)

Long-term exposure limit:

Short-term exposure limit:

Is the substance: (Check for an orange "CHIP" square on the product data sheet or packaging.)

Extremely flammable? **Y/N**	Oxidising? **Y/N**	Very toxic? **Y/N**	Sensitising? **Y/N**
Highly flammable? **Y/N**	Harmful? **Y/N**	Corrosive? **Y/N**	Other? (specify below.)
Flammable? **Y/N**	Toxic? **Y/N**	Irritant? **Y/N**	

Is the substance hazardous to health when:

In contact with skin? **Y/N**	Breathed in? **Y/N**	Other (Specify below)
In contact with eyes? **Y/N**	Swallowed? **Y/N**	

How should the substance be used? (e.g. diluted in water, applied with a brush, sprayed, etc.)

How much is used every week? (state quantity in litres or kilos etc. as appropriate)

Who is exposed to the substance? (e.g. those using it, visitors, service users, etc.)

Does the substance present additional risks to certain groups or individuals?
(e.g. young people, expectant mothers)

Can a less hazardous substance be used to do the same job? Y/N
(if you don't know, please contact your supplier for further information)

What controls are required for this substance, other than personal protective equipment (PPE)?
(e.g. well-ventilated areas, not in spray/mist form, mechanical ventilation, authorised persons only)

Is any PPE required when using the substance?

Eye protection? **Y/N** (state type required)

Gloves? **Y/N**
(state type required)

Overalls/clothing? **Y/N** (state type required)

Mask/respirator? **Y/N**
(state type required)

Other? (state type required)

How should the substance be stored? (e.g. locked cupboard, away from other substances, etc.)

Have persons using this substance been provided with information or training on its use? Y/N

(As a minimum ensure a copy of this assessment is in a known and readily accessible location.)

Spillages: How should an accidental release/spillage of this substance be dealt with?

First aid: What actions should be taken if the substance is:

a) Swallowed?	b) In contact with eyes?
c) In contact with skin?	d) Inhaled?

e) Other? (please specify)

Fire precautions: What actions should be taken in the event of fires involving this substance?

Chemical reactions: Is there any other substance that this substance must not come into contact with?

Disposal: How should the substance be disposed of (or not disposed of)?

Health surveillance: Do staff using the substance require any health surveillance?

Are all the controls detailed above currently in place? Y/N

If these controls are not in place or additional controls are required, state action to be taken. Please note - COSHH substances must NOT be used if adequate control measures are not in place.

Remedial actions required	Date for completion

Are hazards to health adequately controlled with all control measures in place? Y/N

Assessor(s) name:	**Assessor(s) signature:**	**Date:**
The Manager should sign below to show that the assessment is a correct and reasonable reflection of the hazards and of the control measures and actions required.		
Manager's name:	**Manager's signature:**	**Date:**
Remedial actions complete: (Date)	**Manager's signature:**	**Review Date**

A copy of the product Material Hazard Data Sheet must be attached to this assessment.

Handling and storage of chemical substances

The handling and storage of chemical substances may present risks to staff which, left unmanaged, could cause accidents and potentially put you on the wrong side of the law.

Managing the risks

To help you identify the hazards associated with handling and storage operations involving chemicals etc. and the appropriate ways of controlling them, use our example **Risk Assessment - Handling and Storage of Chemical Substances**. It covers the generic hazards associated with this type of activity and suggests control measures to reduce risks to an acceptable level.

Note. This risk assessment only deals with the risks involved with handling and storage of chemical substances. You should prepare a separate assessment for using the substances as required by the **Control of Substances Hazardous to Health Regulations 2002 (as amended 2004)**.

You should ensure that your document only addresses "significant" hazards, i.e. any that could, and more importantly are likely to, cause an accident or injury.

Make your instructions clear

Don't include activities in your document that simply don't need to be there. Work to the principle that if there is any chance of your staff being unaware of the safe way of doing something, then you will need to make it clear in your document. Finally, always ensure that any control measures you identify and follow only go so far "as is reasonably practicable".

Note. The list of potential hazards is not exhaustive. For your risk assessment to be considered suitable and sufficient in the eyes of the law it must accurately reflect the "significant" hazards found in your workplace.

RISK ASSESSMENT - HANDLING AND STORAGE OF CHEMICAL SUBSTANCES

ACTIVITY	PERSON AT RISK	SIGNIFICANT HAZARDS	RISK*			RISK CONTROL MEASURES	RESIDUAL RISK**		
			L	S	DR		L	S	DR
Handling corrosive chemicals without personal protection	Staff	Corrosive chemicals coming into contact with the skin or eyes etc. may cause serious chemical burns	4	4	16	• All staff to be trained to check the labels on all chemical products and how to handle corrosive chemicals. • Staff to be provided with the necessary personal protective equipment (PPE) such as arm-length rubber gloves, eye protection, PVC overalls or aprons, Wellington boots and respirators etc. • Staff to be instructed on what action to take in an emergency. • Emergency showers, eyewash stations to be provided accordingly.	3	2	6
Handling flammable chemicals	As above	Handling flammable chemicals near to a source of ignition may lead to fires resulting in serious burns and property damage	4	4	16	• All staff to be trained to check the labels on chemical products and how to handle flammable chemicals. • All flammable chemicals to be stored in suitable containers and kept in a suitable locked storage area. • Flammable liquids only to be dispensed using non-metallic equipment to prevent sparks causing ignition. • All areas where flammable chemicals are stored to be classed as "No Smoking" or naked lights areas and to be signed accordingly.	3	2	6
Handling toxic chemicals	As above	Ingesting or inhaling toxic chemicals may lead to serious ill-health	3	4	12	• All staff to be trained to check the labels on chemical products and how to handle toxic chemicals. • Staff to be provided with the necessary PPE such as respirators etc. • All staff to be instructed not to eat or drink in areas where toxic chemicals are used or stored. • All staff to be expected to observe good hygiene practices, e.g. washing before meals etc.	3	2	6

RISK ASSESSMENT - HANDLING AND STORAGE OF CHEMICAL SUBSTANCES

ACTIVITY	PERSON AT RISK	SIGNIFICANT HAZARDS	RISK*			RISK CONTROL MEASURES	RESIDUAL RISK**		
			L	S	DR		L	S	DR
Handling chemicals that have carcinogenic properties	Staff	Inhalation, ingestion or absorption of such chemicals into the body may lead to cancers forming	4	5	20	• All staff to be trained in the handling and storing of carcinogenic chemical substances. • Staff to be instructed on what action to take in an emergency. • Such chemicals to be stored in a designated area. • All staff to be provided with the necessary PPE such as coveralls, gloves and respirator etc. • No eating or drinking to be allowed in areas where such substances are stored. • All staff to be expected to observe good hygiene practices, e.g. washing etc. before meals.	2	3	6
Spillages of hazardous chemicals	As above	Spillages of hazardous chemicals may affect staff causing ill-health	3	4	12	• Staff to be instructed on the action to take in the event of spillages. • Spill kits to be provided and be regularly checked.	2	2	4

LIKELIHOOD (L) = Frequent (5) - Probable (4) - Occasional (3) - Improbable (2) - Remote (1)
SEVERITY (S) = Catastrophic (5) - Major (4) - Reportable (3) - Serious (2) - Minor (1)
Degree of Risk (DR) = LIKELIHOOD x SEVERITY
* Numbers used are for illustrative purposes only.
** Residual risk is the level of risk that remains after suitable and sufficient control measures are introduced.

Signed originator.. Job title..

Date completed.. Date for revision...

Liquid spillages

There are hazards and risks present when dealing with liquid spillages which, left unmanaged, could cause accidents and potentially put you on the wrong side of the law.

Managing the risks

To help you identify the hazards and appropriate ways of controlling them, use our example **Risk Assessment - Liquid Spillages** document. It covers the generic hazards associated with such work and suggests control measures to reduce risks to an acceptable level.

You should ensure your document only addresses "significant" hazards, i.e. any that could and more importantly are likely to, cause an accident or injury. For example, your risk assessment doesn't need to cover activities such as the minor spillage of a cup of coffee, or anything similar (although you must have systems in place to deal with such incidents).

Making your instructions clear

There is no point putting activities on the document that simply don't need to be there. Work to the principle that if there is any chance of your staff being unaware of the safe way of preventing spillages or clearing up such spillages, then you will need to make it clear on your document. Finally, always ensure any control measures you identify and follow only go so far "as is reasonably practicable".

Note. The list of potential hazards is not exhaustive as you are in the best position to know which products you use that are likely to be hazardous when spilled. For your risk assessment to be considered suitable and sufficient in the eyes of the law it must accurately reflect the "significant" hazards associated with the tasks found in your workplace.

RISK ASSESSMENT - LIQUID SPILLAGES

ACTIVITY	PERSON AT RISK	SIGNIFICANT HAZARDS	RISK*			RISK CONTROL MEASURES	RESIDUAL RISK**		
			L	S	DR		L	S	DR
Handling, carrying or decanting liquids	Staff members	Liquids spilled on floors in the workplace can cause a slipping hazard	4	3	12	• Staff to be trained in the methods of decanting liquids. • All liquids to be carried in suitable containers and not over-filled. • All spillages to be cleaned up immediately or warning signs (barriers, cones etc.) to be placed in the spillage area.	3	1	3
Handling, carrying or decanting hazardous liquids	As above	The spillage of some hazardous liquids can cause ill-health (from fumes, skin contact, etc.)	4	4	16	• Staff to be trained in dealing with hazardous liquid spillages. • COSHH assessments and manufacturers' safety precautions to be briefed to staff handling hazardous liquids. • Suitable spill kits to be made available. • Appropriate personal protective equipment (PPE) to be worn at all times when handling hazardous liquids.	3	2	6
Handling, carrying or decanting flammable liquids	As above	The spillage of flammable liquids may give rise to a flammable atmosphere	4	5	20	• Staff to be trained in dealing with flammable liquid spillages. • Spillage areas to be kept well ventilated until properly cleaned. • Suitable spill kits to be made available. • Company fire precautions to be observed. • Appropriate PPE to be worn at all times when handling flammable liquids.	3	2	6
Dealing with oil spillages	Maintenance staff	Regular contact with oil may cause damage to the skin	4	3	12	• Maintenance personnel to be trained in dealing with oil spillages. • Oil spillage kits to be readily available. • Tanks and containers to be bunded to contain leakages. • Appropriate PPE to be worn at all times.	3	1	3
Cleaning up blood spillages	Staff members or cleaners	Contact with blood spillages may lead to contracting Hepatitis B, C or D and HIV viruses	4	4	16	• All personnel involved in cleaning up blood spillages to be trained in the relevant precautions to be taken. • Good hygiene practices to be followed. • Spillages of blood to be treated first with hypochlorite granules prior to cleaning up. • Appropriate PPE to be worn at all times.	3	2	6

RISK ASSESSMENT - LIQUID SPILLAGES

ACTIVITY	PERSON AT RISK	SIGNIFICANT HAZARDS	RISK*			RISK CONTROL MEASURES	RESIDUAL RISK**		
			L	S	DR		L	S	DR
Dealing with raw sewage spillages	Maintenance staff	Working with raw sewage spillages may lead to ill-health	4	3	12	• Staff who work with sewage to wear the appropriate PPE, i.e. rubber gloves and Wellington boots, coveralls and face mask. • Good hygiene practices to be maintained, e.g. washing of hands and forearms before eating, smoking etc. • If operative suffers a cut, then consideration must be given to a hospital visit for a Tetanus injection.	3	1	3
Absorbing liquid spilt onto solid medium	Staff	With hazardous liquids there is a possible hazardous reaction and possible increase in ignition risk	4	3	12	• MSDS for chemical compatibility to be consulted and sorbent materials etc. chosen accordingly. In general: - corrosives: use polypropylene-based absorbents - strong oxidising solutions: use mineral-based absorbents - for flammables, bear in mind that wicking effect (high surface area of absorbents, and evaporation) may contribute further to formation of flammable atmosphere and therefore to risk of ignition. • If liquid is unknown, it is highly unlikely to be a strong oxidising solution (would be readily apparent by reaction with floor or ground): test with small quantity of absorbent material; maintain awareness of possible fumes given off, and take appropriate precautions if detected. • Remember, packaging of waste arising must also be resistant to spilt liquid.	3	1	3

LIKELIHOOD (L) = Frequent (5) - Probable (4) - Occasional (3) - Improbable (2) - Remote (1)
SEVERITY (S) = Catastrophic (5) - Major (4) - Reportable (3) - Serious (2) - Minor (1)
Degree of Risk (DR) = LIKELIHOOD x SEVERITY
* Numbers used are for illustrative purposes only. ** Residual risk is the level of risk that remains after suitable and sufficient control measures are introduced

Signed originator.. Job title..

Date completed.. Date for revision..

Safe use of basic cleaning materials

The misuse of basic cleaning materials can prove harmful, leading to skin conditions as well as other forms of ill-health. Where such materials have warning labels on their packaging, they will require a full assessment under the Control of Substances Hazardous to Health Regulations 2002 (as amended) (COSHH). However, this risk assessment deals with the general precautions to be taken when storing, using and disposing of such materials to prevent harm to members of staff who may come into contact with them.

Managing the risks

To help you to identify the common hazards associated with storing, using and disposing of basic cleaning materials and the appropriate ways of controlling them, use our example **Risk Assessment - Safe Use of Basic Cleaning Materials**. It covers the generic hazards associated with these types of activities and suggests control measures to reduce such risks to an acceptable level. You should ensure that your document only addresses "significant" hazards, i.e. any that could, and more importantly are likely to, cause an accident or injury.

Make your instructions clear

Don't include activities in your document that simply don't need to be there. Work to the principle that if there is any chance of your staff being unaware of the safe way of doing something, then you will need to make it clear in your document. Finally, always ensure that any control measures you identify and follow are decided upon the principle of "so far as is reasonably practicable".

Note. The list of potential hazards is not exhaustive. However, for your risk assessment to be considered suitable and sufficient in the eyes of the law it must accurately reflect the "significant" hazards found when using basic cleaning materials.

Note. This risk assessment only deals with the general risks associated with basic cleaning materials. Where chemical-based cleaning materials are considered to be hazardous, then a separate assessment conducted under COSHH will be needed.

RISK ASSESSMENT - SAFE USE OF BASIC CLEANING MATERIALS

ACTIVITY	PERSON AT RISK	SIGNIFICANT HAZARDS	RISK*			RISK CONTROL MEASURES	RESIDUAL RISK**		
			L	S	DR		L	S	DR
Storage of cleaning materials	Users, other staff	Incorrect storage may lead to ingestion of some harmful substances causing skin burns or poisoning	3	4	12	• Staff to ensure that harmful cleaning substances are only stored in the containers that they are received in, i.e. approved and suitably marked containers. • No decanting of cleaning materials into other containers such as drinks bottles etc. to be allowed.	3	2	6
As above	As above	Incorrect storage may lead to fire or explosion causing burns and property damage	3	4	12	• Staff to follow the manufacturer's instructions for the storage of all cleaning materials. • All cleaning materials to be stored in a secure area.	3	1	3
Use of cleaning materials	As above	Incorrect use of cleaning materials may lead to ill-health or skin conditions	4	3	12	• Staff to follow the manufacturer's instructions for the use of cleaning materials. • Staff to be provided with all necessary personal protective equipment as specified by the manufacturer.	3	1	3
As above	As above	Mixing of different types of cleaning materials may lead to ill-health etc.	4	3	12	• Staff to be instructed not to mix different types of cleaning materials.	3	1	3
As above	As above	Incorrect application of some cleaning products may cause eye or skin damage etc.	4	4	16	• Staff who use cleaning products that are corrosive to wear the correct types of hand and eye protection. • Where cleaning products give off fumes that may affect breathing, staff to ensure that suitable ventilation exists before use.	3	2	6

RISK ASSESSMENT - SAFE USE OF BASIC CLEANING MATERIALS

ACTIVITY	PERSON AT RISK	SIGNIFICANT HAZARDS	RISK*			RISK CONTROL MEASURES	RESIDUAL RISK**		
			L	S	DR		L	S	DR
Use of cleaning materials	Users, other staff	Some cleaning materials, when in contact with the skin, may cause skin damage leading to dermatitis etc.	4	3	12	• Staff to be made aware of cleaning products that may damage the skin and to be provided with suitable gloves etc. • Where possible alternative products to be sourced that are less hazardous. • Staff to regularly check their skin for signs of damage such as cracking, flaking or reddening.	3	2	6
As above	As above	Decanting cleaning materials may cause spillages, which may be harmful to health	4	3	12	• Cleaning materials to be purchased in suitable sized containers to prevent the need for decanting. • All spillages of cleaning materials to be cleaned up immediately by following the supplier's/manufacturer's guidelines.	3	1	3
Disposal of cleaning material containers	As above	Incorrect disposal may lead to environmental issues	4	3	12	• Used containers to be disposed of in accordance with the manufacturer's instructions.	3	3	9

LIKELIHOOD (L) = Frequent (5) - Probable (4) - Occasional (3) - Improbable (2) - Remote (1)
SEVERITY (S) = Catastrophic (5) - Major (4) - Reportable (3) - Serious (2) - Minor (1)
Degree of Risk (DR) = LIKELIHOOD x SEVERITY
* Numbers used are for illustrative purposes only.
** Residual risk is the level of risk that remains after suitable and sufficient control measures are introduced.

Signed originator.. Job title..

Date completed.. Date for revision...

Transporting small quantities of chemicals, paints and solvents

Many chemicals, paints and solvents could be hazardous if they come into contact with each other or are spilled during transportation. Failure to manage the risks associated with their transportation may lead to staff being injured or suffering from ill-health.

MANAGING THE RISKS

To help you to identify the hazards associated with the transportation of small quantities of chemical substances and the appropriate ways of controlling them, use our example **Risk Assessment - Transporting Small Quantities of Chemicals, Paints and Solvents**. It covers the generic hazards associated with this type of activity and suggests control measures to reduce risks to an acceptable level. You should ensure that your document only addresses "significant" hazards, i.e. any that could, and more importantly are likely to, cause an accident or injury.

MAKE YOUR INSTRUCTIONS CLEAR

Don't include activities in your document that simply don't need to be there. Work to the principle that if there is any chance of your staff being unaware of the safe way of doing something, then you will need to make it clear in your document. Finally, always ensure that any control measures you identify and follow are decided upon the principle of "so far as is reasonably practicable".

Note. The list of potential hazards is not exhaustive. However, for your risk assessment to be considered suitable and sufficient in the eyes of the law it must accurately reflect the "significant" hazards found when your staff transport chemical substances.

Note. This risk assessment only deals with the generic risks associated with the transportation of small quantities of chemical substances. Your assessment should take into consideration the actual substances your staff are transporting as well as the dangers damage to containers and spillages could cause.

RISK ASSESSMENT - TRANSPORTING SMALL QUANTITIES OF CHEMICALS, PAINTS AND SOLVENTS

ACTIVITY	PERSON AT RISK	SIGNIFICANT HAZARDS	RISK*			RISK CONTROL MEASURES	RESIDUAL RISK**		
			L	S	DR		L	S	DR
Action prior to loading vehicles	Staff	Failure to be aware of the hazardous nature of chemical substances etc. may lead to ill-health	3	3	9	• Staff to be supplied with the Material Safety Data Sheet (MSDS) for all substances that they will be transporting. • Supervisors/Managers to ensure that staff understand the information on the MSDS regarding transportation. • Staff to be made aware of action to be taken in the event of a spillage.	3	2	6
Packaging of chemical substances	As above	Unsafe packaging may lead to spillages resulting in ill-health	3	4	12	• All chemical substances to be transported in their original containers. • Original outer packaging, complete with original labels and hazard warnings to be used. • Caps and stoppers on bottles and lids on tins etc. to be in a secure position. • Glass bottles to be supported with bubble wrap or a similar packaging material in a robust outer container with a lid fastened closed. The outer container to be labelled indicating the contents and the hazard it presents.	3	3	9
Loading vehicles	As above	Failure to secure loads in vehicles may lead to spillages resulting in ill-health	3	3	9	• All containers of chemical substances to be secured within the vehicle to prevent damage and spillages.	3	1	3

RISK ASSESSMENT - TRANSPORTING SMALL QUANTITIES OF CHEMICALS, PAINTS AND SOLVENTS

ACTIVITY	PERSON AT RISK	SIGNIFICANT HAZARDS	RISK*			RISK CONTROL MEASURES	RESIDUAL RISK**		
			L	S	DR		L	S	DR
Transporting chemical substances etc.	Staff	Failure to deal with spillages may lead to ill-health	3	3	9	• Spillage kits to be made available for use in an emergency. • Staff to be trained on the action to be taken in the event of a spillage. • Staff to be issued with the relevant personal protective equipment for use when handling spillages.	3	2	6
Security of chemical substances in transportation	Staff	Failure to secure vehicles may lead to attempted theft and/ or arson	3	3	9	• Vehicles to be kept locked at all times when unattended. • Chemical substances not to be left in vehicles overnight unless they are parked securely.	3	2	6

LIKELIHOOD (L) = Frequent (5) - Probable (4) - Occasional (3) - Improbable (2) - Remote (1)
SEVERITY (S) = Catastrophic (5) - Major (4) - Reportable (3) - Serious (2) - Minor (1)
Degree of Risk (DR) = LIKELIHOOD x SEVERITY
* Numbers used are for illustrative purposes only.
** Residual risk is the level of risk that remains after suitable and sufficient control measures are introduced.

Signed originator.. Job title...

Date completed.. Date for revision...

Use and storage of petrol

Petrol is a highly flammable substance and as such should be handled, used and stored with great care.

Managing the risks

To help you identify the hazards and the appropriate ways of controlling them, use our example **Risk Assessment - Use and Storage of Petrol**. It covers the generic hazards associated with this type of activity and suggests control measures to reduce risks to an acceptable level.

You should ensure that your document only addresses "significant" hazards, i.e. any that could and, more importantly are likely to, cause an accident or injury.

Make your instructions clear

Don't include activities in your document that simply don't need to be there. Work to the principle that if there is any chance of your staff being unaware of the safe way of doing something, then you will need to make it clear in your document. Finally, always ensure any control measures you identify and follow only go so far "as is reasonably practicable".

Note. The list of potential hazards is not exhaustive. However, for your risk assessment to be considered suitable and sufficient in the eyes of the law it must accurately reflect the "significant" hazards found in your workplace.

RISK ASSESSMENT - USE AND STORAGE OF PETROL

ACTIVITY	PERSON AT RISK	SIGNIFICANT HAZARDS	RISK*			RISK CONTROL MEASURES	RESIDUAL RISK**		
			L	S	DR		L	S	DR
Filling containers at petrol stations	Employee	Spillages, use of incorrect or damaged containers creating a fire hazard	3	4	12	• Fuel containers should not be overfilled. Spillages to be reported to petrol station manager to allow immediate clean up. • Only approved containers, in good condition, suitably marked and with tightly fitting caps to be used.	1	2	2
Decanting petrol from container to fuel tank	User	Spilled fuel on ground or on clothes. Fire hazard if fuel is ignited	3	4	12	• Spillages to be prevented by careful pouring, using a plastic funnel that will not generate sparks. • If spilled onto floor, clean up to be immediate and with careful disposal of cleaning materials. • No smoking or naked lights and refuel in the open air only. • If fuel is spilled onto clothes, they are to be changed immediately.	2	2	4
Safe storage of petrol (1)	Occupiers of building	Wrong type of containers may leak and no adequate flameproof storage on site	4	4	16	• No more than 2x10 litres of petrol in approved metal containers to be stored, and no more than 2x5 litres in approved plastic containers. • If storing inside the building, to be stored in an approved flameproof cupboard, suitably marked “Flammable Liquids”. Store cupboards to be placed away from any heat or naked flame sources and kept locked. • Petrol not to be stored with other flammable substances.	2	2	4
Safe storage of petrol (2)	As above	Leaking containers creating a fire hazard	3	4	12	• Condition of containers to be regularly checked for damage. • Caps to be fitted properly and tightly. • Damaged or leaking containers to be replaced immediately.	2	2	4

RISK ASSESSMENT - USE AND STORAGE OF PETROL

ACTIVITY	PERSON AT RISK	SIGNIFICANT HAZARDS	RISK*			RISK CONTROL MEASURES	RESIDUAL RISK**		
			L	S	DR		L	S	DR
Carrying petrol in vehicles	Driver, passengers	Leaking containers creating a fire hazard	3	4	12	• All petrol containers to be kept secure in the boot or rear of the vehicle. • Caps of all containers to be regularly checked for tightness. • Only approved containers for petrol to be used. • Any damaged or leaking containers to be replaced immediately.	2	2	4

LIKELIHOOD (L) = Frequent (5) - Probable (4) - Occasional (3) - Improbable (2) - Remote (1)
SEVERITY (S) = Catastrophic (5) - Major (4) - Reportable (3) - Serious (2) - Minor (1)
Degree of Risk (DR) = LIKELIHOOD x SEVERITY
* Numbers used are for illustrative purposes only.
** Residual risk is the level of risk that remains after suitable and sufficient control measures are introduced.

Signed originator.. Job title..

Date completed.. Date for revision...

Using oils and greases

The use of lubricants such as oils and greases in the workplace may present risks to staff which, left unmanaged, could cause ill-health and potentially put you on the wrong side of the law.

Managing the risks

To help you identify the hazards associated with the use of oils and greases and the appropriate ways of controlling them, use our example **Risk Assessment - Using Oils and Greases**. It covers the generic hazards associated with these substances and suggests control measures to reduce risks to an acceptable level.

Make your instructions clear

Don't include activities in your document that simply don't need to be there. Work to the principle that if there is any chance of your staff being unaware of the safe way of doing something, then you will need to make it clear in your document. Finally, always ensure that any control measures you identify and follow only go so far "as is reasonably practicable".

Note. The list of potential hazards is not exhaustive. However, for your risk assessment to be considered suitable and sufficient in the eyes of the law it must accurately reflect the "significant" hazards found when using oils and greases in your workplace.

RISK ASSESSMENT - USING OILS AND GREASES

ACTIVITY	PERSON AT RISK	SIGNIFICANT HAZARDS	RISK*			RISK CONTROL MEASURES	RESIDUAL RISK**		
			L	S	DR		L	S	DR
Using lubricating oils and greases (general)	Staff	Oils and greases in contact with the skin may lead to dermatitis or other skin conditions	4	3	12	• All staff to receive training in the handling and use of oils and greases. • All staff to be issued with the relevant personal protective equipment (PPE), e.g. suitable gloves and coveralls. • Staff to have access to washing facilities and will be informed of basic hygiene practices.	3	2	6
Using lubricating oils by spraying	As above	Oil, if sprayed in mist form, may enter eyes causing eye injuries	4	3	12	• All staff to be issued with eye protection and respiratory protection when lubricating oils are sprayed. • Staff to have access to washing facilities and will be informed of basic hygiene practices.	3	2	6
Dealing with spillages of oils and greases	As above	Spillages of oils and greases present a slipping hazard which may lead to injuries from falls	3	3	9	• All staff to be trained in dealing with spillages. • Spillages kits to be available at locations where oils and greases are used. • Suitable containers to be provided in which to place cleaning materials after use and the contents to be disposed of in accordance with the company's environmental procedures.	2	2	4
Working in areas where oils and greases are used	As above	Contaminated floor surfaces may cause slipping accidents resulting in injuries	3	3	9	• Staff to be issued with protective footwear with slip resistant soles. • Staff to report slippery floor surfaces to supervisors who will arrange suitable cleaning of such areas.	2	2	4
Storage of oils and greases	As above	Oils and greases stored near to heat sources may result in fires causing burns and property damage	3	4	12	• Staff to ensure that oils and greases are stored in approved containers. • Suitable fire extinguishers to be provided adjacent to oils and grease storage facilities. • Staff to be trained in the action to take in the event of a fire.	2	2	4

LIKELIHOOD (L) = Frequent (5) - Probable (4) - Occasional (3) - Improbable (2) - Remote (1)

SEVERITY (S) = Catastrophic (5) - Major (4) - Reportable (3) - Serious (2) - Minor (1) Degree of Risk (DR) = LIKELIHOOD x SEVERITY

* Numbers used are for illustrative purposes only. ** Residual risk is the level of risk that remains after suitable and sufficient control measures are introduced.

Signed originator.. Job title..

Date completed.. Date for revision..

General

Risk assessment - blank

Although carrying out risk assessments is a legal requirement, it can be confusing for those unaware of what's really required. To help you complete the process use our blank form.

Risk management

Under the **Management of Health and Safety at Work Regulations 1999** all employers are required to carry out risk assessments of all work activities conducted by its employees. To help you complete the process, use our **Risk Assessment - Blank** document, following the guidance below.

Identify the activity (column 1)

Here you must identify the activities being carried out. You only need to cover those activities where you consider the possibility of the risk of harm to be high.

Person at risk (column 2)

Here you need to consider who is at risk from the hazards identified. This may include colleagues, customers, contractors, visitors and the general public etc. You will also need to consider young persons and new or expectant mothers.

Significant Hazards (column 3)

Here you must identify the hazards associated with the work operation to be carried out and in the place where it is to be done. Trivial hazards can be ignored and concentration given to significant hazards which could result in serious harm or affect several people. All aspects of work activity should be considered and a systematic approach adopted that deals with both routine and non-routine tasks.

Risk factors (column 4 - 3 sections)

A calculation now needs to be carried out to determine the degree of risk by taking into account the possible severity of any harm that could be caused and the likelihood of it happening. This will result in a risk score that will determine whether or not further action needs to be taken. Using the information at the bottom of the form you must decide on the likelihood of the risk causing harm (L) and on the severity of that harm (S). By multiplying the two figures together you will obtain the degree of risk (DR) i.e. L x S = DR.

Control measures (column 5)

The law says that you must do what is reasonably practicable to keep both the work and the workplace safe. This means instituting control measures and precautions to eliminate or reduce risk to the lowest possible level. Two questions need to be asked here: **a)** can I get rid of the hazard altogether?; **b)** if not, how can I control the risks so that harm is unlikely? The control measures that you have detailed should be recorded on the form in this column.

Residual risk (column 6 - 3 sections)

You can then re-calculate the residual risk i.e. the risk that remains after the control measures have been applied. You can do this by repeating the calculation for degree of risk mentioned above. If you still consider the residual risk to be high then you should reconsider your control measures until you decide that the residual risk is at an acceptable level.

Note. The use of Personal Protective Equipment (PPE) should only be recommended as a control measure when some residual risk still remains or is specifically required by other legislation/customer site rules. All other avenues should be explored to reduce risk to a minimum before considering PPE.

Recording the findings

By fully completing our risk assessment template you have done this. However, risk assessment is more than just completing a form. The assessment should be both suitable and sufficient. The information relating to the risk assessment, such as the control measures, need to be brought to the attention of and discussed with all of the people that may be involved in the work process. Afterwards consider giving all of these people a personal copy and keeping a record of the signatures of acceptance.

Keeping copies will help to show that you have done what the law requires. These may play an important part of an investigation should an accident occur. Such documents may also need to be disclosed in the event of any action for civil liability.

Review

In some instances the assessments may need to be reviewed and updated. This is particularly relevant if new hazards are encountered or if the work process or venue changes. However, this does not have to be done for every trivial change. It is considered to be good practice to review assessments from time to time to ensure that any precautions put in place are still working effectively.

RISK ASSESSMENT - BLANK

ACTIVITY	PERSON AT RISK	SIGNIFICANT HAZARDS	RISK*			RISK CONTROL MEASURES	RESIDUAL RISK**		
			L	S	DR		L	S	DR
						•			
						•			
						•			
						•			

LIKELIHOOD (L) = Frequent (5) - Probable (4) - Occasional (3) - Improbable (2) - Remote (1)
SEVERITY (S) = Catastrophic (5) - Major (4) - Reportable (3) - Serious (2) - Minor (1)
Degree of Risk (DR) = LIKELIHOOD x SEVERITY
* Numbers used are for illustrative purposes only.
** Residual risk is the level of risk that remains after suitable and sufficient control measures are introduced

Signed originator.. Job title...

Date completed... Date for revision...

Attendance at external events

Many companies arrange external events for their employees for a number of different reasons - to enhance training skills, encourage "team building" or as a means of collective reward etc.

Managing the risks

To help you identify the hazards associated with external events and appropriate ways of controlling them, use our example **Risk Assessment - Attendance at External Events**. It covers the generic hazards associated with this type of activity and suggests control measures to reduce risks to an acceptable level. However, because such events can take so many different forms you should ensure that your assessment addresses the specific risks associated with the type of event that you are considering for your employees.

Note. If your event is to be run by an external provider, ask them to supply their risk assessments and details of insurance held.

You should ensure that your document only addresses "significant" hazards, i.e. any that could, and more importantly are likely to, cause an accident or injury.

Make your instructions clear

Don't include activities in your document that simply don't need to be there. Work to the principle that if there is any chance of your staff being unaware of the safe way of doing something, then you will need to make it clear in your document. Finally, always ensure that any control measures you identify and follow only go so far "as is reasonably practicable".

Note. The list of potential hazards is not exhaustive. However, for your risk assessment to be considered suitable and sufficient in the eyes of the law it must accurately reflect the "significant" hazards that could be encountered at an external event.

RISK ASSESSMENT - ATTENDANCE AT EXTERNAL EVENTS

ACTIVITY	PERSON AT RISK	SIGNIFICANT HAZARDS	RISK*			RISK CONTROL MEASURES	RESIDUAL RISK**		
			L	S	DR		L	S	DR
Indoor events held in unfamiliar surroundings	Attendees	Fire, incidents, unfamiliar surroundings, no knowledge of first aid trained staff	3	4	12	• Before event starts all staff and guests to be given details of the fire instructions. • All staff and guests to be shown fire exit routes and fire assembly points. • A register to be kept of all staff and guests in attendance on a daily basis and a roll call to be held at assembly point in the event of evacuation due to fire. • Event organiser to ensure emergency procedures are in place and that they are briefed out to all attendees. • A nominated person to be held responsible for taking charge in an emergency. • Event organiser to ensure all attendees are kept aware of any significant hazards, or changes that may affect them during the event. • All attendees to be made aware of first aid trained staff.	3	2	6
External events involving sporting activities	As above	Attendees with health problems or disabilities may be subject to harm when participating in unsuitable events	4	4	16	• Organisers to check with location regarding the suitability of attendees for such events. • Attendees to be given the opportunity to discuss event suitability. • Location to provide their own risk assessments prior to event taking place.	3	2	6
External events involving motor vehicles etc.	As above	Injuries may occur if attendees fall from vehicles etc.	4	5	20	• Organisers to ensure the suitability of the event vehicles etc. by checking maintenance logs. • Organisers to ask location to provide relevant risk assessments and control measures in place relating to any such events.	3	2	6

RISK ASSESSMENT - ATTENDANCE AT EXTERNAL EVENTS

ACTIVITY	PERSON AT RISK	SIGNIFICANT HAZARDS	RISK*			RISK CONTROL MEASURES	RESIDUAL RISK**		
			L	S	DR		L	S	DR
External events (general)	Attendees	Injuries may occur if incorrect or no protective equipment is provided	3	4	12	• Organiser to check with location to determine what personal protective equipment (PPE) is required and who will provide it. • No event to commence without the proper equipment.	2	2	4

LIKELIHOOD (L) = Frequent (5) - Probable (4) - Occasional (3) - Improbable (2) - Remote (1)
SEVERITY (S) = Catastrophic (5) - Major (4) - Reportable (3) - Serious (2) - Minor (1)
Degree of Risk (DR) = LIKELIHOOD x SEVERITY
* Numbers used are for illustrative purposes only.
** Residual risk is the level of risk that remains after suitable and sufficient control measures are introduced.

Signed originator.. Job title..

Date completed.. Date for revision...

First aid requirements

Employers are legally obliged to provide first aid facilities in the workplace (Health and Safety (First Aid) Regulations 1981). A failure to do so will potentially put you on the wrong side of the law.

Managing the risks

To help you, use our example **Risk Assessment - First Aid Requirements** document. It covers the generic hazards associated with first aid requirements and suggests control measures to reduce risks to an acceptable level. You should ensure that your document only addresses "significant" hazards, i.e. any that could and more importantly are likely to, lead to an injured person suffering through lack of proper first aid treatment.

Appointments

Your first aid assessment may indicate that you do not require a qualified first aider, but as a minimum, you should appoint someone to take charge (and summon professional help) if someone is injured or falls ill, and to look after your first aid equipment. This individual is known as an "appointed person". However, the assessment may indicate that trained first aiders are needed and the number you require will depend upon your assessment and the number of employees.

Note. For your risk assessment to be considered suitable and sufficient in the eyes of the law it must accurately reflect the "significant" hazards found in your workplace.

Further information

We also recommend that you take a look at the leaflet issued by the HSE "First Aid at Work - Your questions answered", leaflet ref: INDG214, which will help you to assess your first aid provision and explain the difference between appointed persons and trained first aid personnel. You can download a free copy of the document from: http://www.hse.gov.uk/pubns/indg214.pdf.

RISK ASSESSMENT - FIRST AID REQUIREMENTS

ACTIVITY	PERSON AT RISK	SIGNIFICANT HAZARDS	RISK*			RISK CONTROL MEASURES	RESIDUAL RISK**		
			L	S	DR		L	S	DR
Failure to nominate a first aider or an "appointed person"	Injured person or person suffering from severe-ill health	No one trained to summon professional help in an emergency may lead to further complications or a fatality	4	5	20	• First aiders and an appointed person to be nominated in accordance with the **Health and Safety (First Aid) Regulations 1981**. • Appointed person to be trained to summon for professional help (doctor, ambulance etc.) in the event of an accident or case of severe ill-health. • First aiders to be trained in either First Aid at Work (FAW) or in Emergency First Aid at Work (EFAW) and will give treatment relative to their qualifications (see attached table).	3	2	6
As above	As above	No one available to offer immediate treatment in the case of an injured person or a person suffering from severe ill-health could lead to further complications or a fatality	4	5	20	• Where the first aid assessment indicates that a first aid person(s) should be nominated (either because of the risk level or the number of employees), then they are to be both nominated and trained in accordance with the **Health and Safety (First Aid) Regulations 1981** either in FAW or EFAW. • Arrangements to be made for first aid cover if the first aid person is away.	3	2	6
First aid boxes not provided or contents stock low	Injured person	Unable to treat a wound quickly may lead to further complications	4	3	12	• Suitable first aid boxes to be provided, marked and readily accessible. • First aid box stocks to be checked regularly by an appointed person or first aider and should be replenished accordingly.	1	1	1

RISK ASSESSMENT - FIRST AID REQUIREMENTS

ACTIVITY	PERSON AT RISK	SIGNIFICANT HAZARDS	RISK*			RISK CONTROL MEASURES	RESIDUAL RISK**		
			L	S	DR		L	S	DR
Lack of first aid provision for lone workers	Anyone working alone or at a remote location	Injured person unable to self-administer basic first aid treatment leading to untreated wounds etc.	4	4	16	• A basic first aid kit to be provided for lone workers who work remote from the company base. • Lone workers within the company to be given access to first aid kits. • Lone workers to be instructed on summoning for help in an emergency when any injury requires other than basic treatment (e.g. plaster or dressing for minor cuts and grazes etc.).	3	2	6
Lack of first aid provision for shift workers	Anyone working shifts	No immediate treatment available in the case of an injured person or a person suffering from severe ill-health could lead to further complications or a fatality	4	5	20	• Appointed persons to be nominated from amongst the shift working staff to summon professional help in an emergency. • If work is of medium to high risk or staff numbers are high, then trained first aid personnel (either FAW or EFAW) to be nominated for shift workers.	3	2	6
Working with hazardous substances	Staff	Hazardous substances may cause ill-health or physical injury if they come into contact with staff	4	4	16	• Special first aid facilities to be provided in these instances, e.g. eye wash facilities etc. • First aid personnel to be trained to deal with such situations.	3	2	6

RISK ASSESSMENT - FIRST AID REQUIREMENTS

ACTIVITY	PERSON AT RISK	SIGNIFICANT HAZARDS	RISK*			RISK CONTROL MEASURES	RESIDUAL RISK**		
			L	S	DR		L	S	DR
Dealing with body fluid spillages, e.g. blood, vomit	First aid staff	Contact with bodily fluids may cause ill-health	3	3	9	• Disposable aprons to be provided for first aid personnel. • First aid personnel to be trained in dealing with bodily fluids. • Good hygiene practices to be enforced.	3	1	3
Dealing with multiple injuries	As above	Lack of first aid equipment may lead to wounds being untreated	3	3	9	• First aid equipment to be provided in accordance with the requirements of the **Health and Safety (First Aid) Regulations 1981** and the associated Approved Code of Practice. • The provision of equipment to match the degree of risk and numbers of employees in accordance with the guidance in the HSE leaflet INDG214 (rev1) First Aid at Work - your questions answered.	2	2	4

LIKELIHOOD (L) = Frequent (5) - Probable (4) - Occasional (3) - Improbable (2) - Remote (1)
SEVERITY (S) = Catastrophic (5) - Major (4) - Reportable (3) - Serious (2) - Minor (1)
Degree of Risk (DR) = LIKELIHOOD x SEVERITY
* Numbers used are for illustrative purposes only.
** Residual risk is the level of risk that remains after suitable and sufficient control measures are introduced.

Signed originator.. Job title..

Date completed.. Date for revision..

RECORD OF FIRST AID PROVISION

You should make a record of the first aid provisions you have decided upon as a result of your first aid requirements risk assessment.

First aid personnel	Required Yes/No	Number needed
First aider with a First Aid at Work (FAW) certificate		
First aider with an Emergency First Aid at Work (EFAW) certificate		
First aider with additional training (specify) (Required to deal with specific high-risk activities)		
Appointed persons		
First aid equipment and facilities		
First aid containers		
Additional equipment (specify)		
Travel first aid kits		
First aid room		

Note. The minimum first aid provision for each worksite is:
(a) an appointed person to take charge of first aid arrangements;
(b) a suitably stocked first aid box;
(c) information for employees about the first aid arrangements.

Name of person completing this form: ....

Date completed:...

Lone working

People who work on their own should be at no more risk than other employees.

Being safe whilst on your own

Lone working brings its own specific risks, which could cause accidents and potentially put you on the wrong side of the law. To ensure that this doesn't happen, you should complete a risk assessment for lone worker activities, which identifies all "significant" hazards and appropriate "reasonable" ways of reducing the risks to an acceptable level.

Managing the risks

To help you identify the hazards and appropriate ways of controlling them, use our example **Risk Assessment - Lone Working** document. It covers the generic hazards found with most lone working activities and suggests control measures to reduce risks to an acceptable level.

You should ensure your own document only addresses "significant" hazards, i.e. any that, could and more importantly are likely to, cause an accident or injury.

Making your instructions clear

There is no point putting activities on the document that simply don't need to be there. Work to the principle that if there is any chance of your staff being unaware of the safe way of working on their own, then you will need to make it clear on your document. Finally, always ensure any control measures you identify and follow only go so far "as is reasonably practicable".

Note. The list of potential hazards is not exhaustive, as you will know the requirements of lone working as it affects your business better than we do. However, for your risk assessment to be considered suitable and sufficient in the eyes of the law it must accurately reflect the "significant" hazards found in your workplace.

RISK ASSESSMENT - LONE WORKING

ACTIVITY	PERSON AT RISK	SIGNIFICANT HAZARDS	RISK*			RISK CONTROL MEASURES	RESIDUAL RISK**		
			L	S	DR		L	S	DR
Working at remote locations	Operative	Difficulties in dealing with an emergency situation, e.g. accident requiring medical attention	4	3	12	• Lone workers to have a basic first aid kit with them and instructed in basic first aid practices. • Lone workers to have means of summoning medical assistance, e.g. mobile phone, pager etc.	3	2	6
Lone working involving manual handling	As above	If work involves manual handling, it may be beyond an individual's capabilities and cause personal injuries	4	3	12	• Lone workers to be trained in manual handling techniques where required. • Lone worker should be able to summon assistance if the load is beyond personal capabilities. • Mechanical aids to be provided where relevant.	2	2	4
Lone working in public areas	As above	Lone working in public areas may give rise to violence to staff	3	3	9	• Lone workers to receive training in dealing with members of the public, particularly those who may be violent. • Lone workers to be able to summon assistance, e.g. via mobile phone, personal alarm etc.	3	1	3
Working away from normal workplace	As above	Lone working in isolation may give rise to stress	3	3	9	• Supervisors to keep in regular contact with lone workers and to visit them on regular occasions. • Lone workers to have regular contact with their company base.	3	1	3
Lone workers who handle cash	As above	Poor security measures when handling cash may lead to attempted robbery	3	4	12	• Arrangements to be made for money to be kept secure. • Lone workers to be issued with personal attack alarms. • Lone workers to be trained in cash handling.	3	2	6

RISK ASSESSMENT - LONE WORKING

ACTIVITY	PERSON AT RISK	SIGNIFICANT HAZARDS	RISK*			RISK CONTROL MEASURES	RESIDUAL RISK**		
			L	S	DR		L	S	DR
Lone female workers	Operative	Lone female workers may be at a greater risk of personal injury	4	4	16	• Arrangements to be made for closer supervision of lone female workers. • Good communications to be provided, e.g. mobile phones, personal attack alarms etc.	3	2	6
Lone workers with medical conditions	As above	Some medical conditions may increase the risks of the job	3	4	12	• Lone workers to complete a health questionnaire before commencing work. • Lone workers to have the ability to call for medical assistance if required, e.g. via mobile phone, pager etc.	3	2	6

LIKELIHOOD (L) = Frequent (5) - Probable (4) - Occasional (3) - Improbable (2) - Remote (1)
SEVERITY (S) = Catastrophic (5) - Major (4) - Reportable (3) - Serious (2) - Minor (1)
Degree of Risk (DR) = LIKELIHOOD x SEVERITY
* Numbers used are for illustrative purposes only.
** Residual risk is the level of risk that remains after suitable and sufficient control measures are introduced

Signed originator.. Job title...

Date completed.. Date for revision..

Manual handling

Manual handling occurs in most aspects of work. Carried out using the wrong techniques or attempting to move items beyond the capacity of the employee will almost certainly lead to accidents.

Managing the risks

To help you identify the hazards and appropriate ways of controlling them, use our example **Risk Assessment - Manual Handling** document. It covers the generic hazards found with most manual handling tasks and suggests control measures to reduce risks to an acceptable level.

You should ensure that your document only addresses "significant" hazards, i.e. any that could and more importantly are likely to, cause an accident or injury. For example, your risk assessment doesn't need to cover activities such as placing small packs of photocopying paper into the stationery cupboard or similar activities.

Make your instructions clear

There is no point putting activities on the document that simply don't need to be there. Work to the principle that if there is any chance of your staff being unaware of the safe way of carrying out a manual handling task, then you will need to make it clear on your document. Finally, always ensure any control measures you identify and follow only go so far "as is reasonably practicable".

Note. The list of potential hazards is not exhaustive, as you know your workplace better than we do. For your risk assessment to be considered suitable and sufficient in the eyes of the law it must accurately reflect the "significant" hazards found with manual handling operations in your workplace.

RISK ASSESSMENT - MANUAL HANDLING

ACTIVITY	PERSON AT RISK	SIGNIFICANT HAZARDS	RISK*			RISK CONTROL MEASURES	RESIDUAL RISK**		
			L	S	DR		L	S	DR
Moving loads	Operative(s)	Incorrect manual handling techniques (lifting, pushing, pulling etc.)	4	3	12	• Operatives to receive training in manual handling techniques and to be adequately supervised. • Refresher training to be given where needed or when the job changes.	3	1	3
As above	As above	Weight and size of load is excessive leading to back, arm injuries etc.	4	3	12	• Reduce weight of load where possible by breaking it down. • Use of suitable mechanical aids to assist with lifting and moving. • The use of more than one person to move the load to be considered.	3	1	3
As above	As above	Environmental factors (poor lighting, uneven floors etc.)	3	2	6	• Lighting must be adequate. • Checks that floors are free from debris and that all obstacles are removed.	2	1	2
As above	As above	Falling loads leading to bodily injuries	4	3	12	• Loads should be stable and secured where necessary to mechanical aids. • Suitable personal protective equipment to be worn, e.g. safety boots/ shoes, gloves, etc.	3	1	3
As above	As above	Moving loads repetitively leading to muscular injuries	4	3	12	• Working practices to be reviewed to reduce repetitive handling of loads. • Allowance made for adequate rest breaks or changes in tasks. • Mechanisation of the task to be considered.	3	1	3

RISK ASSESSMENT - MANUAL HANDLING

ACTIVITY	PERSON AT RISK	SIGNIFICANT HAZARDS	RISK*			RISK CONTROL MEASURES	RESIDUAL RISK**		
			L	S	DR		L	S	DR
Moving loads	Operative(s)	Some operatives may have health conditions that affect their capacity to move or lift loads, leading to injuries, ill-health etc.	3	4	12	• Working practices for women who may be pregnant to be reviewed. • Working practices for operatives who may have physical weaknesses or disabilities to be reviewed. • Sufficient information to be provided on the tasks that such operatives are given.	3	1	3
As above	As above	Mechanical aids in poor condition may lead to them failing and causing injuries	4	3	12	• All mechanical aids to be checked and maintained on a regular basis. • Stipulated safe working loads to be adhered to. • Operatives to be trained in their use and know how to report faults.	3	1	3

LIKELIHOOD (L) = Frequent (5) - Probable (4) - Occasional (3) - Improbable (2) - Remote (1)
SEVERITY (S) = Catastrophic (5) - Major (4) - Reportable (3) - Serious (2) - Minor (1)
Degree of Risk (DR) = LIKELIHOOD x SEVERITY
* Numbers used are for illustrative purposes only.
** Residual risk is the level of risk that remains after suitable and sufficient control measures are introduced

Signed originator.. Job title..

Date completed.. Date for revision..

Manual handling - team lifting

When using more than one person to assist with the manual handling of loads it could, if carried out incorrectly, lead to accidents involving serious personal injuries.

Managing the risks

To help you to identify the hazards associated with carrying out the movement of loads using teams of two or more people and the appropriate ways of controlling them, use our example **Risk Assessment - Manual Handling - Team Lifting**. It covers the generic hazards associated with this type of activity and suggests control measures to reduce risks to an acceptable level. You should ensure that your document only addresses "significant" hazards, i.e. any that could, and more importantly are likely to, cause an accident or injury.

Make your instructions clear

Don't include activities in your document that simply don't need to be there. Work to the principle that if there is any chance of your staff being unaware of the safe way of doing something, then you will need to make it clear in your document. Finally, always ensure that any control measures you identify and follow are decided upon the principle of "so far as is reasonably practicable".

Note. The list of potential hazards is not exhaustive. However, for your risk assessment to be considered suitable and sufficient in the eyes of the law it must accurately reflect the "significant" hazards found when carrying out team lifting operations.

Note. This risk assessment only deals with the generic risks associated with this type of activity. As loads will vary in weight and size, as will the individual's lifting capabilities, you should ensure that your assessment deals specifically with the items that are required to be handled. You should also take into account the work environment and ensure that it is suitable for the manual handling operation to take place.

RISK ASSESSMENT - MANUAL HANDLING - TEAM LIFTING

ACTIVITY	PERSON AT RISK	SIGNIFICANT HAZARDS	RISK*			RISK CONTROL MEASURES	RESIDUAL RISK**		
			L	S	DR		L	S	DR
Team lifting	Staff	Failure to assess manual handling operations using mechanical aids may lead to accidents resulting in physical injuries	3	4	12	• Before carrying out manual handling operations the task is to be assessed for moving using mechanical aids. • Manual handling of loads to be carried out only as a last resort.	3	2	6
As above	As above	Restricted space can affect manoeuvrability leading to poor access to the load, resulting in strains and sprains to the body	3	4	12	• All work areas to be suitable for a team lift with adequate space being provided for the handlers to gain good access to the load.	3	2	6
As above	As above	Failure to provide suitable handholds for the load may lead to it slipping when lifted causing physical injuries	3	4	12	• All loads requiring a team lift to be fitted with adequate handholds to allow team members to grasp the load securely. • Where handholds cannot be provided, then suitable slings etc. are to be used.	3	2	6
As above	As above	Failure to plan a route for the movement of the load may lead to the load falling due to obstacles being present resulting in physical injuries	3	4	12	• The route to be taken is to be inspected to ensure all obstacles are removed where possible. • A lifting plan to be prepared and communicated to all lifting team members.	3	2	6

RISK ASSESSMENT - MANUAL HANDLING - TEAM LIFTING

ACTIVITY	PERSON AT RISK	SIGNIFICANT HAZARDS	RISK*			RISK CONTROL MEASURES	RESIDUAL RISK**		
			L	S	DR		L	S	DR
As above	As above	Failure to select team members with similar lifting capabilities may make the lifting operation unstable resulting in physical injuries	3	4	12	• Lifting team members to be selected so that they are of a similar build and physical capability.	3	2	6
As above	As above	Failure to nominate one person to take charge of the lifting process may lead to poor communication between team members and cause the load to fall resulting in physical injuries	3	4	12	• A team leader to be nominated to control all aspects of the manual handling operation. • Team leaders to communicate lifting and moving instructions to other team members.	3	2	6
As above	As above	Lack of training in manual handling techniques may lead to physical injuries	3	4	12	• All staff who will be involved in manual handling operations to be trained to carry out such work.	3	2	6
Lifting and moving awkward loads	As above	Failure to take into account awkward loads which are uneven in weight distribution may lead to the load falling causing physical injuries	3	4	12	• All loads to be assessed for weight before lifting. • Where weight distribution is such that one end of a load is heavier than the other, then the strongest team members to lift at the heavier end.	3	2	6

LIKELIHOOD (L) = Frequent (5) - Probable (4) - Occasional (3) - Improbable (2) - Remote (1)
SEVERITY (S) = Catastrophic (5) - Major (4) - Reportable (3) - Serious (2) - Minor (1) Degree of Risk (DR) = LIKELIHOOD x SEVERITY
* Numbers used are for illustrative purposes only. ** Residual risk is the level of risk that remains after suitable and sufficient control measures are introduced.

Signed originator.. Job title..

Date completed... Date for revision..

Pregnant staff

There are specific risks and hazards present in the working environment that may affect women that are either pregnant or of childbearing age.

Managing the risks

To help you identify the hazards and appropriate ways of controlling them, use our example **Risk Assessment - Pregnant Staff** document. It covers the generic hazards associated with pregnancy and suggests control measures to reduce the risks to an acceptable level.

You should ensure that your document only addresses "significant" hazards, i.e. any that could and more importantly are likely to, cause an accident or injury.

Make your instructions clear

Don't include activities in your document that simply don't need to be there. Work to the principle that if there is any chance of pregnant staff being unaware of the safe way of doing something, then you will need to make it clear on your document. Finally, always ensure any control measures you identify and follow only go so far "as is reasonably practicable".

Note. The list of potential hazards is not exhaustive, as you know your workplace and staff better than we do. However, for your risk assessment to be considered suitable and sufficient in the eyes of the law it must accurately reflect the "significant" hazards found in your workplace.

RISK ASSESSMENT - PREGNANT STAFF

ACTIVITY	PERSON AT RISK	SIGNIFICANT HAZARDS	RISK*			RISK CONTROL MEASURES	RESIDUAL RISK**		
			L	S	DR		L	S	DR
Manual handling	Staff members who are pregnant	Postural problems through excessive manual handling operations may increase as pregnancy progresses	4	4	16	• All manual handling tasks to be re-assessed for pregnant women. • The nature of the tasks may need to be altered to reduce the risk of injury. • The amount of physical work to be reduced accordingly and lifting aids to be provided. • Any specific recommendations from a GP to be observed.	3	2	6
Work where there is a risk of exposure to shocks, vibration or sudden movements	As above	Regular exposure can increase risk of miscarriage. Long-term exposure to vibration may lead to risk of premature birth or low birth weight	4	4	16	• Work likely to involve uncomfortable whole body vibration to be avoided, especially at low frequencies. Also, where the abdomen is exposed to shock or jolts.	3	2	6
Work activities causing physical fatigue	As above	Fatigue caused by excessive standing and/or by physical work may lead to miscarriage, premature birth or low birth weight	4	4	16	• Hours of work and type of work activity should be reviewed to minimise the risk. • Pregnant staff should have some control over their work patterns. • Seating to be provided where possible and additional rest breaks should be considered.	3	2	6

RISK ASSESSMENT - PREGNANT STAFF

ACTIVITY	PERSON AT RISK	SIGNIFICANT HAZARDS	RISK*			RISK CONTROL MEASURES	RESIDUAL RISK**		
			L	S	DR		L	S	DR
Using chemical agents during the work process	Staff members who are pregnant	Use of chemical substances that may cause ill-health etc. to pregnant women	4	4	16	• The use of substances labelled as being likely to cause injury to a pregnant woman, nursing mother, unborn child or child of a nursing mother should be avoided. • COSHH assessments and Material Hazard Data Sheets to be obtained to indicate safe use of chemical substances.	3	2	6
Work with display screen equipment	As above	Stress, anxiety or postural issues may occur causing health problems	3	3	9	• Workstations to be assessed taking into account pregnant workers (additional space etc.). • Sufficient rest breaks to be taken away from the screen. • Work tasks to be reviewed to alleviate stressful situations.	3	1	3
Working in extremes of heat and cold	As above	Pregnant women may be more susceptible to heat stress and breast-feeding may become impaired	3	2	6	• Pregnant staff not to be placed in areas where temperatures are either too hot or too cold. • Additional rest and refreshment breaks to be provided.	3	1	3

LIKELIHOOD (L) = Frequent (5) - Probable (4) - Occasional (3) - Improbable (2) - Remote (1)
SEVERITY (S) = Catastrophic (5) - Major (4) - Reportable (3) - Serious (2) - Minor (1)
Degree of Risk (DR) = LIKELIHOOD x SEVERITY
* Numbers used are for illustrative purposes only. ** Residual risk is the level of risk that remains after suitable and sufficient control measures are introduced

Signed originator.. Job title...

Date completed... Date for revision...

Site-specific risks

When you arrive at an unfamiliar site, you'll often be faced with unexpected hazards that won't be covered on your generic site risk assessment. If left unmanaged, these could cause accidents leading to serious personal injuries.

What to do?

Although the tasks your staff complete are likely to be very familiar and can be covered in a generic risk assessment, the site on which they're working can often throw up some unexpected hazards that need to be dealt with. So to record which hazards are present, their associated risks and, most importantly, how you will manage them, e.g. by issuing appropriate personal protective equipment, use our **Risk Assessment - Site-Specific Risks**.

How to fill it in?

The boxes on the form are largely self-explanatory. The first section includes space to identify the location of the site, your emergency arrangements - including first aid trained staff etc. The second part is designed to record any hazards found.

Note. You should ensure that your document only addresses "significant" hazards, i.e. any that could, and more importantly are likely to, cause an accident or injury.

Training record

Any members of staff who may be exposed to the hazards identified should be briefed on how to avoid injury. The final part of the document provides space to record who has received the briefing.

Get a signature. Make sure all members of staff enter their names and sign this document. This is your record that you've assessed the risks properly, and that they have been briefed accordingly.

RISK ASSESSMENT - SITE SPECIFIC RISKS

Site details		
Site address:	Client contact details:	Brief description of work:
Date of assessment:	Duration of work:	Contract manager:
Completed by:	Signature:	Contract reference:
Emergency/first aid arrangements		
Site first aiders:	Nearest hospital:	Location of first aid kit:

Site-specific risks							
Hazards	L	S	DR	Control measures/action required	L	S	RR

Likelihood (L): Frequent (5) - Probable (4) - Occasional (3) - Improbable (2) - Remote (1). Degree of Risk (DR): Likelihood X Severity.	Severity (S): Catastrophic (5) - Major (4) - Reportable (3) - Serious (2) - Minor (1). Residual Risk (RR): Likelihood X Severity after control measures applied.
Generic risk assessments that apply to work:	

All staff/sub-contractors involved in the work to be briefed on site-specific risks, prior to starting any work

Staff name	Signature*	Date

* By signing this document, you're agreeing that you have received and understood a briefing on the site-specific risks and the appropriate control measures necessary to reduce them.

Working out of hours

Working outside of the normal working hours may present risks to staff, which left unmanaged, could cause accidents and potentially put you on the wrong side of the law.

Managing the risks

To help you identify the hazards associated with such activities and the appropriate ways of controlling them, use our example **Risk Assessment - Working Out of Hours**. It covers the generic hazards associated with this type of activity and suggests control measures to reduce risks to an acceptable level. You can then add to this document items that are specific to your workplace and activities. You should ensure your document only addresses "significant" hazards, i.e. any that could, and more importantly are likely to, cause an accident or injury.

Note. You should also refer to your existing risk assessments, including your fire risk assessment, which are associated with the work being carried out. In many cases there will only be a requirement to add additional control measures for hazards that may result specifically from out-of-hours working.

Make your instructions clear

Don't include activities in your document that simply don't need to be there. Work to the principle that if there is any chance of your staff being unaware of the safe way of doing something, then you will need to make it clear in your document. Finally, always ensure that any control measures you identify and follow are decided upon the principle of "so far as is reasonably practicable".

Note. The list of potential hazards is not exhaustive. However, for your risk assessment to be considered suitable and sufficient in the eyes of the law it must accurately reflect the "significant" hazards found when working outside of normal working hours in your workplace environment.

RISK ASSESSMENT - WORKING OUT OF HOURS

ACTIVITY	PERSON AT RISK	SIGNIFICANT HAZARDS	RISK*			RISK CONTROL MEASURES	RESIDUAL RISK**		
			L	S	DR		L	S	DR
Lone working and out of normal working hours in an office	Staff member	Difficulties in dealing with an emergency situation, e.g. accident requiring medical attention	4	3	12	• Lone workers to have access to first aid facilities and instructed in basic first aid practices. • Lone workers to have means of summoning medical assistance, e.g. telephone, mobile phone, etc.	3	2	6
Lone workers with medical conditions	As above	Some medical conditions may increase the risks of the job	3	4	12	• Lone workers to complete a health questionnaire before commencing work. • Lone workers to have the ability to call for medical assistance if required e.g. Telephone, Mobile phone, etc.	3	2	6
Lone workers who handle cash	As above	Poor security measures when handling cash may lead to attempted robbery	3	4	12	• Arrangements to be made for money to be kept secure. • Lone workers to be issued with personal attack alarms where considered necessary. • Lone workers to be trained in cash handling.	3	2	6
Lone working involving manual handling	As above	If work involves manual handling it may be beyond an individual's capabilities causing personal injuries	4	3	12	• Lone workers to be trained in manual handling techniques where required. • Lone workers to be instructed not to attempt to move loads that are beyond personal capabilities. • Mechanical aids to be provided where relevant.	2	2	4

Note: Reference to be made to company general office work risk assessment and any other relevant risk assessments, including the fire risk assessment.

RISK ASSESSMENT - WORKING OUT OF HOURS

ACTIVITY	PERSON AT RISK	SIGNIFICANT HAZARDS	RISK*			RISK CONTROL MEASURES	RESIDUAL RISK**		
			L	S	DR		L	S	DR
Security of premises when working out of normal working hours	Staff member	Failure to secure premises may lead to intruders entering the building	3	3	9	• Staff to be instructed to ensure all external doors are kept locked. • Staff to be instructed to summon assistance by telephone (police, their manager etc.) if intruders are suspected of entering the building.	2	2	4
Access and egress to premises	As above	Increased likelihood of slips, trips and falls during hours of darkness	3	4	12	• External lighting to be regularly checked and maintained so that roads and pathways are suitably illuminated.	3	1	3
Electrical equipment	As above	Failure to switch off electrical equipment may lead to out-of-hours fires starting	3	4	12	• Staff to be instructed to switch off all unnecessary equipment before leaving the premises.	2	2	4

LIKELIHOOD (L) = Frequent (5) - Probable (4) - Occasional (3) - Improbable (2) - Remote (1)
SEVERITY (S) = Catastrophic (5) - Major (4) - Reportable (3) - Serious (2) - Minor (1)
Degree of Risk (DR) = LIKELIHOOD x SEVERITY
* Numbers used are for illustrative purposes only.
** Residual risk is the level of risk that remains after suitable and sufficient control measures are introduced.

Signed originator.. Job title..

Date completed.. Date for revision..

Machinery

Drilling holes in textured coatings

Textured coatings are usually found as a type of decorative finish to walls and ceilings. Failure to take the proper precautions when drilling into them could lead to dust, which may contain asbestos, being inhaled by staff and others.

Managing the risks

To help you identify the hazards associated with drilling into textured coatings or asbestos cement sheets and the appropriate ways of controlling them, use our example **Risk assessment - Drilling Holes in Textured Coatings**. It covers the generic hazards associated with this type of activity and suggests control measures to reduce risks to an acceptable level.

Note. The **Control of Asbestos Regulations 2006** removed the reference to textured coatings, contained in the previous regulations. However, that does not mean it is safe to drill or cut them without taking some precautions against the release of fibres. Therefore, you will still need to assess the risks and have a safe system of work in place.

You should ensure that your document only addresses "significant" hazards, i.e. any that could, and more importantly are likely to, cause an accident or injury.

Make your instructions clear

Don't include activities in your document that simply don't need to be there. Work to the principle that if there is any chance of your staff being unaware of the safe way of doing something, then you will need to make it clear in your document. Finally, always ensure that any control measures you identify and follow only go so far "as is reasonably practicable".

Note. The list of potential hazards is not exhaustive. For your risk assessment to be considered suitable and sufficient in the eyes of the law it must accurately reflect the "significant" hazards found in your workplace.

RISK ASSESSMENT - DRILLING HOLES IN TEXTURED COATINGS

ACTIVITY	PERSON AT RISK	SIGNIFICANT HAZARDS	RISK*			RISK CONTROL MEASURES	RESIDUAL RISK**		
			L	S	DR		L	S	DR
Drilling holes in textured coatings	Staff, others present	Failure to restrict access to work area may lead to respiratory problems caused by inhaling dust	4	3	12	• Work area to be segregated to prevent others entering. • Work area to be designated and signs displayed to warn others. • Barrier tape etc. to be used to indicate work area where it cannot be locked off.	3	1	3
As above	As above	Furniture and fittings in the work area may become contaminated with dust	4	3	12	• All furniture and fittings to be removed from work area where possible. • Any furniture and fittings that remain to be covered with 500 gauge polythene sheeting secured with duct tape. • Sheeting to be cleaned with damp rags when work is complete and disposed of as asbestos waste.	3	1	3
As above	Staff	Failure to wear the correct personal protective equipment (PPE) may lead to dust being inhaled and clothing becoming contaminated	4	3	12	• Staff carrying out the work to wear: - disposable overall with a hood - boots without laces - suitable respiratory equipment - eye protection. • Overalls to be disposed of as asbestos waste. • Boots to be wiped clean with a damp rag and the rag disposed of as asbestos waste.	2	1	2

RISK ASSESSMENT - DRILLING HOLES IN TEXTURED COATINGS

ACTIVITY	PERSON AT RISK	SIGNIFICANT HAZARDS	RISK*			RISK CONTROL MEASURES	RESIDUAL RISK**		
			L	S	DR		L	S	DR
Drilling holes in textured coatings	Staff	Failure to treat work area may lead to dust being released causing respiratory problems	4	4	16	• Staff to follow the safe system of work provided. • The drilling area to be treated with wallpaper paste (or other binding agent) before drilling to prevent fibre release. • All drilling residue to be cleaned up with wet rags, which are to be disposed of as asbestos waste.	3	2	6
As above	As above	Failure to use the correct type of drill and bits may lead to excessive dust release	3	3	9	• Drills to only be used at their lowest speed. • Hole cutters to be used for holes over 20mm in diameter. • All tools to be cleaned afterwards with a damp rag and the rag disposed of as asbestos waste.	2	1	2
As above	As above	Failure to clean area after work may lead to residual dust in the work area	4	2	8	• Work area to be cleaned with a "Type H" vacuum cleaner when work is completed. • Surfaces to be wiped clean with damp rags and the rags disposed of as asbestos waste.	3	1	3

LIKELIHOOD (L) = Frequent (5) - Probable (4) - Occasional (3) - Improbable (2) - Remote (1)
SEVERITY (S) = Catastrophic (5) - Major (4) - Reportable (3) - Serious (2) - Minor (1)
Degree of Risk (DR) = LIKELIHOOD x SEVERITY
* Numbers used are for illustrative purposes only.
** Residual risk is the level of risk that remains after suitable and sufficient control measures are introduced.

Signed originator.. Job title..

Date completed.. Date for revision..

Machinery maintenance

Maintaining machinery can be a hazardous activity. For example, contact could be made from moving parts as safety guards may have been removed. Left unmanaged, this could cause accidents and potentially put you on the wrong side of the law. To ensure this doesn't happen, you should complete a risk assessment for regular maintenance tasks which identifies all "significant" hazards and appropriate "reasonable" ways of reducing risks to an acceptable level.

Managing the risks

To help you identify the hazards associated with machinery maintenance and the appropriate ways of controlling them, use our example **Risk Assessment - Machinery Maintenance**. It covers the generic hazards associated with this type of activity and suggests control measures to reduce risks to an acceptable level. For specific hazards concerning a particular machine we have also provided a blank section for you to complete if necessary.

Make your instructions clear

Work to the principle that if there is any chance of your staff being unaware of the safe way of doing something, then you will need to make it clear in your document. Always ensure that any control measures you identify and follow are decided upon the principle of "so far as is reasonably practicable". **Note 1.** The list of potential hazards is not exhaustive. However, for your risk assessment to be considered suitable and sufficient in the eyes of the law it must accurately reflect the "significant" hazards found when carrying out maintenance activities on your machinery. **Note 2.** This risk assessment only deals with generic maintenance activities. Where other in-depth maintenance activities occur then this assessment should be extended to deal with the more serious risks involved. In some instances a permit-to-work system may also be needed.

RISK ASSESSMENT - MACHINERY MAINTENANCE

ACTIVITY	PERSON AT RISK	SIGNIFICANT HAZARDS	RISK*			RISK CONTROL MEASURES***	RESIDUAL RISK**		
			L	S	DR		L	S	DR
General machinery maintenance	Maintenance staff	Maintenance staff may suffer injuries from moving machinery parts	3	5	15	• All dangerous parts of machinery to be guarded to manufacturers' standards. • Machinery guards to be inspected every month and maintained in good condition. • All new machinery to be checked before first use to ensure it has the CE standard mark, a "Declaration of Conformity" and there are no obvious accessible dangerous moving parts. • Ensure siting of the machine does not cause additional hazards, e.g. feed tables, etc.	3	2	6
Removing guards on machinery	As above	As above	3	4	12	• All machinery to be isolated from its electrical supply and locked off before any guards are removed or disconnected. • Only trained staff to remove machinery guarding. • All guards to be replaced after work has been completed and before restoring any power supplies.	3	2	6
Setting up power presses	As above	Maintenance staff and press setters may suffer crushing injuries from presses	3	4	12	• Staff who are trained to set tools and carry out daily checks of power press guards to ensure that setters on the shop floor carry out daily checks of power press guards.	3	2	6
Machinery lubrication	Maintenance staff, operatives	Contact with moving parts may lead to injuries	3	3	9	• Lubrication of machinery to be carried out only by trained personnel. • All machinery to be isolated from its electrical supply and locked off where possible.	3	1	3

RISK ASSESSMENT - MACHINERY MAINTENANCE

ACTIVITY	PERSON AT RISK	SIGNIFICANT HAZARDS	RISK*			RISK CONTROL MEASURES***	RESIDUAL RISK**		
			L	S	DR		L	S	DR
Work area access	Maintenance staff	Slips, trips and falls could lead to injuries	3	2	6	• Good housekeeping practices to be enforced. • Spillages (oils, water, grease etc.) to be cleaned up immediately.	3	1	3
Sharpening machinery cutting tools; using an abrasive wheel	As above	Maintenance staff and others nearby may suffer serious impact injuries if abrasive wheel fractures during use	3	3	9	• Only maintenance staff that are trained to mount and use abrasive wheels to carry out this operation. • All staff to wear eye protection when using abrasive wheels. • All staff to ensure that there is no loose clothing that may become entangled in the abrasive wheel.	3	1	3
Moving machinery	As above	Maintenance staff who move machinery may suffer strain injuries	4	3	12	• All manual handling of machinery to be planned. • Mechanical aids to be used where possible. • Only staff trained in manual handling to carry out this task.	3	2	6
Work on electrical controls	As above	Danger of electric shock to staff	3	4	12	• Regular checks to be made to ensure that electrical controls are free from damage. • Only trained staff to work on electrical controls.	3	2	6

LIKELIHOOD (L) = Frequent (5) - Probable (4) - Occasional (3) - Improbable (2) - Remote (1)
SEVERITY (S) = Catastrophic (5) - Major (4) - Reportable (3) - Serious (2) - Minor (1) Degree of Risk (DR) = LIKELIHOOD x SEVERITY
* Numbers used are for illustrative purposes only. ** Residual risk is the level of risk that remains after suitable and sufficient control measures are introduced.
*** One of the following control measures will be used. It will be the decision of manager of the works which one it will be.

Signed originator.. Job title...

Date completed... Date for revision...

ADDITIONAL MAINTENANCE ACTIVITIES

The assessment documented above is generic in nature and identifies some of the common risks associated with machinery maintenance and suggests suitable control measures to minimise such risks. You can add to this accordingly, depending upon your own findings.

However, machinery maintenance activities can vary considerably depending upon the type of machinery and the level of maintenance required. Therefore, a more detailed assessment of the specific risks associated with each particular machine should be carried out and the additional control measures should be identified prior to any machinery maintenance work commencing.

You can use the following blank risk assessment form to document such risks and the control measures necessary to mitigate them.

Because maintenance activities can vary, it is recommended that a new form is completed each time a maintenance activity takes place.

RISK ASSESSMENT - MACHINERY MAINTENANCE   MACHINE ....

ACTIVITY	PERSON AT RISK	SIGNIFICANT HAZARDS	RISK*			RISK CONTROL MEASURES***	RESIDUAL RISK**		
			L	S	DR		L	S	DR

LIKELIHOOD (L) = Frequent (5) - Probable (4) - Occasional (3) - Improbable (2) - Remote (1)
SEVERITY (S) = Catastrophic (5) - Major (4) - Reportable (3) - Serious (2) - Minor (1)
Degree of Risk (DR) = LIKELIHOOD x SEVERITY
* Numbers used are for illustrative purposes only.
** Residual risk is the level of risk that remains after suitable and sufficient control measures are introduced.
*** One of the following control measures will be used. It will be the decision of manager of the works, which one it will be.

Signed originator.. Job title..

Date completed.. Date for revision...

Safe use of angle grinders/cutters

Angle grinders/cutters etc. appear simple to use. However, used incorrectly and with the wrong type of cutting or grinding disc and accidents may result.

Managing the risks

To help you identify the hazards associated with the use of angle grinders/cutters and the appropriate ways of controlling them, why not use our example **Risk Assessment - Safe use of Angle Grinders/Cutters**. It covers the generic hazards associated with this type of activity and suggests control measures to reduce risks to an acceptable level.

You should ensure that your document only addresses "significant" hazards, i.e. any that could, and more importantly are likely to, cause an accident or injury.

Make your instructions clear

Don't include activities in your document that simply don't need to be there. Work to the principle that if there is any chance of your staff being unaware of the safe way of doing something, then you will need to make it clear in your document. Finally, always ensure that any control measures you identify and follow only go so far "as is reasonably practicable".

Note. The list of potential hazards is not exhaustive. However, for your risk assessment to be considered suitable and sufficient in the eyes of the law it must accurately reflect the "significant" hazards found in your workplace.

RISK ASSESSMENT - SAFE USE OF ANGLE GRINDERS/CUTTERS

ACTIVITY	PERSON AT RISK	SIGNIFICANT HAZARDS	RISK*			RISK CONTROL MEASURES	RESIDUAL RISK**		
			L	S	DR		L	S	DR
Maintenance of angle grinders/ cutters	Staff	Failure to keep grinders/cutters well maintained may lead to safety features not working	4	4	16	• All angle grinders and cutters to be checked before use. • Any equipment with damaged guards, flexes etc. not to be used, should be taken out of service and labelled for repair. • All electrically operated tools to have a test label fitted and to be regularly tested. • A register to be maintained of all grinders/cutters including their maintenance schedule.	3	2	6
Use of grinders/ cutters (general)	User	Failure to use grinders and cutters with the correct type of disc may lead to discs shattering and causing cuts etc.	4	4	16	• Staff to be trained in the characteristics of each types of disc and their purpose. • All work to be assessed and the correct type of cutting or grinding disc to be used. • Grinding discs not to be used for cutting procedures.	3	2	6
As above	As above	Failure to keep guards in place when using grinder/cutter may lead to injuries if the disc shatters	4	4	16	• All users to be trained to be aware of the importance of ensuring all guards are in place. • All users to wear eye protection to prevent damage to eyes from broken discs.	3	2	6
As above	As above	Worn equipment may lead to excessive vibration which may cause injuries	3	3	9	• Only equipment with a low level of vibration to be purchased. • All equipment to be regularly assessed and maintained to reduce vibration levels.	2	2	4

RISK ASSESSMENT - SAFE USE OF ANGLE GRINDERS/CUTTERS

ACTIVITY	PERSON AT RISK	SIGNIFICANT HAZARDS	RISK*			RISK CONTROL MEASURES	RESIDUAL RISK**		
			L	S	DR		L	S	DR
Maintenance of angle grinders/ cutters	Staff	Failure to keep grinders/cutters well maintained may lead to safety features not working	4	4	16	• All angle grinders and cutters to be checked before use. • Any equipment with damaged guards, flexes etc. not to be used, should be taken out of service and labelled for repair. • All electrically operated tools to have a test label fitted and to be regularly tested. • A register to be maintained of all grinders/cutters including their maintenance schedule.	3	2	6
Use of grinders/ cutters (general)	User	Failure to use grinders and cutters with the correct type of disc may lead to discs shattering and causing cuts etc.	4	4	16	• Staff to be trained in the characteristics of each types of disc and their purpose. • All work to be assessed and the correct type of cutting or grinding disc to be used. • Grinding discs not to be used for cutting procedures.	3	2	6
As above	As above	Failure to keep guards in place when using grinder/cutter may lead to injuries if the disc shatters	4	4	16	• All users to be trained to be aware of the importance of ensuring all guards are in place. • All users to wear eye protection to prevent damage to eyes from broken discs.	3	2	6
As above	As above	Worn equipment may lead to excessive vibration which may cause injuries	3	3	9	• Only equipment with a low level of vibration to be purchased. • All equipment to be regularly assessed and maintained to reduce vibration levels.	2	2	4

Safe use of bench grinders (abrasive wheels)

Bench grinders (or abrasive wheels) can be found in most workshops and whilst they appear to be a simple piece of equipment, if used incorrectly or by untrained staff, injuries could result.

Managing the risks

To help you identify the hazards associated with the use of bench grinders and the appropriate ways of controlling them, use our example **Risk Assessment - Safe use of Bench Grinders (Abrasive Wheels)**. It covers the generic hazards associated with this type of activity and suggests control measures to reduce risks to an acceptable level.

Note. The use of grinding machines or abrasive wheels is covered by the **Provision and Use of Work Equipment Regulations 1998**. Only trained operatives must be allowed to use, change and mount grinding wheels.

You should ensure that your document only addresses "significant" hazards, i.e. any that could, and more importantly are likely to, cause an accident or injury.

Make your instructions clear

Don't include activities in your document that simply don't need to be there. Work to the principle that if there is any chance of your staff being unaware of the safe way of doing something, then you will need to make it clear in your document. Finally, always ensure that any control measures you identify and follow only go so far "as is reasonably practicable".

Note. The list of potential hazards is not exhaustive. For your risk assessment to be considered suitable and sufficient in the eyes of the law it must accurately reflect the "significant" hazards found in your workplace.

RISK ASSESSMENT - SAFE USE OF BENCH GRINDERS (ABRASIVE WHEELS)

ACTIVITY	PERSON AT RISK	SIGNIFICANT HAZARDS	RISK*			RISK CONTROL MEASURES	RESIDUAL RISK**		
			L	S	DR		L	S	DR
Use of a bench grinder (abrasive wheel) general	User	Untrained staff using a bench grinder may lead to personal injuries	4	3	12	• Only staff that have been trained to use a bench grinder. • A notice to be supplied adjacent to the machine listing those members of staff who have been trained. • Supervisors to monitor grinder use.	3	2	6
As above	As above	If the work rest is not close to the wheel, the work piece may be drawn into the wheel causing hand injuries	4	3	12	• The work rest to be checked to ensure that it is as close to the wheel as is practical. • Work rests to be securely tightened to prevent movement during use. • Work rests to be adjusted as the wheel wears down.	3	1	3
As above	As above	Removal of the wheel guard during use may cause particles of metal to enter the eye	4	4	16	• Wheel guards to be secured in position and properly adjusted before the wheel is run. • Wheel guards to be inspected before the wheel is run.	3	2	6
As above	As above	Hazardous floor area around the grinder may lead to user falling against the wheel and sustaining injuries	3	4	12	• Floor areas around a grinder to be kept clear of obstacles. • Wet or greasy floors to be cleaned before using grinder.	3	2	6
As above	As above	Use of a worn grinding wheel may cause it to run unevenly and to shatter causing injuries to user	3	3	9	• Wheels to be inspected for wear before use. • Only trained operatives to change or dress a worn wheel.	3	1	3
As above	As above	Grinding on the side area of a wheel may cause it to shatter causing injuries to the user	4	3	12	• Under no circumstances should grinding take place using the side of the wheel.	3	2	6

RISK ASSESSMENT - SAFE USE OF BENCH GRINDERS (ABRASIVE WHEELS)

ACTIVITY	PERSON AT RISK	SIGNIFICANT HAZARDS	RISK*			RISK CONTROL MEASURES	RESIDUAL RISK**		
			L	S	DR		L	S	DR
Use of a bench grinder (abrasive wheel) general	User	Stopping wheels by area of a wheel may cause it to shatter causing injuries to the user	3	3	9	• Wheels not to be stopped by applying pressure to them. • Wheels to be allowed to run down and stop of their own accord.	3	1	3
As above	As above	Wheel spindles may overheat and cause the motor to catch fire	4	3	12	• Only wheels of the correct type to be fitted to the grinder. • Wheel speeds to match that of the grinder motor.	2	2	4
As above	As above	Use of an incorrect type of wheel may lead to it shattering causing injuries	4	4	16	• Only wheels of the correct type to be fitted to the grinder. • Wheel speeds to match that of the grinder motor.	3	2	6
As above	As above	Failure to wear the correct personal protective equipment PPE may lead to injuries	4	3	12	• All users to wear eye protection. • All users to wear respiratory protection when grinding creates a dust. • User to ensure that clothing is worn so that there is no risk of entanglement.	3	2	6

LIKELIHOOD (L) = Frequent (5) - Probable (4) - Occasional (3) - Improbable (2) - Remote (1)
SEVERITY (S) = Catastrophic (5) - Major (4) - Reportable (3) - Serious (2) - Minor (1) Degree of Risk (DR) = LIKELIHOOD x SEVERITY
* Numbers used are for illustrative purposes only.
** Residual risk is the level of risk that remains after suitable and sufficient control measures are introduced.

Signed originator.. Job title..

Date completed.. Date for revision..

Safe use of chainsaws

Failure to ensure that the risks associated with chainsaw use are reduced to an acceptable level, may lead to an accident, which invariably will put you on the wrong side of the law.

Managing the risks

To help you identify the hazards associated with chainsaw use and the appropriate ways of controlling them, use our example **Risk Assessment - Safe Use of Chainsaws**. It covers the generic hazards associated with this type of activity and then suggests control measures to reduce risks to an acceptable level.

You should ensure that your document only addresses "significant" hazards, i.e. any that could, and more importantly are likely to, cause an accident or injury.

Make your instructions clear

Don't include activities in your document that simply don't need to be there. Work to the principle that if there is any chance of your staff being unaware of the safe way of doing something, then you will need to make it clear in your document. Finally, always ensure that any control measures you identify and follow only go so far "as is reasonably practicable".

Note. The list of potential hazards is not exhaustive. For your risk assessment to be considered suitable and sufficient in the eyes of the law it must accurately reflect the "significant" hazards found in your workplace.

RISK ASSESSMENT - SAFE USE OF CHAINSAWS

ACTIVITY	PERSON AT RISK	SIGNIFICANT HAZARDS	RISK*			RISK CONTROL MEASURES	RESIDUAL RISK**		
			L	S	DR		L	S	DR
Use of a chainsaw (general)	User	Excessive noise and vibration when using a chainsaw may cause health problems	4	3	12	• Only chainsaws with low noise/low vibration levels to be purchased for use. • Users to wear hearing protection and gloves. • Chainsaws to be well maintained to reduce noise and vibration levels.	3	2	6
As above	As above	Failure to wear the correct personal protective equipment (PPE) may lead to severe personal injuries	4	5	20	• All chainsaw users to use the appropriate PPE. • All chainsaw users to be provided with PPE as follows: safety helmet, hearing protection, eye/face protection, chainsaw jackets, gloves, leg protection and chainsaw boots. • All staff to be instructed on the correct use of PPE. • All worn or damaged PPE to be changed as required.	3	3	9
Maintaining a chainsaw	As above	Failure to keep a chainsaw maintained may lead to injuries during use	4	4	16	• All chainsaws to be inspected daily by the user before use. • All safety devices and guards to be checked daily before use. • Only competent staff to maintain chainsaws. • Users to be trained in chain sharpening techniques and chain and guide bar maintenance to keep the saw in a safe working condition.	3	2	6
Use of petrol driven chainsaws	As above	Incorrect filling methods may lead to fire (including on clothing) and subsequent burns	3	4	12	• Petrol to only be stored in cans that are purposely designed for chainsaw filling, labelled and fitted with a secure cap. • An auto-filler to be used when decanting petrol to avoid overfilling. • Fuel containers to be kept clear of any possible source of ignition.	2	2	4

RISK ASSESSMENT - SAFE USE OF CHAINSAWS

ACTIVITY	PERSON AT RISK	SIGNIFICANT HAZARDS	RISK*			RISK CONTROL MEASURES	RESIDUAL RISK**		
			L	S	DR		L	S	DR
Use of a chainsaw (general)	User	Failure to administer first aid in the event of an accident may lead to major loss of blood and possibly life	3	5	15	• Chainsaw users to have first aid training. • A basic first aid kit with at least one large dressing to be provided for each chainsaw user. • Access to be available to a larger first aid kit, usually on the company vehicle or carried out to remote sites. • Supervisors to be instructed on how to summon for medical assistance in the event of a serious accident.	3	2	6
Use of chainsaws at height	As above	Use of incorrect access method may lead to accidents and personal injuries	3	4	12	• Ladders not to be used as access for chainsaw work. • Work from platforms to only be carried out by trained personnel. • Rope access work to only be carried out by staff who have a competence certificate in arboriculture work.	3	2	6
Using a chainsaw for tree work	As above	Users who are not competent in tree work are susceptible to accidents	4	4	16	• Only users who have a certificate of competence to use chainsaws on tree work. • All users to receive regular refresher training.	3	2	6

LIKELIHOOD (L) = Frequent (5) - Probable (4) - Occasional (3) - Improbable (2) - Remote (1)
SEVERITY (S) = Catastrophic (5) - Major (4) - Reportable (3) - Serious (2) - Minor (1)
Degree of Risk (DR) = LIKELIHOOD x SEVERITY
* Numbers used are for illustrative purposes only. ** Residual risk is the level of risk that remains after suitable and sufficient control measures are introduced.

Signed originator.. Job title..

Date completed.. Date for revision...

Safe use of electric drills

Portable electric drills are useful tools and, with care, they can be among the safest. But electric drills can be dangerous if not handled carefully.

Managing the risks

To help you identify the hazards associated with the use of electric drills and the appropriate ways of controlling them, use our example **Risk Assessment - Safe use of Electric Drills**. It covers the generic hazards associated with this type of activity and suggests control measures to reduce risks to an acceptable level.

Note. If you intend on using an electric drill whilst working above ground level then also refer to our **Risk Assessment - Working at Height**.

You should ensure your document only addresses "significant" hazards, i.e. any that could, and more importantly are likely to, cause an accident or injury.

Make your instructions clear

Don't include activities in your document that simply don't need to be there. Work to the principle that if there is any chance of your staff being unaware of the safe way of doing something, then you will need to make it clear in your document. Finally, always ensure any control measures you identify and follow only go so far "as is reasonably practicable".

Note. The list of potential hazards is not exhaustive. However, for your risk assessment to be considered suitable and sufficient in the eyes of the law it must accurately reflect the "significant" hazards found in your workplace.

RISK ASSESSMENT - SAFE USE OF ELECTRIC DRILLS

ACTIVITY	PERSON AT RISK	SIGNIFICANT HAZARDS	RISK*			RISK CONTROL MEASURES	RESIDUAL RISK**		
			L	S	DR		L	S	DR
Using a mains powered electric drill (general)	User	Damaged electrical cable or drill casing may lead to electric shock	4	4	16	• All electric drills to be PAT tested and carry a label indicating the test date. • Users to inspect the drill and cable for damage before use. • All extension cables to be checked before use.	3	2	6
As above	As above	A damaged drill switch or trigger lock may lead to the drill not stopping when required to, causing wrist injuries	4	3	12	• The switch and trigger locks on drills to be checked for damage prior to use. • Drills with damaged switches to be taken out of service and marked for repair.	2	2	4
As above	As above	Use of an electric drill outside in wet or damp conditions may cause electric shock	3	4	12	• Mains powered drill used externally to be protected by a residual current circuit breaker (RCCB). • All RCCBs to be tested before use. • Alternatively, staff to use a double insulated drill for external work.	2	2	4
As above	As above	Failing to turn off the drill before changing drill bits may lead to it starting without warning causing injuries to hands	3	3	9	• Users to switch off and unplug drills before changing drill bits.	2	1	2

RISK ASSESSMENT - SAFE USE OF ELECTRIC DRILLS

ACTIVITY	PERSON AT RISK	SIGNIFICANT HAZARDS	RISK*			RISK CONTROL MEASURES	RESIDUAL RISK**		
			L	S	DR		L	S	DR
Using a mains powered electric drill (general)	User	Exerting excessive pressure when drilling may cause drill to break and puncture skin	3	3	9	• Users to ensure that the correct pressure is applied relative to the material being drilled.	2	1	2
As above	As above	Using a blunt drill bit may cause it to slip causing hand injuries	4	2	8	• User to ensure that all drill bits are kept in a serviceable condition. • When drilling into metal a starting point to be made using a centre punch.	3	1	3
As above	As above	Failure to wear the correct personal protective equipment (PPE) may lead to eye or body injuries	4	4	16	• Users to wear eye protection when using a drill. • Users to avoid wearing loose clothing that may become entangled. • Users to wear respiratory protection if work is dusty.	3	2	6

LIKELIHOOD (L) = Frequent (5) - Probable (4) - Occasional (3) - Improbable (2) - Remote (1)
SEVERITY (S) = Catastrophic (5) - Major (4) - Reportable (3) - Serious (2) - Minor (1)
Degree of Risk (DR) = LIKELIHOOD x SEVERITY
* Numbers used are for illustrative purposes only.
** Residual risk is the level of risk that remains after suitable and sufficient control measures are introduced.

Signed originator.. Job title...

Date completed.. Date for revision...

Safe use of electric welding equipment

If electric welding equipment is used incorrectly, then this could lead to incidents involving fire, resulting in burns and other serious personal injuries.

Managing the risks

To help you to identify the hazards associated with using electric welding equipment and the appropriate ways of controlling them, use our example **Risk Assessment - Safe Use of Electric Welding Equipment**. It covers the generic hazards associated with this type of activity and suggests control measures to reduce risks to an acceptable level. You should ensure that your document only addresses "significant" hazards, i.e. any that could, and more importantly are likely to, cause an accident or injury.

Make your instructions clear

Don't include activities in your document that simply don't need to be there. Work to the principle that if there is any chance of your staff being unaware of the safe way of doing something, then you will need to make it clear in your document. Finally, always ensure that any control measures you identify and follow are decided upon the principle of "so far as is reasonably practicable".

Note. The list of potential hazards is not exhaustive. However, for your risk assessment to be considered suitable and sufficient in the eyes of the law it must accurately reflect the "significant" hazards found when using electric welding equipment.

RISK ASSESSMENT - SAFE USE OF ELECTRIC WELDING EQUIPMENT

ACTIVITY	PERSON AT RISK	SIGNIFICANT HAZARDS	RISK*			RISK CONTROL MEASURES	RESIDUAL RISK**		
			L	S	DR		L	S	DR
Use of electric welding equipment	Other people in the vicinity	Failure to erect barriers etc. may lead to eye injuries from the UV light	3	3	9	• Welders to ensure that barriers are erected around the welding area to protect passers by and others in the area from the UV light.	3	1	3
As above	Users, other people in the vicinity	Failure to observe fire precautions may lead to fires causing injuries	3	5	15	• Welders to ensure that the work area is kept clear of combustible material. • Welders to ensure that a fire extinguisher is readily available in the work area and is to hand. • At least one staff member to remain in the welding area for one hour after welding has ceased to ensure that there is no residual fire risk from smouldering materials.	3	2	6
As above	Users	Failure to wear the correct personal protective equipment (PPE) may lead to personal injuries from the welding process	3	5	15	• All welders to use appropriate PPE (welding face mask or goggles, fire retardant overalls and gloves etc.) before commencing work. • All welding PPE to be maintained in a good serviceable condition.	3	2	6
As above	As above	Failure to continue to wear eye protection until work is complete may lead to eye damage	3	4	12	• All welders to ensure that their eye protection is in place before they strike an arc. • All welders to ensure that their eye protection remains in place until after the arc has extinguished.	3	2	6

RISK ASSESSMENT - SAFE USE OF ELECTRIC WELDING EQUIPMENT

ACTIVITY	PERSON AT RISK	SIGNIFICANT HAZARDS	RISK*			RISK CONTROL MEASURES	RESIDUAL RISK**		
			L	S	DR		L	S	DR
Use of electric welding equipment	Users	Failure to observe that equipment insulation is in good order and that earthing arrangements are satisfactory may lead to electric shock	3	4	12	• Users to ensure that all insulation and earthing arrangements are maintained to a high standard, regularly checked, and defective equipment taken out of service until repaired. • Users to ensure that any faulty equipment is reported immediately to their supervisor/manager.	3	2	6
As above	As above	The securing of an earth lead to pipework containing flammable liquids or gases may lead to fire and serious personal injuries	3	5	15	• Users to ensure that all earth leads are never connected to electrical conduits or to pipes containing flammable liquids or gases.	3	3	9
As above	As above	Working in damp conditions may lead to electric shock	4	4	16	• Users to ensure that arc welding is never carried out in damp or wet surroundings, and the operator's hands and clothing is kept dry.	3	3	9

RISK ASSESSMENT - SAFE USE OF ELECTRIC WELDING EQUIPMENT

ACTIVITY	PERSON AT RISK	SIGNIFICANT HAZARDS	RISK*			RISK CONTROL MEASURES	RESIDUAL RISK**		
			L	S	DR		L	S	DR
Use of electric welding equipment	Users	Uninsulated parts of the electrode holder may come into contact with an earth leading to a flash that could result in eye damage	4	4	16	• Users to ensure that they prevent the uninsulated part of the electrode holder from coming into contact with the earthed workpiece or the earthing clamp, whilst the current is switched on.	3	3	9
As above	As above	Faulty welding equipment may lead to electric shock etc.	3	3	9	• Electric arc welding equipment to be subject to inspection and test, as required by the Electricity at Work Regulations and the results to be kept on file.	3	1	3

LIKELIHOOD (L) = Frequent (5) - Probable (4) - Occasional (3) - Improbable (2) - Remote (1)
SEVERITY (S) = Catastrophic (5) - Major (4) - Reportable (3) - Serious (2) - Minor (1)
Degree of Risk (DR) = LIKELIHOOD x SEVERITY
* Numbers used are for illustrative purposes only.
** Residual risk is the level of risk that remains after suitable and sufficient control measures are introduced.

Signed originator.. Job title..

Date completed.. Date for revision..

Safe use of garden equipment

Failure to observe the correct operating procedures when using garden equipment may lead to accidents resulting in serious personal injuries.

MANAGING THE RISKS

To help you to identify the hazards associated with the operation of garden equipment and the appropriate ways of controlling them, use our example **Risk Assessment - Safe Use of Garden Equipment.** It covers the generic hazards associated with this type of activity and suggests control measures to reduce risks to an acceptable level. You should ensure that your document only addresses "significant" hazards, i.e. any that could, and more importantly are likely to, cause an accident or injury.

MAKE YOUR INSTRUCTIONS CLEAR

Don't include activities in your document that simply don't need to be there. Work to the principle that if there is any chance of your staff being unaware of the safe way of doing something, then you will need to make it clear in your document. Finally, always ensure that any control measures you identify and follow are decided upon the principle of "so far as is reasonably practicable".

Note. The list of potential hazards is not exhaustive. However, for your risk assessment to be considered suitable and sufficient in the eyes of the law it must accurately reflect the "significant" hazards in your workplace when using garden equipment.

Note. This risk assessment deals with the generic risks associated with basic garden equipment, including hand-operated lawnmowers, hedge trimmers, and strimmers. It does not refer to other types of mower or tractor, or specialised equipment such as chainsaws, rotavators etc. Such equipment should be the subject of a separate risk assessment.

RISK ASSESSMENT - SAFE USE OF GARDEN EQUIPMENT

ACTIVITY	PERSON AT RISK	SIGNIFICANT HAZARDS	RISK*			RISK CONTROL MEASURES	RESIDUAL RISK**		
			L	S	DR		L	S	DR
Using lawn mowers - general	Staff	Failure to ensure lawned areas are free from stones and other obstacles may lead to physical injuries	3	3	9	• Lawned areas to be checked for loose stones and other obstacles before mowing starts. • Staff to be issued with personal protective equipment, such as eye protection, gloves etc., which is to be worn at all times during mowing operations. • Staff to be made aware of the dangers of coming into contact with dog faeces. • Staff to watch out for electrical services etc. laid across the ground.	3	1	3
As above	As above	Operating mowers without guards fitted may lead to physical injuries	3	3	9	• Staff to ensure that all guards fitted to mowers are in good condition prior to work starting. • Staff to ensure that all guards are in position prior to work starting.	3	1	3
As above	As above	Contact between mower blades and the feet may lead to lacerations	3	4	12	• All staff to be supplied with protective footwear to prevent injuries to feet. • Supervisors to check that footwear is being worn at all times when using mowers.	3	2	6
As above	As above	The incorrect method of working on sloping or wet ground may lead to slips, trips and falls resulting in physical injuries	3	3	9	• Mowing on sloping ground to be carried out across the slope. • Protective footwear to have suitable soles to give good grip on wet grass etc.	3	1	3

RISK ASSESSMENT - SAFE USE OF GARDEN EQUIPMENT

ACTIVITY	PERSON AT RISK	SIGNIFICANT HAZARDS	RISK*			RISK CONTROL MEASURES	RESIDUAL RISK**		
			L	S	DR		L	S	DR
Using lawn mowers - general	Staff	Excessive noise and vibration may lead to hearing impairment and/or vibration white finger	3	4	12	• All mowers to be assessed for noise and vibration levels on an annual basis. • Manufacturer's data to be used when purchasing new machines to enable the choice of equipment with the lowest levels of noise and vibration. • Machines to be regularly maintained to reduce noise and vibration levels.	3	2	6
Use of an electric mower	Staff	Failure to disconnect the electrical supply before working on the blades may lead to serious cuts etc.	3	4	12	• Staff to ensure that the electrical supply has been disconnected before attempting to work on the blades. • Staff to ensure the blades have stopped rotating before attempting to work on them. • Only trained staff to be allowed to carry out mower maintenance.	3	2	6
As above	As above	Failure to manage the electrical supply to the mower may lead to fatal electrical shocks	3	5	15	• All electric operated mowers to be powered from an RCD to protect against electric shock. • Staff to be aware of the position of power cables and flexes during the mower operation.	3	3	9
Use of a petrol driven mower	As above	Failure to store fuel safely may lead to fires or explosions resulting in loss of life	3	5	15	• Petrol to only be kept in approved containers. • Petrol to be stored in a nominated safe place. • Only sufficient petrol for one day's work to be carried.	3	2	6
As above	As above	Failure to refuel the mower correctly may lead to fire or explosions resulting in loss of life	3	5	15	• Engines to be switched off before refuelling. • Engine and exhaust to be allowed to cool down before refuelling. • Refuelling to take place in designated areas only. • Only trained staff to refuel mowers	3	2	6

RISK ASSESSMENT - SAFE USE OF GARDEN EQUIPMENT

ACTIVITY	PERSON AT RISK	SIGNIFICANT HAZARDS	RISK*			RISK CONTROL MEASURES	RESIDUAL RISK**		
			L	S	DR		L	S	DR
Use of electric hedge trimmers	Staff	Failure to disconnect the electrical supply before working on the blades may lead to serious cuts etc.	3	4	12	• Staff to ensure that the electrical supply has been disconnected before attempting to work on the blades. • Staff to ensure the blades have stopped moving before attempting to work on them. • Only trained staff to be allowed to carry out hedge trimmer work and maintenance.	3	2	6
As above	As above	Failure to manage the electrical supply to the hedge trimmer may lead to fatal electrical shocks	3	5	15	• All electric-operated hedge trimmers to be powered from an RCD to protect against electric shock. • Staff to be aware of the position of power cables and flexes during the trimming operation.	3	3	9
As above	As above	Falls when using a hedge trimmer at height may lead to serious physical injuries	3	4	12	• Staff to use extension handles for trimming above head height. • Hedge trimmers not to be used from stepladders.	3	2	6
Use of petrol driven hedge trimmers	As above	Failure to store fuel safely may lead to fires or explosions resulting in loss of life	3	5	15	• Petrol to only be kept in approved containers. • Petrol to be stored in a nominated safe place. • Only sufficient petrol for one day's work to be carried.	3	2	6
As above	As above	Failure to refuel the mower correctly may lead to fire or explosions resulting in loss of life	3	5	15	• Engines to be switched off before refuelling. • Engine and exhaust to be allowed to cool down before refuelling. • Refuelling to take place in designated areas only. • Only trained staff to refuel hedge trimmers.	3	2	6

RISK ASSESSMENT - SAFE USE OF GARDEN EQUIPMENT

ACTIVITY	PERSON AT RISK	SIGNIFICANT HAZARDS	RISK*			RISK CONTROL MEASURES	RESIDUAL RISK**		
			L	S	DR		L	S	DR
Use of electric strimmers	Staff	Failure to disconnect the electrical supply before working on the blades may lead to serious cuts etc.	3	3	9	• Staff to ensure that the electrical supply has been disconnected before attempting to work on the blades. • Staff to ensure the motor has stopped rotating before attempting to replace blades etc. • Only trained staff to be allowed to carry out strimmer maintenance.	3	2	6
As above	As above	Failure to manage the electrical supply to the strimmer may lead to fatal electrical shocks	3	5	15	• All electric-operated strimmers to be powered from an RCD to protect against electric shock. • Staff to be aware of the position of power cables and flexes during the strimming operation.	3	3	9
Use of petrol driven strimmers	As above	Failure to store fuel safely may lead to fires or explosions resulting in loss of life	3	5	15	• Petrol to only be kept in approved containers. • Petrol to be stored in a nominated safe place. • Only sufficient petrol for one day's work to be carried.	3	3	9

RISK ASSESSMENT - SAFE USE OF GARDEN EQUIPMENT

ACTIVITY	PERSON AT RISK	SIGNIFICANT HAZARDS	RISK*			RISK CONTROL MEASURES	RESIDUAL RISK**		
			L	S	DR		L	S	DR
Use of petrol driven strimmers	Staff	Failure to refuel the strimmer correctly may lead to fire or explosions resulting in loss of life	3	5	15	• Engines to be switched off before refuelling. • Engine and exhaust to be allowed to cool down before refuelling. • Refuelling to take place in designated areas only. • Only trained staff to refuel strimmers.	3	2	6

LIKELIHOOD (L) = Frequent (5) - Probable (4) - Occasional (3) - Improbable (2) - Remote (1)
SEVERITY (S) = Catastrophic (5) - Major (4) - Reportable (3) - Serious (2) - Minor (1)
Degree of Risk (DR) = LIKELIHOOD x SEVERITY
*Numbers used are for illustrative purposes only.
** Residual risk is the level of risk that remains after suitable and sufficient control measures are introduced.

Signed originator... Job title..

Date completed... Date for revision..

Safe use of hand tools

Accidents caused by the incorrect use of hand tools are common in the workplace.

Managing the risks

To help you identify the hazards and appropriate ways of controlling them, use our example **Risk Assessment - Safe use of Hand Tools** document. It covers the generic hazards found with the use of most of the common types of hand tools and suggests control measures to reduce risks to an acceptable level.

You should ensure that your document only addresses "significant" hazards, i.e. any that could and more importantly are likely to, cause an accident or injury.

Make your instructions clear

Work to the principle that if there is any chance of your staff being unaware of the safe way of using particular hand tools, then you will need to make it clear on your document. Finally, always ensure any control measures you identify and follow only go so far "as is reasonably practicable".

Note. The list of potential hazards is not exhaustive, as you will know your workplace and the hand tools your staff use, better than we do. However, for your risk assessment to be considered suitable and sufficient in the eyes of the law it must accurately reflect the "significant" hazards found in your workplace.

RISK ASSESSMENT - SAFE USE OF HAND TOOLS

ACTIVITY	PERSON AT RISK	SIGNIFICANT HAZARDS	RISK*			RISK CONTROL MEASURES	RESIDUAL RISK**		
			L	S	DR		L	S	DR
Using a screwdriver	Operative	Choosing the wrong type may cause tool to slip leading to piercing injuries	3	4	12	• The correct type of screwdriver for the job to be chosen, e.g. using a Posidrive head for a Posidrive screw as opposed to a Philips head. • Longer length screwdrivers require less force to tighten or slacken screws, which will require less physical effort and thus giving more control.	2	1	2
Using hand tools during electrical work	As above	Using un-insulated hand tools on electrical work may lead to electrical shock or burn injuries	4	4	16	• Only insulated tools to be used when working on electrical equipment. • Insulation must be in good condition. • Mains supplies to be turned off before commencing work where possible. • (Note - a separate risk assessment and a safe system of work will be required for live working.)	3	2	6
Using pliers or gripping tools	As above	Using an incorrect or damaged tool may cause it to slip leading to cuts and bruising	3	3	9	• The correct type and size of tool for the task in hand to be chosen. • Pliers and gripping tools to be maintained in a good condition.	3	1	3
Sawing metal, wood etc.	As above	Using incorrect type of saw can lead to saw jamming or jumping out causing cuts to hand/wrists	4	3	12	• The correct saw for the task in hand to be used, e.g. hacksaw for metal cutting, wood saw for woodcutting etc. • A good cutting technique to be used, i.e. even, steady strokes with even pressure.	3	1	3

RISK ASSESSMENT - SAFE USE OF HAND TOOLS

ACTIVITY	PERSON AT RISK	SIGNIFICANT HAZARDS	RISK*			RISK CONTROL MEASURES	RESIDUAL RISK**		
			L	S	DR		L	S	DR
Sawing metal, wood etc.	Operative	Using saws with damaged blades such as missing or broken teeth can lead to the saw jumping out of workpiece and causing cuts to hands/wrists	4	3	12	• The condition of saw blades to be checked before use. • Saws with damaged blades should not be used. • Periodic hand tool checks to be introduced and faulty or damaged items to be replaced.	3	1	3
Using electric saws	As above	Missing guards or damaged blades, cables etc. on electrical saws can lead to injuries to hands, eyes etc.	4	5	20	• Guards to always be fitted and in position. • Blades to be checked for type and damage before use. • The condition of electrical cables to be checked and taken out of service if damaged. • Eye protection to be worn.	3	1	3
Using a hammer	As above	Use of hammers with loose heads can lead to impact injuries	4	2	8	• Hammer shafts to be in good condition and hammer head is securely fixed. • If damaged do not use and replace.	2	1	2
Using files	As above	Using files with damaged handles can lead to cuts to hand	4	2	8	• Always ensure that file handles are secure to the tang. • Files with damaged handles to be replaced.	2	1	2
Using chisels	As above	Incorrect use and storage of chisels or using damaged chisels can lead to personal injuries	4	4	16	• Always use the correct chisel for the job in hand. • Chisels to be well maintained. • Don't strike wood chisels with a hammer (other than types designed for this activity, e.g. mortise chisels). • Keep chisel ends protected when not in use. • Eye protection to be worn where necessary.	2	1	2

RISK ASSESSMENT - SAFE USE OF HAND TOOLS

ACTIVITY	PERSON AT RISK	SIGNIFICANT HAZARDS	RISK*			RISK CONTROL MEASURES	RESIDUAL RISK**		
			L	S	DR		L	S	DR
Using spanners	Operative	Using the wrong sized spanner can lead to it slipping causing hand/ arm injuries	4	3	12	• The correct size and type of spanner to be used; ring spanners will give a better grip than open-ended ones. • Make sure any nuts or bolts have good faces that will allow the spanner to grip. • Don't use excessive pressure and use a releasing agent if nut or bolt is rusted.	3	1	3
Using knives	As above	Incorrect use of knife can lead to cuts to hands/ arms	4	4	16	• Consider using a safer, alternative tool to carry out the task, e.g. a cable stripper, scissors etc. • Cut away from the body and the hand should be kept behind the blade. • Kevlar type gloves to be worn to prevent cuts.	3	1	3

LIKELIHOOD (L) = Frequent (5) - Probable (4) - Occasional (3) - Improbable (2) - Remote (1)
SEVERITY (S) = Catastrophic (5) - Major (4) - Reportable (3) - Serious (2) - Minor (1)
Degree of Risk (DR) = LIKELIHOOD x SEVERITY
* Numbers used are for illustrative purposes only.
** Residual risk is the level of risk that remains after suitable and sufficient control measures are introduced.

Signed originator.. Job title..

Date completed.. Date for revision..

Safe use of lathes

Using a lathe incorrectly can present risks to both the user and other people in the work area. This could lead to a serious accident resulting in significant personal injuries.

MANAGING THE RISKS

To help you identify the hazards associated with using a lathe and the appropriate ways of controlling them, use our example **Risk Assessment - Safe Use of Lathes**. It covers the generic hazards associated with this type of activity and suggests control measures to reduce risks to an acceptable level. You should ensure that your document only addresses "significant" hazards, i.e. any that could, and more importantly are likely to, cause an accident or injury.

Note. This risk assessment only deals with the generic risks associated with lathe use. As lathes differ in both size, type and function you should ensure that relevant training is undertaken before the lathe is used for the first time. Any risks identified by the manufacturer in operating manuals etc. should also be taken into consideration.

MAKE YOUR INSTRUCTIONS CLEAR

Don't include activities in your document that simply don't need to be there. Work to the principle that if there is any chance of your staff being unaware of the safe way of doing something, then you will need to make it clear in your document. Finally, always ensure that any control measures you identify and follow are decided upon the principle of "so far as is reasonably practicable".

Note. The list of potential hazards is not exhaustive. However, for your risk assessment to be considered suitable and sufficient in the eyes of the law it must accurately reflect the "significant" hazards found when using lathes.

RISK ASSESSMENT - SAFE USE OF LATHES

ACTIVITY	PERSON AT RISK	SIGNIFICANT HAZARDS	RISK*			RISK CONTROL MEASURES	RESIDUAL RISK**		
			L	S	DR		L	S	DR
Pre-work check of lathe safety equipment	User	Lathes in an unsafe working condition may lead to personal injury	3	3	9	• All safety equipment on a lathe to be checked to ensure it's in working order.	3	1	3
Work area	As above	Obstructed work areas may lead to slips and trips resulting in personal injury	3	3	9	• Users to ensure that all work areas surrounding the lathe are kept clear of obstructions likely to cause slips and trips. • All work areas surrounding lathes to have a hatched area marked out in yellow to be kept clear at all times.	3	1	3
Use of a lathe	As above	Failure to ensure chuck guard is in place during use may lead to personal injuries caused by physical contact with the chuck	3	4	12	• All chuck guards to be electrically interlocked so that the lathe cannot be operated until the guard is in place. • All interlocks to be of a fail-safe type so that they cannot be over-ridden by users.	2	2	4
As above	As above	Faulty emergency stop buttons or kick bars may lead to the inability to stop the lathe in an emergency causing serious injuries to the user	3	5	15	• All emergency stop buttons and kick bars to be checked before the lathe is used. • All users to report any faulty emergency stop mechanisms to their supervisor/manager.	3	2	6

RISK ASSESSMENT - SAFE USE OF LATHES

ACTIVITY	PERSON AT RISK	SIGNIFICANT HAZARDS	RISK*			RISK CONTROL MEASURES	RESIDUAL RISK**		
			L	S	DR		L	S	DR
Use of a lathe	User	Adjusting belts to alter speeds with the lathe in motion may lead to trapped hands and personal injuries	3	4	12	• Users to ensure that where speed adjustment is carried out by altering drive belts, this will only be done whilst the lathe is stationary. • Belt guards to be fitted with an electric interlock so that the lathe stops if the guard is removed.	3	1	3
As above	User, other people	Failure to clamp work piece securely in the chuck may lead to it coming loose and causing personal injuries to users or others	3	4	12	• Users to ensure that all work pieces are securely held in chucks, between chucks and tail stocks or secured to face plates. • All chuck keys and allen keys etc. to be removed before the lathe is turned on.	3	2	6
As above	As above	Failure to wear close fitting clothing etc. may lead to entanglement and serious personal injuries	3	5	15	• All users to wear close fitting clothing or coveralls that fasten up to the neck. • Long hair to be tied back and/or covered by suitable headwear. • Cloths or rags used to clean up cutting oil to be used only when the lathe is stationary.	3	2	6
As above	As above	Failure to wear eye protection may lead to swarf etc. damaging the eyes	3	4	12	• Users to wear eye protection before the lathe is switched on.	3	1	3

RISK ASSESSMENT - SAFE USE OF LATHES

ACTIVITY	PERSON AT RISK	SIGNIFICANT HAZARDS	RISK*			RISK CONTROL MEASURES	RESIDUAL RISK**		
			L	S	DR		L	S	DR
Use of a lathe	User, other people	Cleaning up swarf by hand may lead to cuts to hands	3	2	6	• Users to clean up swarf using a dustpan and brush.	3	1	3
As above	As above	Failure to wash hands after contact with cutting fluids may lead to skin conditions such as dermatitis etc.	3	3	9	• Users to ensure that cutting fluids are allowed to drain into the reservoir before removing work pieces. • Users to wash their hands after making contact with cutting fluids.	3	1	3
As above	As above	Failure to wait until the lathe has stopped before attempting to remove work pieces may lead to entanglement and injuries to hands	3	4	12	• Users to ensure that the lathe is switched off and has finished rotating before removing work pieces.	3	2	6

LIKELIHOOD (L) = Frequent (5) - Probable (4) - Occasional (3) - Improbable (2) - Remote (1)
SEVERITY (S) = Catastrophic (5) - Major (4) - Reportable (3) - Serious (2) - Minor (1)
Degree of Risk (DR) = LIKELIHOOD x SEVERITY
* Numbers used are for illustrative purposes only. ** Residual risk is the level of risk that remains after suitable and sufficient control measures are introduced.

Signed originator.. Job title..

Date completed... Date for revision..

Safe use of oxy-acetylene welding and cutting equipment

If oxy-acetylene welding and cutting equipment is used incorrectly, this could lead to accidents and fires resulting in serious personal injuries.

Managing the risks

To help you to identify the hazards associated with using oxy-acetylene welding and cutting equipment and the appropriate ways of controlling them, use our example **Risk Assessment - Safe Use of Oxy-acetylene Welding and Cutting Equipment**. It covers the generic hazards associated with this type of activity and suggests control measures to reduce risks to an acceptable level. You should ensure that your document only addresses "significant" hazards, i.e. any that could, and more importantly are likely to cause an accident or injury.

Make your instructions clear

Don't include activities in your document that simply don't need to be there. Work to the principle that if there is any chance of your staff being unaware of the safe way of doing something, then you will need to make it clear in your document. Finally, always ensure that any control measures you identify and follow are decided upon the principle of "so far as is reasonably practicable".

Note. The list of potential hazards is not exhaustive and each place of use will be different. However, for your risk assessment to be considered suitable and sufficient in the eyes of the law it must accurately reflect the "significant" hazards found when using oxy-acetylene welding and cutting equipment in your workplace.

RISK ASSESSMENT - SAFE USE OF OXY-ACETYLENE WELDING AND CUTTING EQUIPMENT

ACTIVITY	PERSON AT RISK	SIGNIFICANT HAZARDS	RISK*			RISK CONTROL MEASURES	RESIDUAL RISK**		
			L	S	DR		L	S	DR
Use of oxy-acetylene welding and cutting equipment	Users, other people in the vicinity	Fire resulting from the incorrect use of the oxy-acetylene equipment, e.g. regulator pressures set wrongly, incorrect torch light up or shutdown causing a backfire or flashback	3	5	15	• Only trained staff to use oxy-acetylene welding and cutting equipment. • All users to carry out a pre-check of the equipment before use. • Pressure gauges to be set as required by the work to be carried out. • Staff to be trained in the action to take in the event of a fire. • Emergency fire fighting equipment to be provided in the vicinity of the work.	3	2	6
As above	As above	The use of faulty equipment may cause fires etc. resulting in loss of life/property damage	3	5	15	• Only equipment procured from a reputable supplier to be used. • Only purpose-designed equipment to be used for the work being carried out. • Staff to be instructed to withdraw faulty items from use and to arrange repair or replacement.	3	2	6
As above	As above	Presence of flammable materials in the work area may lead to accidental ignition resulting in fires	3	5	15	• Staff to ensure that the work area is kept clear of flammable materials. Where this is not possible, staff to use fire screens and/or fire blankets to prevent contact from sparks etc. • Where necessary, staff to work to a permit-to-work system.	3	2	6

RISK ASSESSMENT - SAFE USE OF OXY-ACETYLENE WELDING AND CUTTING EQUIPMENT

ACTIVITY	PERSON AT RISK	SIGNIFICANT HAZARDS	RISK*			RISK CONTROL MEASURES	RESIDUAL RISK**		
			L	S	DR		L	S	DR
Use of oxy-acetylene welding and cutting equipment	Users, other people in the vicinity	Hose damage during welding/cutting operations or leakage due to aging may lead to fuel release and fire causing burn injuries	3	5	15	• Staff to ensure that all gas hoses are in good condition prior to work starting. • Staff to ensure that all gas hoses are positioned out of the line of fire from the torch flame and metal spatter.	3	2	6
As above	As above	Residual hot spots or smouldering material after welding/cutting may lead to fires causing burn injuries	3	5	15	• Staff to carry out post-work inspections to verify no hot spots remain or that any smouldering materials are extinguished.	3	2	6
As above	As above	Oxy-acetylene equipment not fitted with flashback arrestors may lead to gas cylinder fires and explosion with a danger to life and property	3	5	15	• Staff to ensure that flashback arrestors are fitted to both the oxygen and acetylene pressure regulators before use. • Where disposable flashback arrestors are used, staff to replace them after a flashback or back fire. • Resettable flashback arrestors will be set in accordance with the manufacturer's instructions. • Resettable flashback arrestors will be replaced at the manufacturer's recommended intervals. • All causes of flashbacks will be investigated to identify any damage or faults to equipment before the equipment is re-used.	3	2	6

RISK ASSESSMENT - SAFE USE OF OXY-ACETYLENE WELDING AND CUTTING EQUIPMENT

ACTIVITY	PERSON AT RISK	SIGNIFICANT HAZARDS	RISK*			RISK CONTROL MEASURES	RESIDUAL RISK**		
			L	S	DR		L	S	DR
Use of oxy-acetylene welding and cutting equipment	Users, other people in the vicinity	Fires may result if the equipment is not fitted with non return valves or hose check valves	3	4	12	• Non return valves/hose check valves to be fitted on the hose ends connecting to the blowpipe or torch.	3	2	6
As above	As above	Incorrect choice, fitting or setting of pressure regulators may lead to fires	3	5	15	• Only the correct type of pressure regulators to be fitted to gas cylinders. • Staff to be trained in the fitting of regulators and the connecting of hoses etc. • Damaged regulators to be taken out of service and repaired/replaced. • Regulators to be set to the correct working pressures. • Regulators to be changed every five years. • Regulators to have their adjusting screw "backed-off" when not in use.	3	3	9
As above	As above	The use of grease or thread tape when fitting regulators may lead to fires resulting from oxygen/hydrocarbon reaction	3	5	15	• Staff to ensure that grease or thread tape is never applied to screw threads on pressure regulator connections.	2	3	6

RISK ASSESSMENT - SAFE USE OF OXY-ACETYLENE WELDING AND CUTTING EQUIPMENT

ACTIVITY	PERSON AT RISK	SIGNIFICANT HAZARDS	RISK*			RISK CONTROL MEASURES	RESIDUAL RISK**		
			L	S	DR		L	S	DR
Use of oxy-acetylene welding and cutting equipment	Users, other people in the vicinity	Failure to close gas cylinder valves when empty may lead to the risk of accidental fires resulting in property damage etc.	3	5	15	• Staff to ensure that gas cylinder valves are in the closed position when returning them to the cylinder storage area. • Staff to treat all empty cylinders in the same manner as full ones because of the presence of residual gas. • All empty gas cylinders to be returned to the manufacturer on a regular basis. Storage to be kept to a minimum.	3	2	6
As above	As above	Failure to wear the correct types of personal protective equipment (PPE) during welding/ cutting operations may lead to personal injuries, loss of sight etc.	4	4	16	• Staff to be provided with the correct types of PPE for the work that they are carrying out. • Supervisors to ensure that PPE is worn by all staff members during welding/cutting operations. • Staff to report faulty items of PPE and secure immediate replacements.	3	2	6

LIKELIHOOD (L) = Frequent (5) - Probable (4) - Occasional (3) - Improbable (2) - Remote (1)
SEVERITY (S) = Catastrophic (5) - Major (4) - Reportable (3) - Serious (2) - Minor (1)
Degree of Risk (DR) = LIKELIHOOD x SEVERITY
* Numbers used are for illustrative purposes only. ** Residual risk is the level of risk that remains after suitable and sufficient control measures are introduced.

Signed originator.. Job title..

Date completed... Date for revision..

Safe use of pillar and bench mounted drills

If pillar or bench mounted drilling machines are used incorrectly, this could lead to accidents involving serious personal injuries.

Managing the risks

To help you to identify the hazards associated with using pillar or bench mounted drilling machines and the appropriate ways of controlling them, use our example **Risk Assessment - Safe Use of Pillar and Bench Mounted Drills**. It covers the generic hazards associated with this type of activity and suggests control measures to reduce risks to an acceptable level. You should ensure that your document only addresses "significant" hazards, i.e. any that could, and more importantly are likely to, cause an accident or injury.

Make your instructions clear

Don't include activities in your document that simply don't need to be there. Work to the principle that if there is any chance of your staff being unaware of the safe way of doing something, then you will need to make it clear in your document. Finally, always ensure that any control measures you identify and follow are decided upon the principle of "so far as is reasonably practicable".

Note. The list of potential hazards is not exhaustive. However, for your risk assessment to be considered suitable and sufficient in the eyes of the law it must accurately reflect the "significant" hazards found when using pillar or bench mounted drilling machines.

Note. This risk assessment only deals with the generic risks associated with pillar and bench mounted drilling machines. As such equipment differs in size, type and function, you should ensure that relevant training is undertaken before the equipment is used for the first time. Any risks identified by the manufacturer in operating manuals etc. should also be taken into consideration.

RISK ASSESSMENT - SAFE USE OF PILLAR AND BENCH MOUNTED DRILLS

ACTIVITY	PERSON AT RISK	SIGNIFICANT HAZARDS	RISK*			RISK CONTROL MEASURES	RESIDUAL RISK**		
			L	S	DR		L	S	DR
Use of drilling machine	User	Failure to keep work area clear of obstructions may lead to slips, trips and falls resulting in personal injuries	3	3	9	• All floor areas around drilling machines to be kept free of obstructions. • Floor areas around pillar drills to have a marked hatched area to be kept clear at all times.	3	1	3
As above	As above	Attempts to adjust speed of belt-operated machines whilst the machine is running can lead to personal injuries	3	3	9	• All belt mechanisms to have an electrically interlocked guard so that the machine stops when the guard is opened. • All interlocks to be of a type that is incapable of being over-ridden. • All users to be trained on how to change drill-operating speeds safely.	3	1	3
As above	As above	Failure to secure the drilling bit in the chuck may lead to it flying out causing personal injuries	3	4	12	• Users to ensure that all drill bits are secure in the chuck. • All chuck keys to be removed after tightening of the drill bit. • All chuck guards to be in place before the machine is switched on.	3	2	6
As above	As above	Failure to secure work piece may lead to personal injuries if the drill bit jams	3	3	9	• All small work pieces to be held securely in a hand vice. • Larger work pieces to be secured using clamps which will secure the work piece to the machine's work table.	3	1	3

RISK ASSESSMENT - SAFE USE OF PILLAR AND BENCH MOUNTED DRILLS

ACTIVITY	PERSON AT RISK	SIGNIFICANT HAZARDS	RISK*			RISK CONTROL MEASURES	RESIDUAL RISK**		
			L	S	DR		L	S	DR
Use of drilling machine	User	Failure to ensure that bench drills are securely mounted may lead to them moving, causing personal injury	3	3	9	• All bench operated drilling machines to be fixed to the bench surface by bolts so that they remain stable.	2	1	2
As above	As above	Failure to protect the eyes during drilling may lead to eye injuries from swarf	3	4	12	• All drills to be fitted with a chuck guard which will be adjusted so that it gives maximum protection against swarf. • All users to wear eye protection when using drilling machines.	2	2	4
As above	As above	Failure to stop the drill in an emergency may lead to personal injuries	3	4	12	• All drilling machines to be fitted with an emergency stop mechanism - either by the use of a button or a foot operated emergency stop. • All emergency stop mechanisms to be checked before the drill is used and any faults to be reported.	3	2	6

LIKELIHOOD (L) = Frequent (5) - Probable (4) - Occasional (3) - Improbable (2) - Remote (1)
SEVERITY (S) = Catastrophic (5) - Major (4) - Reportable (3) - Serious (2) - Minor (1)
Degree of Risk (DR) = LIKELIHOOD x SEVERITY
* Numbers used are for illustrative purposes only. ** Residual risk is the level of risk that remains after suitable and sufficient control measures are introduced.

Signed originator.. Job title..

Date completed.. Date for revision...

Safe use of pressure washers

If pressure washers are used incorrectly, then this could lead to accidents involving serious electric shock resulting in personal injuries or death.

Managing the risks

To help you to identify the hazards associated with using pressure washers and the appropriate ways of controlling them, use our example **Risk Assessment - Safe Use of Pressure Washers**. It covers the generic hazards associated with this type of activity and suggests control measures to reduce risks to an acceptable level. You should ensure that your document only addresses "significant" hazards, i.e. any that could, and more importantly are likely to, cause an accident or injury.

Make your instructions clear

Don't include activities in your document that simply don't need to be there. Work to the principle that if there is any chance of your staff being unaware of the safe way of doing something, then you will need to make it clear in your document. Finally, always ensure that any control measures you identify and follow are decided upon the principle of "so far as is reasonably practicable".

Note. The list of potential hazards is not exhaustive. However, for your risk assessment to be considered suitable and sufficient in the eyes of the law it must accurately reflect the "significant" hazards found when using pressure washers.

Note. This risk assessment only deals with the generic risks associated with power washers. As such equipment differs in size, type and function you should ensure that relevant training is undertaken before the equipment is used. Any risks identified by the manufacturer in operating manuals etc. should also be taken into consideration.

RISK ASSESSMENT - SAFE USE OF PRESSURE WASHERS

ACTIVITY	PERSON AT RISK	SIGNIFICANT HAZARDS	RISK*			RISK CONTROL MEASURES	RESIDUAL RISK**		
			L	S	DR		L	S	DR
Connecting the electrical supply to a pressure washer	User	Failure to use a residual current device (RCD) may lead to the user receiving a fatal electric shock or burns	4	5	20	• An RCD to be fitted at the point that the washer connects to the mains socket outlet. • RCDs to be tested each time before the washer is used.	3	3	9
Checking of all electrical supply cables to a pressure washer	As above	Failure to check for damaged cables may lead to the user receiving a fatal electric shock or burns	4	4	16	• All associated cables to be examined for damage such as cuts or abrasions before the washer is used and on a daily basis. • All damaged cables to be replaced before the washer is used. • Cables to be routed away from the work area to prevent them getting caught, pulled or driven over.	3	2	6
Inspection of connecting plugs	As above	A damaged plug may lead to the user receiving a fatal electric shock or burns	4	4	16	• All connecting plugs to be examined by the user before the washer is put into service and at least on a daily basis. • All flexes must be secured by the plug top cable-retaining device and no conductors must be outside of the plug top. • Only fuses of the correct capacity to be fitted to the plug.	3	2	6
Inspection of electrical parts of the washer	As above	Exposure to live electrical parts of the washer may lead to the user receiving a fatal electric shock or burns	4	5	20	• All electrical parts of the washer to be inspected before use and at least on a daily basis to ensure that all protective covers etc. are in good condition and free from cracks or breakages. • All faults to be reported and the equipment taken out of service until repaired.	3	3	9

RISK ASSESSMENT - SAFE USE OF PRESSURE WASHERS

ACTIVITY	PERSON AT RISK	SIGNIFICANT HAZARDS	RISK*			RISK CONTROL MEASURES	RESIDUAL RISK**		
			L	S	DR		L	S	DR
Washer maintenance	User, others	Failure to maintain pressure washers may lead to the user receiving a fatal electric shock or burns	3	5	15	• All pressure washers to be inspected each time before use. • All pressure washers to have their insulation and earthing tested by a competent person every three months and more often if the washer is used on a construction site or similar workplace. • A log book to be prepared to indicate such tests have been carried out.	2	2	4
Use of the washer	As above	Coming into contact with high pressure water jets could cause skin damage etc.	4	4	16	• All staff to be trained in the correct use of the pressure washer. • All staff to wear the necessary personal protective equipment (PPE). • Supervisors to regularly check pressure washer is being used correctly.	3	2	6
As above	User	The misuse of washing solutions may lead to skin conditions	4	3	12	• Users to only mix washing solutions in accordance with manufacturers' instructions. • User to wear PPE (suitable gloves etc.) when mixing washing solutions.	3	1	3

LIKELIHOOD (L) = Frequent (5) - Probable (4) - Occasional (3) - Improbable (2) - Remote (1)
SEVERITY (S) = Catastrophic (5) - Major (4) - Reportable (3) - Serious (2) - Minor (1) Degree of Risk (DR) = LIKELIHOOD x SEVERITY
* Numbers used are for illustrative purposes only. ** Residual risk is the level of risk that remains after suitable and sufficient control measures are introduced.

Signed originator.. Job title..

Date completed.. Date for revision..

Using pedestrian-operated pallet trucks

Using pedestrian-operated pallet trucks may present risks to staff which, left unmanaged, could cause accidents and potentially put you on the wrong side of the law.

Managing the risks

To help you identify the hazards associated with using this type of equipment and the appropriate ways of controlling the risks, use our example **Risk Assessment - Using Pedestrian-Operated Pallet Trucks**. It covers the generic hazards associated with this type of activity and suggests control measures to reduce risks to an acceptable level.

You should ensure that your document only addresses "significant" hazards, i.e. any that could, and more importantly are likely to, cause an accident or injury.

Make your instructions clear

Don't include activities in your document that simply don't need to be there. Work to the principle that if there is any chance of your staff being unaware of the safe way of doing something, then you will need to make it clear in your document. Finally, always ensure that any control measures you identify and follow only go so far "as is reasonably practicable".

Note. The list of potential hazards is not exhaustive. However, for your risk assessment to be considered suitable and sufficient in the eyes of the law it must accurately reflect the "significant" hazards found when using this type of equipment.

RISK ASSESSMENT - USING PEDESTRIAN-OPERATED PALLET TRUCKS

ACTIVITY	PERSON AT RISK	SIGNIFICANT HAZARDS	RISK*			RISK CONTROL MEASURES	RESIDUAL RISK**		
			L	S	DR		L	S	DR
Using a standard hydraulic pallet truck	Staff	Failure to use the truck properly may lead to a loaded truck running out of control and overturning with the falling load causing physical injuries	3	3	9	• All staff that operate standard pallet trucks to be trained in their use. • Staff to control the truck movement when it is loaded by using the drive and parking brake mechanisms. • Staff to ensure that the forks are suitably placed under the pallet to be moved.	2	2	4
As above	As above	Overloading a pallet truck may result in the truck failing causing the load to fall resulting in physical injuries	3	3	9	• All pallet trucks to be marked with their safe working load. • All staff to be trained to understand the loading limitations of each truck.	2	2	4
As above	As above	Pallet truck may be run over the user's foot if the user is distracted, resulting in foot injuries	3	3	9	• All staff who use pallet trucks to wear protective footwear. • All staff to receive a toolbox talk on the use of pallet trucks and the need to observe safe working practices.	2	2	4
As above	As above	Mechanical failure of a pallet truck may lead to the load falling resulting in physical injuries	4	3	12	• All pallet trucks to be regularly inspected for wear. • All pallet trucks to be regularly maintained including topping up of hydraulic fluids.	2	2	4

RISK ASSESSMENT - USING PEDESTRIAN-OPERATED PALLET TRUCKS

ACTIVITY	PERSON AT RISK	SIGNIFICANT HAZARDS	RISK*			RISK CONTROL MEASURES	RESIDUAL RISK**		
			L	S	DR		L	S	DR
Improper use of a pallet truck	Staff	Horseplay involving pallet trucks may lead to physical injuries from slips and falls	4	3	12	• All users of pallet trucks to receive training in their use. • Supervisors to regularly check for the misuse of pallet trucks. • Disciplinary action to be taken against staff who misuse pallet trucks.	2	2	4

LIKELIHOOD (L) = Frequent (5) - Probable (4) - Occasional (3) - Improbable (2) - Remote (1)
SEVERITY (S) = Catastrophic (5) - Major (4) - Reportable (3) - Serious (2) - Minor (1)
Degree of Risk (DR) = LIKELIHOOD x SEVERITY
* Numbers used are for illustrative purposes only.
** Residual risk is the level of risk that remains after suitable and sufficient control measures are introduced.

Signed originator.. Job title..

Date completed... Date for revision..

Young persons working in an engineering environment

Under health and safety law a "young person" is defined as anyone under 18 years. Employers are duty-bound to make a specific risk assessment for under-18s that takes particular account of their inexperience, lack of awareness of risks and immaturity. If work tasks for young persons are not managed correctly, then this could lead to accidents involving serious personal injuries.

Managing the risks

To help you to identify the hazards associated with young persons working in an engineering environment and the appropriate ways of controlling them, use our example **Risk Assessment - Young Persons Working in an Engineering Environment**. It covers the generic hazards associated with these types of activity and suggests control measures to reduce risks to an acceptable level. You should ensure your document only addresses "significant" hazards, i.e. any that could, and more importantly are likely to, cause an accident or injury.

Make your instructions clear

Don't include activities in your document that simply don't need to be there. Work to the principle that if there is any chance of young people in your employment being unaware of the safe way of doing something, then you will need to make it clear in your document. Finally, always ensure that any control measures you identify and follow are decided upon the principle of "so far as is reasonably practicable".

Note. Risk assessments for young people should be carried out before they commence work in accordance with the **Health & Safety (Young Persons) Regulations 1997**.

Note. For your risk assessment to be considered suitable and sufficient in the eyes of the law it must accurately reflect the "significant" hazards found in your workplace that may affect young people in your employment. Our risk assessment only deals with the generic risks associated with common activities in the engineering environment and the list of potential hazards is not exhaustive.

Note. Where young people carry out activities that are already covered by your risk assessment process, it may only be necessary to modify existing assessments to take their age and lack of experience into account.

RISK ASSESSMENT - YOUNG PERSONS WORKING IN AN ENGINEERING ENVIRONMENT

ACTIVITY	PERSON AT RISK	SIGNIFICANT HAZARDS	RISK*			RISK CONTROL MEASURES	RESIDUAL RISK**		
			L	S	DR		L	S	DR
Getting around in general	Young people	Slips, trips and falls may lead to personal injuries as a result of soiled floor surfaces	4	3	12	• Young persons to be instructed to report all spillages or soiled floor surfaces, damaged floor coverings etc. to their supervisor. • Young persons to be instructed to be aware of tripping hazards and to report these to their supervisor.	3	2	6
Manual handling	As above	Incorrect manual handling may lead to physical injuries such as back strain, arm injuries etc.	4	4	16	• Manual handling operations to be eliminated where possible. • Induction training for young persons to include an awareness of the company's manual handling procedures and safe lifting practices. • All young persons to receive instruction on manual handling techniques. • Young persons to be made aware of the need to use mechanical aids etc. and to be instructed in their use. • Young persons to be instructed to seek assistance when needed during manual handling operations.	3	2	6
Use of mechanical tools and equipment	As above	Misuse of tools and equipment may lead to physical injuries	3	4	12	• Young persons to only use mechanical equipment such as grinders, drills and compressed air tools etc. under the supervision of trained staff. • Where guards on tools and equipment are provided they are to be kept in good repair and supervisors to check this before allowing young persons to operate such items of equipment. • Young persons to be instructed to report faulty equipment to their supervisor. • Personal protective equipment to be provided and worn for those operations requiring it.	3	2	6

RISK ASSESSMENT - YOUNG PERSONS WORKING IN AN ENGINEERING ENVIRONMENT

ACTIVITY	PERSON AT RISK	SIGNIFICANT HAZARDS	RISK*			RISK CONTROL MEASURES	RESIDUAL RISK**		
			L	S	DR		L	S	DR
Using electrical equipment	Young persons	The use of faulty electrical appliances may lead to electric shock resulting in burns or death	3	5	15	• All portable electrical equipment used by young persons to be regularly PAT tested and carry a label indicating this. • Young persons to be instructed not to use equipment without a PAT tested label. • Young persons to be instructed to take faulty items out of service and report the fact to their supervisor.	3	2	6
Use of handtools	As above	The incorrect use of hand tools may lead to injuries to hands, eyes etc.	3	4	12	• Young persons to only use hand tools that they have been trained to use unless under supervision. • All hand tools to be kept in good repair and young persons to report faulty items to their supervisor.	3	2	6
Action in the event of a fire	As above	Failure to carry out the required actions in the event of a fire may lead to serious injuries or loss of life	3	5	15	• Young persons to be trained in the action to be taken in the event of a fire. • Young persons to take part in regular fire drills to familiarise themselves with the sound of the fire alarm and the actions to be taken when leaving the building and reporting to their assembly point.	3	2	6

LIKELIHOOD (L) = Frequent (5) - Probable (4) - Occasional (3) - Improbable (2) - Remote (1)
SEVERITY (S) = Catastrophic (5) - Major (4) - Reportable (3) - Serious (2) - Minor (1) Degree of Risk (DR) = LIKELIHOOD x SEVERITY
* Numbers used are for illustrative purposes only. ** Residual risk is the level of risk that remains after suitable and sufficient control measures are introduced.

Signed originator.. Job title...

Date completed.. Date for revision...

Office

Display screen equipment (DSE) - workstation assessment

Whenever a new employee starts working with you or there are significant changes to the working environment, you should undertake a workstation assessment. You should also do this if an employee reports health problems they think are related to using the workstation.

DSE QUESTIONNAIRE

The HSE recommends that users are fully involved in the assessment of their workstation under the **Health and Safety (Display Screen Equipment) Regulations 1992**. In fact, it recommends that you start with a questionnaire for staff to complete their own initial assessment. Our **Display Screen Equipment (DSE) - Workstation Assessment** is designed so that you can issue it to each employee and then review the results. The employee works through a series of questions which they can answer with a simple tick.

A MONEY-SAVING DEVICE

Unfortunately, many questionnaires are poorly drafted with the result that you end up offering employees a variety of items which they don't need, such as wrist rests and document holders. With this in mind, our questionnaire is worded so that items are only made available to employees if they are really necessary. Following an introductory section that explains how to use the form, it's broken down into a series of eight sub-sections. These ask questions on the different elements, such as the set up of the workstation, the chair and the work environment.

DISPLAY SCREEN EQUIPMENT - WORKSTATION ASSESSMENT

Instructions to the workstation user:

Please read each question fully and answer by ticking either the "Yes", "No" or "Not Applicable" (N/A) box. If you wish to add any additional information, put a tick in the "Further Information" (FI) box. Then use the Further Information section at the end of the document to record your points. Completed assessments should be sent to .... (insert name).

	Y	N	N/A	FI
A. Software				
• Have you received adequate training in how to use the software?	❑	❑	❑	❑
• Do you find that the software is suitable for the tasks you perform?	❑	❑	❑	❑
B. Posture				
• Can you sit comfortably and easily change your posture?	❑	❑	❑	❑
• Can you adjust your equipment, e.g. your chair, monitor and desk, so that you can achieve a comfortable viewing position?	❑	❑	❑	❑
• Do all of the functions of the chair work, e.g. seat height, back tilt and height, swivel?	❑	❑	❑	❑
• Have you adjusted your chair to support the small of your back?	❑	❑	❑	❑
• Can your chair be positioned close enough to your desk, i.e. the arms don't prevent this?	❑	❑	❑	❑
• Is the chair stable, e.g. on a five-star base?	❑	❑	❑	❑
• Are your feet either flat on the floor, or on a footrest, so that there is not too much pressure from the seat on the backs of the legs?	❑	❑	❑	❑
• When keying, are the forearms approximately level with the keyboard, and the elbow approximately at a right angle?	❑	❑	❑	❑
• If necessary, is there a document holder available? (Select N/A if not needed)	❑	❑	❑	❑
C. Workstation/work surface				
• Is your workstation arranged so that you can work comfortably?	❑	❑	❑	❑
• Is there space in front of the keyboard to support your hands and forearms?	❑	❑	❑	❑
• Do you find your desk large enough for all the necessary equipment and paperwork?	❑	❑	❑	❑
• Is your workstation, including the area beneath, free from obstructions and hazards?	❑	❑	❑	❑

	Y	N	N/A	FI
D. Display screen				
• Is the information displayed on the screen clear and easy to read?	❑	❑	❑	❑
• Is the text size comfortable to read?	❑	❑	❑	❑
• Is the screen clean?	❑	❑	❑	❑
• Can the contrast and brightness be adjusted? (Please check)	❑	❑	❑	❑
• Does the screen swivel and tilt?	❑	❑	❑	❑
• Is the image on the screen stable and flicker free?	❑	❑	❑	❑
• Is the screen at the correct height, i.e. is the top of the screen at eye level?	❑	❑	❑	❑
E. Keyboard				
• Is the keyboard fully functional and the characters clearly readable?	❑	❑	❑	❑
• Is the keyboard separate from the screen?	❑	❑	❑	❑
• Can the tilt of the keyboard be adjusted to suit your needs?	❑	❑	❑	❑
• Do you feel have good keying technique? i.e. not hitting the keys too hard, not resting the wrists whilst typing	❑	❑	❑	❑
F. Mouse, tracker-ball or other pointing device (the pointer)				
• Is the mouse or other pointer fully functional?	❑	❑	❑	❑
• Is the mouse or other pointer positioned close to you?	❑	❑	❑	❑
• Do you have a relaxed arm, straight wrist and do you avoid overreaching when using the pointer?	❑	❑	❑	❑
• Is your forearm and wrist supported whilst using it, e.g. by the desk?	❑	❑	❑	❑
• Does the device work smoothly at a pace which suits you?	❑	❑	❑	❑
• Do you know how to adjust the software settings for speed and accuracy of the pointer?	❑	❑	❑	❑
• If you are left-handed, has the mouse been adjusted to "right-click" for most functions?	❑	❑	❑	❑
G. Environment				
• Is the lighting suitable, e.g. not too bright or too dim?	❑	❑	❑	❑
• Is the screen free from glare and reflections?	❑	❑	❑	❑
• Is the desk surface free from irritating sources of reflection or glare?	❑	❑	❑	❑
• If necessary, are there adjustable window coverings provided?	❑	❑	❑	❑

	Y	N	N/A	FI
• Does the temperature and humidity seem comfortable?	❑	❑	❑	❑
• Are levels of noise comfortable?	❑	❑	❑	❑

H. Eyesight and health

	Y	N	N/A	FI
• Are you aware that you are entitled to a free eye test if you use display screen equipment as a regular and habitual part of your work? (Ask your manager for details.)	❑	❑	❑	❑
• Has this questionnaire covered everything to do with the use of your workstation? If no, please detail any other problems, e.g. discomfort, ill- health, in the section below.	❑	❑	❑	❑
• Have you read the HSE's information leaflet "Working with VDUs"? http://www.hse.gov.uk/pubns/indg36.pdf	❑	❑	❑	❑

Further information (use additional sheet if required):

Name:	Workstation location:
Signature:	Date assessment completed:

For office use only

Manager's name:	
List of actions to be taken:	Sign and date when completed:
Note. Refer to a trained DSE assessor or occupational health specialist if the user is experiencing health problems which appear to be associated with use of the workstation.	

Managing slips, trips and falls in an office environment

Slips, trips and falls can present a major hazard in an office environment. If the risks are not managed properly, this could lead to accidents resulting in personal injuries.

Managing the risks

To help you to identify the hazards associated with getting around in an office environment and the appropriate ways of controlling them, use our example **Risk Assessment - Managing Slips, Trips and Falls in an Office Environment.** It covers the generic hazards and suggests control measures to reduce risks to an acceptable level. You should ensure that your document only addresses "significant" hazards, i.e. any that could, and more importantly are likely to, cause an accident or injury.

Make your instructions clear

Don't include activities in your document that simply don't need to be there. Work to the principle that if there is any chance of your staff being unaware of the safe way of doing something, then you will need to make it clear in your document. Finally, always ensure that any control measures you identify and follow are decided upon the principle of "so far as is reasonably practicable".

Note. The list of potential hazards is not exhaustive. However, for your risk assessment to be considered suitable and sufficient in the eyes of the law it must accurately reflect the "significant" hazards found when getting around in an office environment.

Note. This risk assessment only deals with the generic risks associated with an office environment. Your assessment should deal with the situation within your own offices and any specific risks need to be assessed.

RISK ASSESSMENT - MANAGING SLIPS, TRIPS AND FALLS IN AN OFFICE ENVIRONMENT

ACTIVITY	PERSON AT RISK	SIGNIFICANT HAZARDS	RISK*			RISK CONTROL MEASURES	RESIDUAL RISK**		
			L	S	DR		L	S	DR
Getting around in general	Staff	Failure to ensure floor coverings are in good condition may lead to slips, trips and falls resulting in physical injuries	3	3	9	• All floor coverings to be checked regularly by the office manager/ supervisor. • Faulty floor coverings to be repaired or replaced at the first opportunity. • Staff to be encouraged to report faulty floor coverings. • Temporary signs etc. to be placed to identify hazards until repair/ replacement can take place.	3	1	3
As above	As above	Failure to prevent trailing cables may lead to slips, trips and falls resulting in physical injuries	3	3	9	• All trailing cables to be secured so that they do not present a tripping hazard. • The use of extension leads to be kept to a minimum and when used, cables to be kept away from areas where staff walk.	3	1	3
As above	As above	Failure to clean up spillages may lead to slips and falls resulting in physical injuries	3	3	9	• Staff to be instructed to clean up all spillages immediately after they occur. • Facilities to be made available (mop, bucket etc.) to allow spillages to be cleaned up.	3	1	3
As above	As above	Failure to ensure adequate lighting on staircases etc. may lead to falls resulting in serious injuries	3	4	12	• Lighting on staircases etc. to be regularly checked by supervisors/ managers. • Staff to be encouraged to report faulty lighting fittings to their supervisor/ manager. • Faulty lighting fittings to be repaired.	3	2	6

RISK ASSESSMENT - MANAGING SLIPS, TRIPS AND FALLS IN AN OFFICE ENVIRONMENT

ACTIVITY	PERSON AT RISK	SIGNIFICANT HAZARDS	RISK*			RISK CONTROL MEASURES	RESIDUAL RISK**		
			L	S	DR		L	S	DR
Getting around in general	Staff	Failure to warn staff when floor cleaning takes place may lead to slips and falls resulting in physical injuries	3	3	9	• Cleaning staff to display warning signs of floor cleaning. • Warning signs to be removed only after the floor area is dry. • Where possible, floor cleaning to take place out of hours.	3	1	3
As above	As above	The storage of goods etc. in walkways may lead to tripping hazards resulting in physical injuries from falls	3	3	9	• All goods etc. to be stored in their proper place. • No obstacles to be placed in corridors, staircases, etc.	3	1	3
As above	As above	Use of external access doors may cause wet floors in bad weather leading to slips and falls resulting in physical injuries	3	3	9	• Doormats to be provided at entrance doors to allow people to dry their footwear. • Doormats to be changed regularly. • Cleaning staff to regularly clean up any excess water etc. from entrance areas during bad weather.	3	1	3
As above	As above	Failure of staff to store personal belongings, such as bags etc., away from walkways may lead to trips and falls resulting in physical injuries	3	3	9	• Staff to store personal belongings away from walkways etc. • Where cloakroom facilities are provided, these are to be used.	3	1	3

LIKELIHOOD (L) = Frequent (5) - Probable (4) - Occasional (3) - Improbable (2) - Remote (1)
SEVERITY (S) = Catastrophic (5) - Major (4) - Reportable (3) - Serious (2) - Minor (1) Degree of Risk (DR) = LIKELIHOOD x SEVERITY
* Numbers used are for illustrative purposes only. ** Residual risk is the level of risk that remains after suitable and sufficient control measures are introduced.

Signed originator.. Job title..

Date completed.. Date for revision..

Occupational stress

The HSE defines stress as "the adverse reaction people have to excessive pressure or other types of demand placed on them". So to ensure this doesn't happen you need to identify what could cause this, and then take steps to minimise the risks.

MANAGING THE RISKS

To help you identify the hazards and appropriate ways of controlling them, use our example **Risk Assessment - Occupational Stress** document. It covers the generic causes of stress at work and suggests control measures to reduce the risks to an acceptable level.

You should ensure that your document only addresses "significant" causes of stress. Research has shown that feeling stressed at work is not confined to particular occupations or levels within organisations. Workers with management responsibilities also show stress symptoms. Different individuals may react differently to stress and the same person may react differently to stress at different times.

Always ensure any control measures you identify and follow only go so far "as is reasonably practicable".

Note. The list of potential stress hazards is not exhaustive. For your risk assessment to be considered suitable and sufficient in the eyes of the law it must accurately reflect the "significant" stress related hazards found in your workplace.

RISK ASSESSMENT - OCCUPATIONAL STRESS

ACTIVITY	PERSON AT RISK	SIGNIFICANT HAZARDS	RISK*			RISK CONTROL MEASURES	RESIDUAL RISK**		
			L	S	DR		L	S	DR
Workload demands	Staff member	Workloads are excessive leading to long hours causing ill-health	4	4	16	• Individual workloads to be planned and regularly reviewed. • Staff to be encouraged to discuss workloads with their manager if becoming excessive and they feel unable to cope. • Consideration given to change of duties, either temporarily or permanently.	3	2	6
Personal control over individual workload	As above	Staff having no say in how their workload is managed can lead to them being unable to cope and to sick leave	4	4	16	• Staff to be given an input into the control over their daily tasks, e.g. task variation, flexible meal breaks, work rotation. • Staff to be encouraged to discuss work situations with their manager to alleviate problems. • Managers to regularly review workloads.	3	2	6
Work/life balance	As above	Lack of flexibility in workload can lead to excessive working hours conflicting with private life leading to illness, sick leave etc.	4	3	12	• All staff work commitments to be regularly reviewed and working hours monitored. • Managers to be aware of staff showing extremes of fatigue etc. where it is relative to long working hours. • Staff to be encouraged to raise such issues with their manager.	3	2	6
Personal relationships at work	As above	Poor personal relationships can lead to bullying, harassment etc.	4	4	16	• Managers to be trained to recognise and to adopt a positive attitude towards unacceptable behaviour. • Staff to be encouraged to raise such issues with their manager either in private or at regular team meetings.	3	2	6

RISK ASSESSMENT - OCCUPATIONAL STRESS

ACTIVITY	PERSON AT RISK	SIGNIFICANT HAZARDS	RISK*			RISK CONTROL MEASURES	RESIDUAL RISK**		
			L	S	DR		L	S	DR
Working to incorrect, or without a, job description	Staff member	Staff who do not have or understand their job description may feel isolated, leading to increased stress levels	4	2	8	• All staff to have a current job description and for it to be reviewed on a regular basis with both staff and manager input. • Staff to be given regular feedback on their work performance. • Where necessary, managers to assess the provision of job related training and personal development.	1	2	2
Managing change in the workplace	As above	Staff not kept informed of company changes may feel that their job is in jeopardy leading to increased levels of stress and possibly sick leave	4	2	8	• Change to be managed effectively to prevent it leading to uncertainty and insecurity. • Staff to be kept informed and involved with company or work changes. • Regular team meetings to be held to allow an exchange of information.	1	2	2

LIKELIHOOD (L) = Frequent (5) - Probable (4) - Occasional (3) - Improbable (2) - Remote (1)
SEVERITY (S) = Catastrophic (5) - Major (4) - Reportable (3) - Serious (2) - Minor (1)
Degree of Risk (DR) = LIKELIHOOD x SEVERITY
* Numbers used are for illustrative purposes only. ** Residual risk is the level of risk that remains after suitable and sufficient control measures are introduced

Signed originator.. Job title..

Date completed.. Date for revision..

Office

Although an office is traditionally a low-risk environment, a few hazards do exist. Use our document to identify and manage them.

Managing the risks

As such, we have followed its approach in our example **Risk Assessment - Office** document. It covers the generic hazards found in an office environment and suggests control measures to reduce risks to an acceptable level.

Slips, trips and falls

These risks appear in all workplaces and often result in serious accidents. So you need to ensure that you've implemented appropriate precautions, such as good housekeeping, undamaged flooring, e.g. no loose carpet etc., cables and wires are contained and walkways are kept free from rubbish and not used as storage areas (this is also important when assessing fire-related risks).

Manual handling

Although moving objects etc. aren't often core office activities, it is something that happens in all offices - be it boxes of paper, rubbish bins, water bottles etc. So, you need to ensure that your staff have had basic instruction in lifting techniques. If many items are being moved, make sure you have trolleys or other suitable lifting equipment.

Display screen use

Using a PC for a prolonged period is known to have certain risks associated with it. These include various musculoskeletal problems, eyestrain etc. Identify any general hazards on your office risk assessment and then pick up any specific workstation issues with a display screen risk assessment.

Note. The list of potential hazards is not exhaustive. For your risk assessment to be considered suitable and sufficient in the eyes of the law it must accurately reflect the "significant" hazards associated with your workplace.

RISK ASSESSMENT - OFFICE

ACTIVITY	PERSON AT RISK	SIGNIFICANT HAZARDS	RISK*			RISK CONTROL MEASURES	RESIDUAL RISK**		
			L	S	DR		L	S	DR
Moving around the office	All staff and visitors	Slips, trips and falls as a result of trailing cables, damaged floor coverings, spillages etc.	4	3	12	• Good housekeeping, including cleaning up spillages. • Trailing cables to be managed. • Floors and walkways to be maintained to a satisfactory standard. • Supervisors to regularly check all office areas to ensure standards are maintained.	3	1	3
Manual handling	All staff	Incorrect lifting and handling techniques, lifting excessive or awkward weights etc. leading to back pain	3	3	9	• Mechanical aids to be used where possible, e.g. trolleys. • Loads to be broken down into smaller sizes and weights, e.g. split boxes of copying paper into individual packs. • Manual handling training to be considered for staff if lifting becomes a regular task.	3	1	3
Using Display Screen Equipment (DSE)	Staff who work using computer screens	Staff may suffer from upper limb disorders (RSI), back pain and headaches from incorrect usage, posture, glare etc.	4	2	8	• Seating and screens to be adjustable. • Staff to be educated in setting up their workstations. • Either staff to complete a self-assessment of their workstations or a full DSE assessment should be completed. • Supervisors to carry out regular checks to ensure correct posture. • The screen to be placed between overhead light fittings. Also, direct sunlight should not be allowed to shine on the screen.	3	1	3
Using electrical equipment, e.g. copiers, printers, kettle, toaster etc.	All staff	Staff could be affected by electrical shock or burns through incorrect usage or poorly maintained equipment	4	4	16	• Office equipment to be regularly checked. • PAT testing to be arranged for specific items. • Staff to be encouraged to report faulty equipment to supervisor. • No personal electrical equipment to be brought into the workplace.	3	2	6
Action in the event of fire	All staff and visitors	Staff and visitors trapped in the office may suffer from smoke inhalation, burns and possibly death	3	5	15	• Action in the event of fire to be communicated to all staff. • Evacuation procedures to be placed around the building at strategic points. • Regular fire alarm checks to be carried out. • Fire drill to be regularly carried out. • Fire extinguishers to be provided and maintained on a contract. • Fire exits to be kept clear of obstructions. • Supervisor to walk the building on a regular basis to check that fire instructions are being complied with.	2	2	4

RISK ASSESSMENT - OFFICE

ACTIVITY	PERSON AT RISK	SIGNIFICANT HAZARDS	RISK*			RISK CONTROL MEASURES	RESIDUAL RISK**		
			L	S	DR		L	S	DR
Work causing stress	All staff	Staff could be affected by excessive pressure due to work demands, working long hours, etc. causing anxiety and stress	3	2	6	• Work loads to be agreed with staff and managed in conjunction with supervisor. • Staff to be encouraged to raise issues that affect their well-being at team meetings etc. • A company stress policy to be developed and staff to be kept informed.	3	1	3
Working in the office with poor hygiene and welfare conditions	As above	Poor hygiene and welfare conditions leading to staff discomfort or illness	3	2	6	• Toilets to have a regular supply of hot and cold water complete with soap and towels. • Kitchen area to have a safe supply of mains cold water. • Toilets and kitchen area to be regularly cleaned. • Facilities in the kitchen area provided to store food, drink and kitchen utensils etc.	2	1	2
Working in the office in uncomfortable conditions	As above	General discomfort	3	1	3	• Office temperatures to be monitored and heating provided when cold. • Windows to be openable for ventilation. • No overcrowding.	2	1	2
Use of cleaning chemicals	Cleaner, possibly staff	Skin irritation or eye injury from bleach or acid-based product	3	3	9	• Safer alternatives to be considered. • To be used in accordance with manufacturers' instructions. • Rubber gloves to be used. • Splashes or spillages to be avoided. • Staff to be aware of first aid action.	3	1	3

LIKELIHOOD (L) = Frequent (5) - Probable (4) - Occasional (3) - Improbable (2) - Remote (1)
SEVERITY (S) = Catastrophic (5) - Major (4) - Reportable (3) - Serious (2) - Minor (1) Degree of Risk (DR) = LIKELIHOOD x SEVERITY
* Numbers used are for illustrative purposes only. ** Residual risk is the level of risk that remains after suitable and sufficient control measures are introduced.

Signed originator.. Job title...

Date completed... Date for revision..

Office cleaning

Office cleaning is not usually considered to be hazardous and tends to be overlooked when carrying out the risk assessment process - but it shouldn't be. So use our document to identify what could be dangerous, and what you can do to minimise the risks.

A CLEAN OFFICE

Cleaning is not without its risks, especially if it involves the use of machines, such as floor scrubbers or chemicals etc. Hazards left unmanaged could cause accidents and potentially put you on the wrong side of the law.

To ensure this doesn't happen, you should complete a risk assessment for cleaning in offices, which identifies all "significant" hazards and appropriate "reasonable" ways of reducing risks to an acceptable level.

MANAGING THE RISKS

To help you identify the hazards associated with cleaning in the office environment and the appropriate ways of controlling them, use our example **Risk Assessment - Office Cleaning**. It covers the generic hazards associated with this type of activity and suggests control measures to reduce risks to an acceptable level.

Note. If you use a contract cleaning company, ensure that their staff have been briefed on their risk assessments and ask to see copies.

You should ensure that your document only addresses "significant" hazards, i.e. any that could, and more importantly are likely to, cause an accident or injury

MAKE YOUR INSTRUCTIONS CLEAR

Don't include activities in your document that simply don't need to be there. Work to the principle that if there is any chance of your staff being unaware of the safe way of doing something, then you will need to make it clear in your document. Finally, always ensure that any control measures you identify and follow only go so far "as is reasonably practicable".

Note. The list of potential hazards is not exhaustive. However, for your risk assessment to be considered suitable and sufficient in the eyes of the law it must accurately reflect the "significant" hazards found in your workplace.

RISK ASSESSMENT - OFFICE CLEANING

ACTIVITY	PERSON AT RISK	SIGNIFICANT HAZARDS	RISK*			RISK CONTROL MEASURES	RESIDUAL RISK**		
			L	S	DR		L	S	DR
Getting about in general	Cleaners, staff, etc.	Cleaners and others risk injuries such as fractures and bruising if they trip over objects or slip on spillages or wet floors and fall	4	3	12	• Warning cones or boards to be placed in areas where floor cleaning is in progress. • Good housekeeping to be maintained so that tripping hazards are removed. • Cleaners to use socket outlets nearest to them to minimise trailing leads. • Cleaners to wear suitable footwear to prevent slipping on wet floors.	3	1	3
Contact with chemical substances	Cleaners	Cleaners may suffer skin conditions or eye injury if they come into contact with bleach or other cleaning materials	3	4	12	• All cleaning staff to be trained in the risks, use and storage of cleaning chemicals. • Consideration to be given to the use of non-hazardous cleaning agents where available. • Cleaning chemicals to be stored in a locked area. • Rubber gloves and long handled mops to be provided to minimise hand contact with chemicals. • Where necessary a COSHH assessment to be carried out for any hazardous cleaning agents.	3	2	6
Lifting heavy objects such as rubbish bags, cleaning machines etc.	As above	Cleaners may suffer a back injury when lifting heavy objects incorrectly or awkwardly	4	3	12	• Cleaners to be instructed not to lift heavy rubbish bags and to break the loads down to lessen the weight. • Cleaning machines will be of a wheeled type only to allow ease of movement. For multi-storey buildings, machines to be provided on each floor. • Cleaners to be instructed to ask for assistance when moving heavy boxes etc.	3	2	6
Using cleaning machines	As above	Cleaners and others risk injuries if machine is used improperly	4	3	12	• Correct type of machine to be provided for the work. • Cleaners to be trained in safe machine use. • Machine to be kept maintained and in good condition.	3	1	3

RISK ASSESSMENT - OFFICE CLEANING

ACTIVITY	PERSON AT RISK	SIGNIFICANT HAZARDS	RISK*			RISK CONTROL MEASURES	RESIDUAL RISK**		
			L	S	DR		L	S	DR
Using electrically operated cleaning equipment	Cleaners	Risk of electric shock if machine is faulty or in poor condition	3	4	12	• Register to be maintained of all electrically operated cleaning equipment. • All equipment to be regularly checked by a competent person. • Cleaners to be instructed to place faulty equipment out of use until it is repaired. • Cleaners to carry out basic checks of all leads, plug tops etc. and will report all faulty items.	3	2	6
Lone working	As above	Cleaners working out of hours and alone may suffer sudden illness or have an accident and be unable to summon help	3	3	9	• Cleaners to sign in and out at the reception desk. If not signed out at the end of their shift security staff to look for them.	2	2	4

LIKELIHOOD (L) = Frequent (5) - Probable (4) - Occasional (3) - Improbable (2) - Remote (1)
SEVERITY (S) = Catastrophic (5) - Major (4) - Reportable (3) - Serious (2) - Minor (1)
Degree of Risk (DR) = LIKELIHOOD x SEVERITY
* Numbers used are for illustrative purposes only.
** Residual risk is the level of risk that remains after suitable and sufficient control measures are introduced.

Signed originator.. Job title...

Date completed... Date for revision...

Office storage

Storing items in offices, whether in cabinets, cupboards or on shelves in storage areas, can, if carried out incorrectly, lead to accidents involving personal injuries.

Managing the risks

To help you to identify the hazards associated with safe storage and the appropriate ways of controlling them, use our example **Risk Assessment - Office Storage**. It covers the generic hazards associated with this type of activity and suggests control measures to reduce risks to an acceptable level. You should ensure that your document only addresses "significant" hazards, i.e. any that could and, more importantly are likely to, cause an accident or injury.

Make your instructions clear

Don't include activities in your document that simply don't need to be there. Work to the principle that if there is any chance of your staff being unaware of the safe way of storing items in the office, then you will need to make it clear in your document. Finally, always ensure that any control measures you identify and follow are decided upon the principle of "so far as is reasonably practicable". The list of potential hazards is not exhaustive.

Note. This risk assessment only deals with the generic risks associated with office storage. For your risk assessment to be considered suitable and sufficient in the eyes of the law it must accurately reflect the "significant" hazards found in your office storage areas.

RISK ASSESSMENT - OFFICE STORAGE

ACTIVITY	PERSON AT RISK	SIGNIFICANT HAZARDS	RISK*			RISK CONTROL MEASURES	RESIDUAL RISK**		
			L	S	DR		L	S	DR
Accessing storage at height	Staff	Use of incorrect access equipment may lead to falls causing personal injuries	3	4	12	• High-level storage to be restricted, as far as is reasonably practicable. • All staff to be instructed not to use makeshift access equipment such as chairs, stools etc. • Access equipment such as suitable stepladders, podium steps and/or kick stools will be provided for high-level access.	3	2	6
As above	As above	Use of faulty access equipment may lead to falls causing personal injuries	3	4	12	• Staff to be instructed to visually check all access equipment before use. • All faulty access equipment to be taken out of service and be repaired or replaced. • Regular formal inspections of access equipment to be made at least every six-months and the results recorded. Faulty items to be removed from use and be repaired or replaced.	3	2	6
As above	As above	Inappropriate use of access equipment (overreaching, stretching etc.) may lead to falls causing personal injuries	3	4	12	• Use of access equipment to be restricted to those trained and competent in use. • Staff to be instructed that maximum working height must not be exceeded. • Staff to ensure that they re-position steps rather than overstretch. • Floor surfaces to be suitable to use (firm and even surface) • Staff using access equipment to wear appropriate footwear (low heeled, non-slip soles). • Access equipment to be securely stored when not in use to avoid unauthorised use.	3	2	6

RISK ASSESSMENT - OFFICE STORAGE

ACTIVITY	PERSON AT RISK	SIGNIFICANT HAZARDS	RISK*			RISK CONTROL MEASURES	RESIDUAL RISK**		
			L	S	DR		L	S	DR
Storage - general	Staff	Manual handling of unstable or unwieldy loads may lead to falls causing personal injuries including back injuries etc.	3	4	12	• Staff to ensure that shelves etc. are not overloaded. • Storage to be organised so that heavy/bulky items are stored at lower levels. • Frequently used items to be stored at easily accessible locations. • Staff to be trained in handling and lifting techniques. • Sack trucks, trolleys etc. to be provided for moving heavy items.	3	2	6
As above	As above	Insecure shelving or cabinets etc. may lead to falls causing personal injuries	3	3	9	• All shelving to be checked regularly to ensure that its fixings and brackets etc. are secure. • Staff to report insecure items to their manager who will take the necessary remedial action. • Tall, freestanding cupboards and cabinets to be secured to either the walls or the floor to prevent overturning.	3	1	3

LIKELIHOOD (L) = Frequent (5) - Probable (4) - Occasional (3) - Improbable (2) - Remote (1)
SEVERITY (S) = Catastrophic (5) - Major (4) - Reportable (3) - Serious (2) - Minor (1)
Degree of Risk (DR) = LIKELIHOOD x SEVERITY
* Numbers used are for illustrative purposes only. ** Residual risk is the level of risk that remains after suitable and sufficient control measures are introduced.

Signed originator.. Job title...

Date completed.. Date for revision...

Transport

Access to vehicles whilst loading/unloading

Work that involves the loading or unloading of vehicles could cause fall injuries if the incorrect method of access or egress is used. To ensure that this doesn't happen, you should complete a risk assessment which identifies all "significant" hazards and appropriate "reasonable" ways of reducing such risks to an acceptable level.

Managing the risks

To help you identify the hazards associated with such activities and the appropriate ways of controlling them, use our example **Risk Assessment - Loading and Unloading Vehicles**. It covers the generic hazards associated with this type of activity and suggests control measures to reduce risks to an acceptable level. You can then add to this document items that are specific to your workplace and activities. You should ensure your document only addresses "significant" hazards, i.e. any that could, and more importantly are likely to, cause an accident or injury. **Note.** You should also refer to your existing risk assessments, including your working at height and traffic management risk assessment, which are associated with this type of work.

Make your instructions clear

Work to the principle that if there is any chance of your staff being unaware of the safe way of doing something, then you will need to make it clear in your document. Always ensure that any control measures you identify and follow are decided upon the principle of "so far as is reasonably practicable". **Note.** The list of potential hazards is not exhaustive. However, for your risk assessment to be considered suitable and sufficient in the eyes of the law it must accurately reflect the "significant" hazards found when loading and unloading vehicles

RISK ASSESSMENT - ACCESS TO VEHICLES WHILST LOADING/UNLOADING

ACTIVITY	PERSON AT RISK	SIGNIFICANT HAZARDS	RISK			RISK CONTROL MEASURES	RESIDUAL RISK*		
			L	S	DR		L	S	DR
Climbing into or out of vehicle cab	Driver, others	Incorrect method of access or egress may lead to falls resulting in physical injuries	4	3	12	• Staff who need to access the cab of a vehicle to use the steps provided. No climbing to be undertaken using wheels as a stepping point. Where handholds are provided to assist balance they should be used.	3	1	3
Access to rear of vans with tail lifts	As above	As above	4	3	12	• Controls for tail lifts to be mounted so that they can be accessed from ground level when first lowering the tailboard. • Handrails to be used on the sides of tail lifts to prevent falling when being raised or lowered with driver on board.	3	2	6
Access to the rear of vans with fixed or folding access steps	As above	As above	4	3	12	• Drivers to ensure steps are in position and are resting on a flat surface before accessing them. • Steps to be checked regularly for wear by drivers and supervisors. • Vehicles not to be driven with folding steps in the unfolded position.	3	1	3
Access to trailers and flat-back vehicles	As above	As above	4	4	16	• Loading to be carried out by mechanical means whenever possible, e.g. forklift trucks, thus avoiding the need for access. • Whenever possible, loading bays of the same height as the vehicle to be used to prevent climbing. • If rear of vehicle must be accessed, then a ladder or stepladder to be provided.	3	2	6

RISK ASSESSMENT - ACCESS TO VEHICLES WHILST LOADING/UNLOADING

ACTIVITY	PERSON AT RISK	SIGNIFICANT HAZARDS	RISK			RISK CONTROL MEASURES	RESIDUAL RISK*		
			L	S	DR		L	S	DR
Access to the tops of vehicles, e.g. tankers, HGVs	Drivers, others	Failing to access the vehicle in the correct manner may lead to falls from height causing serious physical injuries	4	4	16	• Access to the tops of vehicles to be by a well-constructed ladder. • Where such ladders are fixed to the vehicle, they will be properly fixed and adequately maintained. • Where walkways on vehicles are provided, they will be made of non-slip material such as grating etc. Where possible, permanent handrails to be provided. Alternatively, collapsible handrails to be used.	3	3	9
Access to vehicles when delivering to customers' premises	Drivers, others	As above	4	4	16	• Where access to vehicles for loading /unloading purposes is required at customers' premises, drivers will be issued with suitable steps or stepladders. • For heavy or unwieldy loads customers will be notified in advance of the need to make any additional equipment available and to maintain a clear and safe access area for all vehicles.	3	3	9

RISK ASSESSMENT - ACCESS TO VEHICLES WHILST LOADING/UNLOADING

ACTIVITY	PERSON AT RISK	SIGNIFICANT HAZARDS	RISK			RISK CONTROL MEASURES	RESIDUAL RISK*		
			L	S	DR		L	S	DR
Walking in vehicle loading and unloading areas	All staff	Slips, trips and falls caused by spillages of diesel fuel, oily surfaces etc. may cause physical injury	4	3	12	• Staff to be reminded regularly to report any unsafe ground conditions. • Temporary marking of spillages to be carried out with signs, cones etc. until they can be cleaned. • A dressing of sand to be applied to diesel or oil spillages prior to cleaning. • Supervisors to check areas for contaminated surfaces and arrange cleaning.	3	2	6

LIKELIHOOD (L) = Frequent (5) - Probable (4) - Occasional (3) - Improbable (2) - Remote (1)
SEVERITY (S) = Catastrophic (5) - Major (4) - Reportable (3) - Serious (2) - Minor (1) Degree of Risk (DR) = LIKELIHOOD x SEVERITY
* Numbers used are for illustrative purposes only. ** Residual risk is the level of risk that remains after suitable and sufficient control measures are introduced.

Signed originator.. Job title..

Date completed.. Date for revision...

Changing wheels on vehicles

Changing a wheel on a vehicle can present risks to drivers which, left unmanaged, can cause accidents and potentially put you on the wrong side of the law.

Managing the risks

To help you identify the hazards associated with changing wheels on vehicles and the appropriate ways of controlling them, use our example **Risk Assessment - Changing Wheels on Vehicles**. It covers the generic hazards associated with this type of activity and suggests control measures to reduce risks to an acceptable level.

Note. This risk assessment only deals with the changing of wheels on cars and light vehicles. For larger vehicles and heavy goods vehicles where specialist equipment may be needed, it is recommended that the services of a garage or tyre replacement company be utilised. Your company Driving at Work Policy should specify the method to be adopted. You should ensure your document only addresses "significant" hazards, i.e. any that could, and more importantly are likely to, cause an accident or injury.

Make your instructions clear

Don't include activities in your document that simply don't need to be there. Work to the principle that if there is any chance of your staff being unaware of the safe way of doing something, then you will need to make it clear in your document. Finally, always ensure that any control measures you identify and follow only go so far "as is reasonably practicable".

Note. The list of potential hazards is not exhaustive. However, for your risk assessment to be considered suitable and sufficient in the eyes of the law it must accurately reflect the "significant" hazards found when changing wheels on vehicles.

RISK ASSESSMENT - CHANGING WHEELS ON VEHICLES

ACTIVITY	PERSON AT RISK	SIGNIFICANT HAZARDS	RISK*			RISK CONTROL MEASURES	RESIDUAL RISK**		
			L	S	DR		L	S	DR
Preparing to change a wheel	Driver	Not ensuring vehicle is on hard standing may result in the failure of the vehicle jack	3	2	6	• Vehicle to be parked on a hard ground surface with handbrake applied, in gear and engine switched off before attempting to jack it up. • If this is not possible then a solid board should be used to rest the jack on and to spread the weight.	2	1	2
As above	As above	If the vehicle is parked by the roadside there may be a danger of being hit by other road users	3	4	12	• Vehicle to be parked away from the dangers of other road users. • Vehicle hazard warning lights to be used where fitted. • If on the motorway, vehicle to be parked on hard shoulder as far away from the roadway as possible and a warning triangle to be used to alert other motorists.	2	2	4
Use of vehicle jack	As above	Use of a faulty vehicle jack may lead to vehicle slipping and injuring staff	4	2	8	• Vehicle jacks to be checked on a regular basis to ensure that they operate correctly. • Hydraulic jacks to have their fluid level checked on a regular basis and topped up where necessary.	2	1	2
Loosening of wheel nuts	As above	Use of incorrect or worn tools may lead to abrasions to hands or back injuries	4	3	12	• Correct type and size of wheel brace to be used. • If nuts are very tight, use a piece of metal tubing to gain extra leverage. • If wheel nuts refuse to move, call for assistance from a garage or tyre fitting company.	3	1	3
Lifting off wheel	As above	Incorrect lifting technique may lead to back injury	4	3	12	• The wheel to be grasped firmly and lifted from the wheel studs with the knees bent and the back kept straight. Assistance to be sought if necessary. • Wheel to be rolled to one side not carried.	3	1	3

RISK ASSESSMENT - CHANGING WHEELS ON VEHICLES

ACTIVITY	PERSON AT RISK	SIGNIFICANT HAZARDS	RISK*			RISK CONTROL MEASURES	RESIDUAL RISK**		
			L	S	DR		L	S	DR
Refitting replacement wheel	Driver	Incorrect lifting technique may lead to back injury	4	3	12	• Wheel to be rolled into position not carried • The wheel to be grasped firmly and lifted onto the wheel studs with the knees bent and the back kept straight. Assistance to be sought if necessary.	3	1	3
Tightening wheel nuts	As above	Failure to tighten wheel sufficiently may lead to it becoming loose and causing an accident	3	4	12	• Wheel nuts to be tightened by hand initially whilst rotating the wheel to ensure that it is in its proper position. • Final tightening to be done using wheel brace on diagonally opposite nuts. If possible use a torque wrench to get the correct tightness.	2	2	4
Removing vehicle jack	As above	Failure to lower vehicle down steadily may result in it dropping and causing injuries	3	3	9	• The jack to be released slowly to ensure that it is completely free of the vehicle before it is removed.	2	1	2

LIKELIHOOD (L) = Frequent (5) - Probable (4) - Occasional (3) - Improbable (2) - Remote (1)
SEVERITY (S) = Catastrophic (5) - Major (4) - Reportable (3) - Serious (2) - Minor (1)
Degree of Risk (DR) = LIKELIHOOD x SEVERITY
* Numbers used are for illustrative purposes only.
** Residual risk is the level of risk that remains after suitable and sufficient control measures are introduced.

Signed originator.. Job title..

Date completed.. Date for revision..

Control of third party drivers on company premises

Failure to control the actions of third party drivers, whether they are delivery drivers, contractors or visitors to your premises, may lead to accidents resulting in personal injury as well as vehicle or property damage.

Managing the risks

To help you to identify the hazards associated with the control of third party drivers and the appropriate ways of controlling them, use our example **Risk Assessment - Control of Third Party Drivers on Company Premises**. It covers the generic hazards associated with this type of activity and suggests control measures to reduce risks to an acceptable level. You should ensure that your document only addresses "significant" hazards, i.e. any that could, and more importantly are likely to, cause an accident or injury.

Make your instructions clear

Don't include activities in your document that simply don't need to be there. Work to the principle that if there is any chance of your staff being unaware of the safe way of doing something, then you will need to make it clear in your document. Finally, always ensure that any control measures you identify and follow are decided upon the principle of "so far as is reasonably practicable".

Note. The list of potential hazards is not exhaustive. However, for your risk assessment to be considered suitable and sufficient in the eyes of the law it must accurately reflect the "significant" hazards in your workplace when third party drivers are on your premises.

Note. This risk assessment deals with the generic risks associated with the movement of vehicles belonging to third party drivers and their relationship with people on your site (staff, others). You should also ensure that your staff are aware of the movement of vehicles around your premises and the hazards that this presents.

RISK ASSESSMENT - CONTROL OF THIRD PARTY DRIVERS ON COMPANY PREMISES

ACTIVITY	PERSON AT RISK	SIGNIFICANT HAZARDS	RISK*			RISK CONTROL MEASURES	RESIDUAL RISK**		
			L	S	DR		L	S	DR
Access to premises by third party drivers	Drivers, staff, other people	Lack of site knowledge may lead to accidents involving vehicles and people resulting in serious injuries	3	5	15	• Site entrance to be signed to indicate the reporting point for visiting drivers. • All drivers to be given instructions on goods delivery/ collection points.	3	3	9
Driving on company premises	As above	Driving too fast on company premises may lead to accidents involving vehicles and people resulting in serious injuries	4	4	16	• Site speed limit to be restricted to 10mph for all vehicles. • All staff and visiting drivers to be made aware of site speed limits.	3	3	9
As above	As above	Failure to drive on recognised roadways may lead to accidents involving vehicles and people resulting in serious injuries	4	4	16	• All traffic routes to be suitably signposted. • All site entrances and exits to be suitably signposted. • Loading/unloading bays to be suitably signposted.	3	3	9
Parking in loading and unloading bays	As above	Failure to park in the correct parking places may lead to vehicle accidents resulting in injuries to drivers, etc.	3	4	12	• Visiting drivers to be informed of parking areas for loading and unloading of vehicles. • Parking of vehicles to be allowed in designated areas only when loading or unloading vehicles.	3	2	6
Staff parking	As above	Failure to park in the correct parking places may lead to vehicle accidents	3	4	12	• All parking areas to be signposted. • Staff to be given a designated parking area.	3	2	6

RISK ASSESSMENT - CONTROL OF THIRD PARTY DRIVERS ON COMPANY PREMISES

ACTIVITY	PERSON AT RISK	SIGNIFICANT HAZARDS	RISK*			RISK CONTROL MEASURES	RESIDUAL RISK**		
			L	S	DR		L	S	DR
Use of contractors' vehicles on site	Drivers, staff, other people	Conflict between contractors' vehicles and other vehicles may lead to accidents involving personal injury	3	4	12	• Contractors working on site to be provided with a designated parking area. • Contractors to be given details of the site traffic management plan. • Contractors to be made aware of site speed limits.	3	2	6
Reversing of vehicles	Staff, other people	Failure to observe the presence of other vehicles or people may lead to accidents resulting in physical injuries	3	5	15	• Reversing to be carried out only with the use of a trained banksman. • The banksman to wear high visibility clothing during reversing operations.	3	2	6

LIKELIHOOD (L) = Frequent (5) - Probable (4) - Occasional (3) - Improbable (2) - Remote (1)
SEVERITY (S) = Catastrophic (5) - Major (4) - Reportable (3) - Serious (2) - Minor (1)
Degree of Risk (DR) = LIKELIHOOD x SEVERITY
* Numbers used are for illustrative purposes only.
** Residual risk is the level of risk that remains after suitable and sufficient control measures are introduced.

Signed originator.. Job title..

Date completed... Date for revision..

Driving at work

It's been widely reported that driving vehicles whilst at work is more dangerous than actually being in a workplace. So use our document to highlight the risks and also what you can do to manage them.

On the road

You should assess the risks of driving and implement suitable control measures, so that risks faced by your staff are minimised so far as is reasonably practicable.

Managing the risks

To help you identify the hazards and appropriate ways of controlling them, use our example **Risk Assessment - Driving at Work** document. It covers the generic hazards associated with driving a normal vehicle on UK roads and suggests control measures to reduce risks to an acceptable level. This risk assessment should be used in conjunction with a Driving at Work Policy.

Note. The list of potential hazards is not exhaustive. For your risk assessment to be considered suitable and sufficient in the eyes of the law it must accurately reflect the "significant" hazards associated with driving at work.

RISK ASSESSMENT - DRIVING AT WORK

ACTIVITY	PERSON AT RISK	SIGNIFICANT HAZARDS	RISK*			RISK CONTROL MEASURES	RESIDUAL RISK**		
			L	S	DR		L	S	DR
Driving on company business (general)	Drivers, passengers and third parties	Potential for fatality or serious injury in the event of a road accident	3	4	12	• Check all driving licences annually. Drivers should only be permitted to drive on company business if they hold a valid UK driving licence that explicitly covers the type of vehicle which they're required to drive. • Implement a driving at work policy. • Consider defensive or advanced driver training for key drivers. • UK speed limits to be adhered to at all times.	3	3	9
Driving during adverse weather conditions	As above	Increased potential for road accident leading to serious or fatal injury	3	4	12	• The vehicle should be maintained and ready for winter conditions. • Consider restricting vehicle use during extreme conditions. • Drivers to check weather reports before attempting long journeys. • The use of public transport to be considered.	3	3	9
Driving for extended periods	As above	Increased potential for road accident if driver is suffering from fatigue	3	4	12	• Suitable maximum driving periods to be set. • Break periods to be set (example: 15 minutes rest after 2.5 hours driving). • Drive share on long journeys to be considered (where "passenger" can also drive). • Driving is prohibited when drivers are suffering from extreme fatigue. It's the driver's responsibility to stop and rest.	2	3	6
Driving when under the influence of alcohol or drugs	As above	Impaired reaction times may lead to increased risk of serious road accident	3	4	12	• Driving under the influence of drugs or alcohol will be classed as gross misconduct. • Drivers are prohibited from drinking any alcohol in the preceding eight hours before driving. • Drivers should not drive if they are taking prescribed medication which is known to cause drowsiness.	1	2	2

RISK ASSESSMENT - DRIVING AT WORK

ACTIVITY	PERSON AT RISK	SIGNIFICANT HAZARDS	RISK*			RISK CONTROL MEASURES	RESIDUAL RISK**		
			L	S	DR		L	S	DR
Driving a poorly maintained vehicle	Driviers, passengers and third parties	Increased risk of road accident or breakdown. Potential for serious or fatal injury when stopped on hard shoulder	3	2	6	• A maintenance schedule for vehicle to be in place and enforced. • Spot check employees' own vehicles which are used on company business. • Pre-drive checklist to be used to spot common faults prior to journey (lights not working, tyre under inflated etc.). • Emergency procedure to be communicated to all drivers for use in breakdown.	2	2	4
Driving when using mobile telephone	As above	Use of phone may be illegal and could distract driver leading to increased potential for road accident	3	2	6	• Drivers should not use a mobile telephone or similar device whilst driving. Driver to stop and phone caller back when safe to do so.	1	2	2

LIKELIHOOD (L) = Frequent (5) - Probable (4) - Occasional (3) - Improbable (2) - Remote (1)
SEVERITY (S) = Catastrophic (5) - Major (4) - Reportable (3) - Serious (2) - Minor (1)
Degree of Risk (DR) = LIKELIHOOD x SEVERITY
* Numbers used are for illustrative purposes only.
** Residual risk is the level of risk that remains after suitable and sufficient control measures are introduced.

Signed originator.. Job title..

Date completed.. Date for revision..

Forklift truck operations

The use of forklift trucks can present risks in the workplace to both drivers and pedestrians alike which, left unmanaged, could cause accidents and potentially put you on the wrong side of the law.

Managing the risks

To help you identify the hazards and appropriate ways of controlling them, use our example **Risk Assessment - Forklift Truck Operations** document. It covers the generic hazards associated with the use of forklift trucks and then suggests control measures to reduce risks to an acceptable level.

You should ensure that your document only addresses "significant" hazards, i.e. any that could and more importantly are likely to, cause an accident or injury.

Make your instructions clear

There is no point putting activities on the document that simply don't need to be there. Work to the principle that if there is any chance of your staff being unaware of the safe way of operating a forklift truck, then you will need to make it clear on your document. Having said that, your truck drivers must be suitably trained so that they are competent to drive the type of lift truck that you have provided for them. Where you have prepared risk assessments, then you must bring them to their attention.

Finally, always ensure any control measures you identify and follow only go so far "as is reasonably practicable".

Note. The list of potential hazards is not exhaustive. For your risk assessment to be considered suitable and sufficient in the eyes of the law it must accurately reflect the "significant" hazards associated with the use of the particular types of lift trucks in your workplace.

RISK ASSESSMENT - FORKLIFT TRUCK OPERATIONS

ACTIVITY	PERSON AT RISK	SIGNIFICANT HAZARDS	RISK*			RISK CONTROL MEASURES	RESIDUAL RISK**		
			L	S	DR		L	S	DR
Driving a forklift truck	Driver, other staff, members of the public	Accidents occurring when a truck is being driven by an untrained driver may lead to injuries to the driver and others	4	5	20	• Only trained drivers to be allowed to operate forklift trucks. • Licences to be regularly inspected. • Trucks with key operated ignition to have all keys removed when not in use and keys held by a responsible person. • All staff to be kept informed of the company rules regarding truck driving.	3	3	9
As above	As above	Accidents occurring when a truck is being driven too fast for road conditions may lead to overturning	4	5	20	• Signs to be displayed with speed limits. • Drivers to be regularly reminded of the need to obey on-site or off-site speed limits. • Other staff encouraged to report speeding vehicles to their manager.	3	3	9
As above	As above	A truck driven with an insecure load may lead to the load falling and injuring the driver and other people	4	5	20	• Drivers to be trained in the movement of loads. • All loads to be secure on the truck before moving. • Load weight limit of the truck to be observed by the driver at all times. • Road surfaces to be kept in good condition to allow trucks to move smoothly.	3	2	6
As above	As above	A truck being driven up or down a gradient that is too steep may lead to the truck overturning	4	5	20	• All on-site gradients to be checked to ensure that their slope is gentle. • Lift trucks should never be driven up or down gradients that exceed the maximum gradient specified by the manufacturer.	3	3	9

RISK ASSESSMENT - FORKLIFT TRUCK OPERATIONS

ACTIVITY	PERSON AT RISK	SIGNIFICANT HAZARDS	RISK*			RISK CONTROL MEASURES	RESIDUAL RISK**		
			L	S	DR		L	S	DR
Driving a forklift truck in the vicinity of pedestrians	Pedestrians	Pedestrians may be struck by the truck, leading to severe injuries	4	5	20	• Pedestrian and truck routes to be kept segregated where possible. • Signs to be displayed indicating truck usage in area. • Trucks to be fitted with flashing beacons and audible reversing alarms. • In shared work areas pedestrians to wear high visibility clothing.	3	3	9
Failure of lift truck mechanism when in use	Driver, pedestrians	Failure of load bearing parts may lead to load falling from the truck injuring people	3	5	15	• All trucks to undergo periodic thorough examination by a competent person and to be regularly serviced and maintained. • All drivers to carry out pre-work checks and to report any concerns to their manager.	2	3	6
Driving a lift truck	Driver	Truck overturning when being driven too fast or hitting an obstacle may cause injury to the driver	4	5	20	• Rollover cages to be fitted to the truck to protect the driver. • Driver restraining devices to be fitted and worn by all truck drivers.	2	3	6

LIKELIHOOD (L) = Frequent (5) - Probable (4) - Occasional (3) - Improbable (2) - Remote (1)
SEVERITY (S) = Catastrophic (5) - Major (4) - Reportable (3) - Serious (2) - Minor (1)
Degree of Risk (DR) = LIKELIHOOD x SEVERITY
* Numbers used are for illustrative purposes only.
** Residual risk is the level of risk that remains after suitable and sufficient control measures are introduced.

Signed originator.. Job title...

Date completed.. Date for revision..

Loading goods into cars

Loading the boot of a car or other vehicle is a task regularly carried out but seldom thought through - even though there are potential manual handling risks associated with it.

Loading up

Whether it is the "on the road" office, e.g. laptop, multi-media projector, files etc. or that small delivery of goods urgently required by a customer, if handled incorrectly, the result could be severe back pain. Thinking of the risks involved is not something that we normally do until it is too late.

To ensure this type of injury doesn't happen, you should complete a risk assessment for your specific activities, which identifies all "significant" hazards and appropriate "reasonable" ways of reducing risks to an acceptable level.

Managing the risks

To help you identify the hazards associated with loading goods into the boots of cars or the rear of estate vehicles and the appropriate ways of controlling them, use our example **Risk Assessment - Loading Goods into Cars**. It covers the generic hazards associated with this type of activity and then suggests control measures to reduce the risks to an acceptable level.

Note. The **Manual Handling Operations Regulations 1992** apply to all lifting and handling operations and require you to carry out a risk assessment for these activities.

You should ensure that your document only addresses "significant" hazards, i.e. any that could, and more importantly are likely to, cause an accident or injury.

Make your instructions clear

Don't include activities in your document that simply don't need to be there. Work to the principle that if there is any chance of your staff being unaware of the safe way of doing something, then you will need to make it clear in your document. Finally, always ensure that any control measures you identify and follow only go so far "as is reasonably practicable".

Note. The list of potential hazards is not exhaustive. However, for your risk assessment to be considered suitable and sufficient in the eyes of the law it must accurately reflect the "significant" hazards found in your workplace.

RISK ASSESSMENT - LOADING GOODS INTO CARS

ACTIVITY	PERSON AT RISK	SIGNIFICANT HAZARDS	RISK*			RISK CONTROL MEASURES	RESIDUAL RISK**		
			L	S	DR		L	S	DR
Loading and unloading the vehicle	Driver	Carrying heavy items over long distances may cause back pain	4	3	12	• Vehicles to be parked as close to the building location as possible. • A trolley or small-wheeled truck to be used to carry goods from the building to the vehicle. • Loads which are carried manually to be broken down into smaller sizes to reduce weight.	3	1	3
Lifting goods into the vehicle	As above	Incorrect lifting techniques may cause back injuries	4	3	12	• Correct lifting techniques must be used. • If loads are heavy and cannot be broken down assistance must be sought.	3	2	6
As above	As above	Failure to load vehicle correctly may cause it to become unstable when driving	3	4	12	• Vehicles to be loaded so that larger, heavier items are loaded first. • Heavy items to be placed so that weight is over the rear axle. • Vehicles not to be overloaded. • Loads to be secure and in estate vehicles covered by a net.	3	2	6
As above	As above	Carrying extended loads in the rear of a vehicle or on a roof rack may lead to accidents	3	3	9	• Where goods extend beyond the rear of a vehicle (either from the rear or on a roof rack) the goods should have a visible indication of their presence. • Goods on roof racks to be securely fastened. • Only roof racks designed to fit the vehicle to be used.	2	1	2

RISK ASSESSMENT - LOADING GOODS INTO CARS

ACTIVITY	PERSON AT RISK	SIGNIFICANT HAZARDS	RISK*			RISK CONTROL MEASURES	RESIDUAL RISK**		
			L	S	DR		L	S	DR
Driving	Driver	Driving with a heavily loaded vehicle will affect braking distances and may cause accidents	3	3	9	• Drivers to take account of their vehicle weight and the effect that this may have upon stopping distances. • Vehicles not to be overloaded.	2	2	4
As above	As above	Failure to ensure correct tyre pressure on a loaded vehicle may affect steering and lead to accidents	3	2	6	• Vehicle tyre pressure to be checked to match the vehicle laden weight. • Reference to be made to the vehicle handbook for correct tyre pressure.	2	1	2

LIKELIHOOD (L) = Frequent (5) - Probable (4) - Occasional (3) - Improbable (2) - Remote (1)
SEVERITY (S) = Catastrophic (5) - Major (4) - Reportable (3) - Serious (2) - Minor (1)
Degree of Risk (DR) = LIKELIHOOD x SEVERITY
* Numbers used are for illustrative purposes only.
** Residual risk is the level of risk that remains after suitable and sufficient control measures are introduced.

Signed originator.. Job title...

Date completed... Date for revision..

Safe management of grey fleet drivers

Grey fleet drivers use their own vehicles on company business. It is important that businesses manage such operations to the same standards as those for drivers of company-owned vehicles. Failure to do so may lead to road traffic accidents resulting in serious injuries or loss of life.

Managing the risks

To help you to identify the hazards associated with the management of grey fleet drivers and the appropriate ways of controlling them, use our example **Risk Assessment - Safe Management of Grey Fleet Drivers**. It covers the generic hazards associated with this type of activity and suggests control measures to reduce risks to an acceptable level. You should ensure that your document only addresses "significant" hazards, i.e. any that could, and more importantly are likely to, cause an accident or injury.

Make your instructions clear

Don't include activities in your document that simply don't need to be there. Work to the principle that if there is any chance of your staff being unaware of the safe way of doing something, then you will need to make it clear in your document. Finally, always ensure that any control measures you identify and follow are decided upon the principle of "so far as is reasonably practicable".

Note. The list of potential hazards is not exhaustive. However, for your risk assessment to be considered suitable and sufficient in the eyes of the law it must accurately reflect the "significant" hazards of the use of privately owned vehicles on company business.

Note. This risk assessment deals with the generic risks associated with drivers who use their own vehicles on company business. You should also have a private vehicle driving policy that supplements your own assessment of the risks in your particular business.

RISK ASSESSMENT - SAFE MANAGEMENT OF GREY FLEET DRIVERS

ACTIVITY	PERSON AT RISK	SIGNIFICANT HAZARDS	RISK*			RISK CONTROL MEASURES	RESIDUAL RISK**		
			L	S	DR		L	S	DR
Driving a private vehicle on company business	Driver, others	Failure to keep within the vehicle MAM (maximum authorised mass) or gross vehicle weight may lead to steering/braking defects, resulting in road traffic accidents	3	5	15	• All privately owned vehicles used on company business to be suitable for the specified loads to be carried. • Vehicles not to be overloaded. • Drivers to observe the company's driving policy at all times.	3	3	9
As above	As above	Failure to keep the vehicle in a roadworthy condition may lead to road traffic accidents	3	5	15	• All privately owned vehicles used on company business to be maintained in a roadworthy condition and serviced in accordance with the manufacturer's recommendations. • All such vehicles over three years of age to have a current MOT certificate which is to be presented annually for inspection. • Drivers to observe the company's driving policy at all times.	3	3	9
As above	As above	Poor driving standards may lead to road traffic accidents resulting in injuries to drivers and other people	3	5	15	• All drivers to have a current driving licence for the class of vehicle that they are driving. • Drivers' licences to be produced and checked on an annual basis. • Drivers to observe the driving standards set out in the Highway Code.	3	2	6
As above	Drivers	Driver fatigue caused by driving too many hours may lead to road traffic accidents resulting in injuries to drivers and other people	3	5	15	• Drivers' hours to be monitored. • Drivers to be encouraged to take regular breaks when driving long distances or when feeling tired. • Drivers to be briefed on the dangers of driving when tired. • All long journeys to be planned so that regular rest breaks can be taken.	3	2	6

RISK ASSESSMENT - SAFE MANAGEMENT OF GREY FLEET DRIVERS

ACTIVITY	PERSON AT RISK	SIGNIFICANT HAZARDS	RISK*			RISK CONTROL MEASURES	RESIDUAL RISK**		
			L	S	DR		L	S	DR
Driving a private vehicle on company business	Driver, others	Driving under the influence of alcohol or drugs may lead to road traffic accidents resulting in serious injuries to the driver and others	3	5	15	• Drivers to be made aware of the company's driving policy relating to alcohol and drugs. • Drivers to be reminded of the need to inform their managers if they are taking prescription drugs that may affect their driving.	3	3	9
Road traffic accidents whilst driving on company business	As above	Accidents involving other vehicles, property damage etc. may involve police action	3	3	9	• Drivers to report all road traffic accidents to the police. • Drivers to report all road traffic accidents to their manager. • Drivers to report all road traffic accidents that have caused vehicle or property damage to their insurer.	3	2	6

LIKELIHOOD (L) = Frequent (5) - Probable (4) - Occasional (3) - Improbable (2) - Remote (1)
SEVERITY (S) = Catastrophic (5) - Major (4) - Reportable (3) - Serious (2) - Minor (1)
Degree of Risk (DR) = LIKELIHOOD x SEVERITY
* Numbers used are for illustrative purposes only.
** Residual risk is the level of risk that remains after suitable and sufficient control measures are introduced.

Signed originator.. Job title..

Date completed.. Date for revision..

Safety for delivery drivers of vehicles up to 1,500kg (1.5 tonnes)

Drivers of delivery vehicles can be subjected to various hazards in the course of their work which, unless controlled, could lead to accidents involving serious personal injuries.

Managing the risks

To help you to identify the hazards associated with delivery driving and the appropriate ways of controlling them, use our example **Risk Assessment - Safety for Delivery Drivers of Vehicles up to 1,500kg (1.5 Tonnes)**. It covers the generic hazards associated with this type of activity and suggests control measures to reduce risks to an acceptable level. You should ensure that your document only addresses "significant" hazards, i.e. any that could, and more importantly are likely to, cause an accident or injury.

Make your instructions clear

Don't include activities in your document that simply don't need to be there. Work to the principle that if there is any chance of your staff being unaware of the safe way of doing something, then you will need to make it clear in your document. Finally, always ensure that any control measures you identify and follow are decided upon the principle of "so far as is reasonably practicable".

Note. The list of potential hazards is not exhaustive. However, for your risk assessment to be considered suitable and sufficient in the eyes of the law it must accurately reflect the "significant" hazards found as part of your delivery operations.

Note. This risk assessment only deals with the generic risks associated with driving delivery vehicles. As such vehicles differ in size, type and function, you should ensure that all relevant hazards associated with the way you expect your delivery drivers to operate are considered. Any risks identified by the vehicle manufacturer in operating manuals etc. should also be taken into consideration.

RISK ASSESSMENT - SAFETY FOR DELIVERY DRIVERS OF VEHICLES UP TO 1,500KG (1.5 TONNES)

ACTIVITY	PERSON AT RISK	SIGNIFICANT HAZARDS	RISK*			RISK CONTROL MEASURES	RESIDUAL RISK**		
			L	S	DR		L	S	DR
Manual handling (1) loading vehicle	Drivers	Failure to carry out correct manual handling procedures during loading may lead to limb or back injuries	4	4	16	• All delivery drivers to be trained in manual handling procedures. • Drivers to seek assistance when loading heavy goods onto vehicles. • Vehicles to be loaded so that the first delivery items are last to be loaded. • Goods to be spaced equally within the vehicle to allow an even weight distribution. • Delivery vehicles not to be overloaded.	3	3	9
Manual handling (2) unloading vehicle	Driver and assistant	Failure to carry out correct manual handling procedures during unloading may lead to limb or back problems	4	4	16	• All delivery drivers and assistants to be trained in manual handling procedures. • Drivers to seek assistance when unloading heavy goods from vehicles considered to be beyond their lifting capabilities • Mechanical aids to be provided to assist with the movement of goods such as sack trucks etc.	3	3	9
Deliveries to commercial or industrial premises	As above	Failure to be aware of on-site hazards may cause injuries to drivers and their assistants	3	4	12	• Where deliveries are made to commercial or industrial premises, details of any on-site hazards or specific unloading details are to be requested at the time of taking the delivery orders. • Site-specific safety information is to be given to drivers before delivery. • Drivers are to report to a customer's representative before unloading the delivery vehicle. • Drivers must not use customer's forklift trucks to assist unloading unless express permission has been granted and the driver is trained in the use of forklift trucks. • Drivers to have the authority not to unload if delivery site conditions present a hazard and are unsafe.	3	2	6

RISK ASSESSMENT - SAFETY FOR DELIVERY DRIVERS OF VEHICLES UP TO 1,500KG (1.5 TONNES)

ACTIVITY	PERSON AT RISK	SIGNIFICANT HAZARDS	RISK*			RISK CONTROL MEASURES	RESIDUAL RISK**		
			L	S	DR		L	S	DR
Deliveries to residential premises	Driver and assistant	Failure to be aware of any delivery restrictions and hazards may cause injuries to drivers and their assistants	3	4	12	• Where deliveries are made to residential premises, details of any on-site hazards or specific access details are to be requested at the time of taking the delivery orders. • Alternatively, the customer is to be contacted in order to obtain delivery information. • Site-specific safety information is to be given to drivers before delivery commences.	3	2	6
Driving company delivery vehicles	Driver	Failure to drive company vehicles in a safe manner can lead to serious or fatal road traffic accidents	3	5	15	• All drivers of company vehicles to have their driving licences checked on an annual basis by their supervisor/manager. • All drivers to drive company delivery vehicles in accordance with the Highway Code. • All drivers to drive company delivery vehicles in accordance with road traffic and weather conditions. • Drivers to report all accidents, no matter how minor, to their supervisor/manager.	3	3	9
Maintaining delivery vehicles	Driver, company	Failure to keep vehicles adequately maintained may lead to serious or fatal road traffic accidents	3	5	15	• Drivers to ensure that vehicle is in a roadworthy condition before each journey. • Drivers to report all vehicle faults to their supervisor/manager. • Drivers not to drive their vehicle if it is an unroadworthy condition.	3	3	9

RISK ASSESSMENT - SAFETY FOR DELIVERY DRIVERS OF VEHICLES UP TO 1,500KG (1.5 TONNES)

ACTIVITY	PERSON AT RISK	SIGNIFICANT HAZARDS	RISK*			RISK CONTROL MEASURES	RESIDUAL RISK**		
			L	S	DR		L	S	DR
Use of agency drivers	Drivers	Failure to ensure that agency drivers are familiar with the company vehicle may lead to road traffic accidents	3	4	12	• Agency driver's licence to be checked by their supervisor/manager. • Agency drivers to be instructed in the basic operation of the company vehicle they will be expected to drive. • Agency drivers to be instructed in the means of loading and unloading the company vehicle.	3	2	6

LIKELIHOOD (L) = Frequent (5) - Probable (4) - Occasional (3) - Improbable (2) - Remote (1)
SEVERITY (S) = Catastrophic (5) - Major (4) - Reportable (3) - Serious (2) - Minor (1) Degree of Risk (DR) = LIKELIHOOD x SEVERITY
* Numbers used are for illustrative purposes only. ** Residual risk is the level of risk that remains after suitable and sufficient control measures are introduced.

Signed originator.. Job title...

Date completed... Date for revision...

Vehicle movements

Risks associated with vehicle movements on your premises could cause accidents and potentially put you on the wrong side of the law. So use our document to help you identify what's dangerous and also what you can do to minimise the risks.

Managing the risks

To help you identify the hazards and appropriate ways of controlling them, use our example **Risk Assessment - Vehicle Movements** document. It covers the generic hazards found with such activities and then suggests the control measures required to reduce the risks to an acceptable level.

You should ensure that your document only addresses "significant" hazards, i.e. any that could and more importantly are likely to, cause an accident or injury.

Make your instructions clear

There is no point putting activities on the document that simply don't need to be there. Work to the principle that if there is any chance of your staff being unaware of hazards associated with vehicle movements on your site, then you will need to make it clear on your document. Finally, always ensure any control measures you identify and follow only go so far "as is reasonably practicable".

Note. The list of potential hazards is not exhaustive. For your risk assessment to be considered suitable and sufficient in the eyes of the law it must accurately reflect the "significant" hazards found in your workplace associated with the movement of vehicles.

RISK ASSESSMENT - VEHICLE MOVEMENTS

ACTIVITY	PERSON AT RISK	SIGNIFICANT HAZARDS	RISK*			RISK CONTROL MEASURES	RESIDUAL RISK**		
			L	S	DR		L	S	DR
Vehicles entering or leaving premises	Pedestrians, other drivers	Risk of injury from vehicles if unseen by the driver	4	5	20	• Pedestrian and vehicle routes to be marked out to give segregation. • Where possible, barriers to be installed to prevent pedestrians from walking onto areas where vehicles manoeuvre. • Signs to be displayed to indicate the separate areas. • Banksman to be in place to control driver's actions.	3	3	9
Reversing vehicles on site	As above	Risk of injury from reversing vehicles on site	4	4	16	• Avoid the need for reversing by providing one-way traffic systems on site. • Prohibit non-essential staff in designated reversing areas such as loading bays etc. • Reversing only to be carried out with the presence of a second person or Banksman to control pedestrian traffic.	3	2	6
Vehicles driving on site where blind spots exist	As above	Risk of injury from vehicles where blind spots exist on site	3	4	12	• Use of fixed mirrors at blind spots to help driver visibility. • Signs warning of poor visibility to be displayed. • Drivers encouraged to travel slowly and to use their horn when negotiating blind spots.	3	2	6
Vehicles driving on site above speed limit	As above	Risk of injury or vehicle collisions if vehicles are driven too fast on site	4	4	16	• Speed restriction signs to be displayed at relevant points on site. • Ramps to be provided to control speed. • Disciplinary action to be taken against speeding drivers.	3	2	6
Private vehicles and delivery vehicles on site	As above	Risk of pedestrians or drivers being struck by vehicles	3	4	12	• Area set aside for the parking of private vehicles and clearly marked. • Where necessary height restriction to be installed to restrict usage to cars and light vans only. • Car parking areas to be clearly marked.	3	2	6

RISK ASSESSMENT - VEHICLE MOVEMENTS

ACTIVITY	PERSON AT RISK	SIGNIFICANT HAZARDS	RISK*			RISK CONTROL MEASURES	RESIDUAL RISK**		
			L	S	DR		L	S	DR
Loading or unloading vehicles	Drivers	Risk of physical injury when handling loads	3	4	12	• Vehicles to drive close to loading bay so they can be loaded or unloaded on the level where possible. • Forklift trucks operated by trained drivers to be used for lifting heavy goods.	3	2	6
Driving from site onto the highway	As above	Risk of an accident if awareness of other traffic or traffic speed is not observed	3	5	15	• Warning signs to be displayed for vehicles leaving the site. • Halt signs to be in place prior to entering onto the highway. • Drivers to be aware of any local conditions, e.g. blind bends, dual carriageways etc.	3	2	6

LIKELIHOOD (L) = Frequent (5) - Probable (4) - Occasional (3) - Improbable (2) - Remote (1)
SEVERITY (S) = Catastrophic (5) - Major (4) - Reportable (3) - Serious (2) - Minor (1)
Degree of Risk (DR) = LIKELIHOOD x SEVERITY
* Numbers used are for illustrative purposes only.
** Residual risk is the level of risk that remains after suitable and sufficient control measures are introduced

Signed originator.. Job title...

Date completed... Date for revision...

Visiting customer sites

All sites have their particular hazards which you should be aware of before the visit takes place. Make use of our document to ensure the risks are minimised.

Managing the risks

To help you identify the hazards associated with visiting customer sites and the appropriate ways of controlling them, use our example **Risk Assessment – Visiting Customer Sites**. It covers the generic hazards associated with this type of activity and suggests control measures to reduce risks to an acceptable level.

Note. This risk assessment covers the main issues that should be considered when planning visits to customer sites. All sites present different degrees of risk and you should ensure that you obtain information from the customer before preparing your document.

You should ensure your document only addresses "significant" hazards, i.e. any that could, and more importantly are likely to, cause an accident or injury.

Make your instructions clear

Don't include activities in your document that simply don't need to be there. Work to the principle that if there is any chance of your staff being unaware of the safe way of doing something, then you will need to make it clear in your document. Finally, always ensure that any control measures you identify and follow only go so far "as is reasonably practicable".

Note. The list of potential hazards is not exhaustive. However, for your risk assessment to be considered suitable and sufficient in the eyes of the law it must accurately reflect the "significant" hazards found when staff visit a particular site.

RISK ASSESSMENT - VISITING CUSTOMER SITES

ACTIVITY	PERSON AT RISK	SIGNIFICANT HAZARDS	RISK*			RISK CONTROL MEASURES	RESIDUAL RISK**		
			L	S	DR		L	S	DR
Visiting construction sites	Staff	Failure to be aware of site rules may place the staff at risk of physical injuries	4	3	12	• Staff to contact site manager before entering site. • Staff to participate in any site induction training. • Staff to observe site rules at all times.	3	1	3
As above	As above	Failure to observe designated traffic routes may lead to vehicle accidents resulting in physical injuries to staff	4	3	12	• Staff to observe designated vehicle routes at all times. • Staff to park in designated parking areas at all times. • Staff to observe site speed limits.	3	1	3
As above	As above	Failure to observe the movement of construction vehicles may lead to accidents resulting in physical injuries	4	4	16	• Staff to determine with the site manager where vehicle movements are to take place. • Staff to observe all site safety signs and keep clear of areas where vehicle movements are taking place unless they are working in that area.	3	2	6
As above	As above	Failure to wear the correct personal protective equipment (PPE) may lead to physical injuries	4	3	12	• Staff to wear the appropriate PPE as indicated in the site induction training. • Staff to be made aware of the procedure of how to obtain additional items of PPE and to exchange worn or damaged items.	3	1	3
Visiting other company workplaces	As above	Failure to be aware of company H&S rules may place the staff at risk of physical injuries	4	3	12	• Staff to contact company representative on entering the premises. • Staff to participate in any company induction training. • Staff to observe customers' H&S rules at all times.	3	1	3

RISK ASSESSMENT - VISITING CUSTOMER SITES

ACTIVITY	PERSON AT RISK	SIGNIFICANT HAZARDS	RISK*			RISK CONTROL MEASURES	RESIDUAL RISK**		
			L	S	DR		L	S	DR
Visiting other company workplaces	Staff	Failure to be aware of company emergency procedures may lead to injuries in the event of a fire or other emergency	3	5	15	• Staff to ensure that they are made aware of all emergency procedures that exist on the premises. • Staff to respond immediately to any emergency warnings and obey all instructions. • Staff to raise any alarms if an emergency situation arises from their work.	3	2	6
Working in domestic premises	Staff	Failure to be aware of hazards in domestic premises may lead to physical injuries	3	3	9	• Staff to check with occupier that no obvious hazards exist, e.g. dangerous animals, unsafe electrical systems etc.	2	1	2

LIKELIHOOD (L) = Frequent (5) - Probable (4) - Occasional (3) - Improbable (2) - Remote (1)
SEVERITY (S) = Catastrophic (5) - Major (4) - Reportable (3) - Serious (2) - Minor (1)
Degree of Risk (DR) = LIKELIHOOD x SEVERITY
* Numbers used are for illustrative purposes only.
** Residual risk is the level of risk that remains after suitable and sufficient control measures are introduced.

Signed originator.. Job title...

Date completed... Date for revision...

Winter driving

There are many risks associated with driving - even in the best weather conditions. However, the risks are even greater during the winter. To ensure these risks are kept to a minimum make full use of our document.

Managing the risks

To help you identify the hazards associated with driving in the winter months and some appropriate ways of controlling them, use our example **Risk Assessment - Winter Driving**. It covers the generic hazards associated with this type of activity and suggests control measures to reduce the risks to an acceptable level.

You should ensure that your document only addresses "significant" hazards, i.e. any that could, and more importantly are likely to, cause an accident or injury.

Make your instructions clear

Don't include activities in your document that simply don't need to be there. Work to the principle that if there is any chance of your staff being unaware of the safe way of doing something, then you will need to make it clear in your document. Finally, always ensure that any control measures you identify and follow only go so far "as is reasonably practicable".

Note. The list of potential hazards is not exhaustive. For your risk assessment to be considered suitable and sufficient in the eyes of the law it must accurately reflect the "significant" hazards found in your workplace

RISK ASSESSMENT - WINTER DRIVING

ACTIVITY	PERSON AT RISK	SIGNIFICANT HAZARDS	RISK*			RISK CONTROL MEASURES	RESIDUAL RISK**		
			L	S	DR		L	S	DR
Pre-driving vehicle checks	Driver	Failure to ensure vehicle is roadworthy may lead to vehicle accidents with injuries to driver, passengers etc.	4	4	16	• All exterior lights to be checked. • Engine oil and water levels to be checked, including anti-freeze levels. • Water levels in washer bottles to be checked. • Tyres to be checked for condition and pressure. • All windows and mirrors to be cleaned. • Fuel level to be checked.	3	2	6
Driving in heavy rain	As above	Poor visibility may lead to vehicle accidents with injuries to driver, passenger etc.	4	3	12	• Windscreen wipers to be kept in good condition. • Vehicle speed to be adjusted to suit road conditions. • Lights to be used if visibility is poor. • Screen heater to be used to prevent misting.	3	1	3
Driving in fog	As above	As above	4	3	12	• Vehicle speed to be reduced and a longer gap with the vehicle in front to be maintained. • Fog lights (where fitted) to be used. • Vehicle to be driven using dipped headlights. • If visibility becomes extremely poor, the vehicle to be taken off the road until it improves.	3	1	3
Driving in ice or snow	As above	Difficult road conditions may lead to driver losing control of the vehicle	4	4	16	• Drivers to ensure tyres are in good condition and at the correct pressure. • Drivers to drive steadily and where possible keep to salted/gritted roadways. • Drivers to use dipped headlights when driving in snow. • Drivers to ensure windows and mirrors are kept free from ice/snow.	3	2	6

RISK ASSESSMENT - WINTER DRIVING

ACTIVITY	PERSON AT RISK	SIGNIFICANT HAZARDS	RISK*			RISK CONTROL MEASURES	RESIDUAL RISK**		
			L	S	DR		L	S	DR
Driving (general)	Driver	Driving on long journeys at night may lead to tiredness and fatigue causing accidents	3	4	12	• Journeys to be planned to allow for rest breaks. • Drinking coffee or eating high-energy food such as chocolate or boiled sweets to lessen fatigue. • Drivers who begin to feel drowsy to take a break at the soonest opportunity.	3	2	6
As above	As above	Failure to prepare for breakdowns may put driver at risk	3	3	9	• Vehicle to carry a warning triangle to be used in the event of a breakdown. • Vehicle to carry tools for changing a wheel. • Driver to have a torch for use in the dark. • For long journeys vehicles to be equipped with a spare fuel can. • Driver to be aware of emergency telephone numbers in the event of a breakdown.	2	1	2

LIKELIHOOD (L) = Frequent (5) - Probable (4) - Occasional (3) - Improbable (2) - Remote (1)
SEVERITY (S) = Catastrophic (5) - Major (4) - Reportable (3) - Serious (2) - Minor (1)
Degree of Risk (DR) = LIKELIHOOD x SEVERITY
* Numbers used are for illustrative purposes only.
** Residual risk is the level of risk that remains after suitable and sufficient control measures are introduced.

Signed originator.. Job title..

Date completed.. Date for revision..

Working in loading and unloading areas

Working in loading and unloading areas may present risks to staff and others. So use our document to help you identify the hazards and appropriate control measures.

Managing the risks

To help you identify the hazards associated with work in such areas and the appropriate ways of controlling them, use our example **Risk Assessment - Working in Loading and Unloading Areas**. It covers the generic hazards associated with this type of activity and suggests control measures to reduce risks to an acceptable level.

You should ensure that your document only addresses "significant" hazards, i.e. any that could, and more importantly are likely to, cause an accident or injury.

Make your instructions clear

Don't include activities in your document that simply don't need to be there. Work to the principle that if there is any chance of your staff being unaware of the safe way of doing something, then you will need to make it clear in your document. Finally, always ensure that any control measures you identify and follow only go so far "as is reasonably practicable".

Note. The list of potential hazards is not exhaustive. However, for your risk assessment to be considered suitable and sufficient in the eyes of the law it must accurately reflect the "significant" hazards found when working in loading and unloading areas of your workplace.

RISK ASSESSMENT - WORKING IN LOADING AND UNLOADING AREAS

ACTIVITY	PERSON AT RISK	SIGNIFICANT HAZARDS	RISK*			RISK CONTROL MEASURES	RESIDUAL RISK**		
			L	S	DR		L	S	DR
Working in loading and unloading areas (general)	Staff	Failure to observe designated pedestrian routes may lead to accidents with moving vehicles	4	4	16	• All pedestrian routes to be marked accordingly. • Where possible, physical barriers to be erected to prevent pedestrians straying on to vehicle routes. • Information relating to pedestrian routes to be briefed to staff on a regular basis.	3	2	6
As above	As above	Failure to obey site rules may lead to accidents involving vehicles	4	4	16	• Drivers and pedestrians to be given information regarding site rules. • All site speed limits to be adequately signposted. • All routes for vehicles to be adequately signposted. • Parking areas for the loading and unloading of vehicles to be adequately signposted.	3	2	6
As above	As above	Unauthorised drivers of forklift trucks may be involved in accidents resulting in injuries	3	4	12	• All forklift truck drivers to be trained in the use of their truck. • All forklift truck drivers to be authorised by the employer. • All forklift trucks to be parked in the designated area and the keys removed and kept secure when not in use.	2	2	4
As above	As above	Pedestrians may come into contact with reversing vehicles resulting in physical injuries	3	4	12	• Reversing to only take place in designated areas. • All unauthorised staff to be kept out of areas where reversing takes place. • Where necessary, a banksman to control vehicle movements in reversing areas.	2	1	2
Working in loading bays	As above	Failure to observe surroundings when working in or accessing loading bays may lead to falls resulting in personal injuries	3	3	9	• Access points to loading bays to be designated accordingly. • Physical barriers to be erected at the ends of loading bays to prevent falls. • Loading bays to be kept clear of non-essential staff.	2	1	2

RISK ASSESSMENT - WORKING IN LOADING AND UNLOADING AREAS

ACTIVITY	PERSON AT RISK	SIGNIFICANT HAZARDS	RISK*			RISK CONTROL MEASURES	RESIDUAL RISK**		
			L	S	DR		L	S	DR
Working in external areas	Staff	Pedestrians accessing external areas may be subject to collisions with moving vehicles leading to serious injuries	4	4	16	• All unauthorised pedestrians to be kept away from external areas where vehicle movements take place. • All external areas to be well lit to give drivers and pedestrians adequate visibility. • All staff who work in such areas, e.g. loading and unloading, to wear high-visibility clothing.	3	2	6
Loading and unloading vehicles	As above	Staff unloading vehicles incorrectly may lead to manual handling injuries	4	3	12	• All staff who load or unload vehicles to use mechanical aids to lift heavy goods. • All staff who manually load or unload vehicles to have received manual handling training. • All staff who load or unload vehicles to wear personal protective equipment (PPE).	3	2	6
As above	As above	Failure of mechanical aids when loading or unloading goods may lead to injuries to operator	3	3	9	• All mechanical aids to be subject to regular tests and inspection. • Staff to report faulty items to their supervisor for corrective action. • Staff to be trained in the use of mechanical aids.	2	1	2

RISK ASSESSMENT - WORKING IN LOADING AND UNLOADING AREAS

ACTIVITY	PERSON AT RISK	SIGNIFICANT HAZARDS	RISK*			RISK CONTROL MEASURES	RESIDUAL RISK**		
			L	S	DR		L	S	DR
Sheeting and unsheeting of vehicle loads	Vehicle drivers and others	Drivers and others may be injured through contact with other vehicles whilst sheeting or unsheeting a vehicle	3	3	9	• Sheeting and unsheeting of vehicles to take place in an area away from other vehicles. • Areas for sheeting and unsheeting to be protected from strong winds and bad weather.	2	2	4
As above	As above	Falls from the backs of vehicles when sheeting or unsheeting may lead to physical injuries	4	4	16	• Climbing on to vehicles during manual sheeting or unsheeting operations to be forbidden. • Access equipment to be used during manual sheeting and unsheeting operations. • Supervisors to ensure that the rules for sheeting or unsheeting are followed at all times.	3	2	6

LIKELIHOOD (L) = Frequent (5) - Probable (4) - Occasional (3) - Improbable (2) - Remote (1)
SEVERITY (S) = Catastrophic (5) - Major (4) - Reportable (3) - Serious (2) - Minor (1)
Degree of Risk (DR) = LIKELIHOOD x SEVERITY
* Numbers used are for illustrative purposes only.
** Residual risk is the level of risk that remains after suitable and sufficient control measures are introduced.

Signed originator.. Job title..

Date completed.. Date for revision..

Workplace

Changing electric lamps

There are enough risks associated with the changing of electric lamps to make the task dangerous. Failure to ensure that these risks are reduced to an acceptable level may result in accidents, which could put you on the wrong side of the law.

Managing the risks

To help you identify the hazards associated with changing electric lamps and some appropriate ways of controlling them, use our example **Risk Assessment - Changing Electric Lamps**. It covers the generic hazards associated with this type of activity and suggests control measures to reduce the risks to an acceptable level.

Note. Because, invariably, carrying out this task involves some work at height, we suggest you also refer to our **Risk Assessment - Working at Height**.

You should ensure that your document only addresses "significant" hazards, i.e. any that could, and more importantly are likely to, cause an accident or injury.

Make your instructions clear

Don't include activities in your document that simply don't need to be there. Work to the principle that if there is any chance of your staff being unaware of the safe way of doing something, then you will need to make it clear in your document. Finally, always ensure that any control measures you identify and follow only go so far "as is reasonably practicable".

Note. The list of potential hazards is not exhaustive. For your risk assessment to be considered suitable and sufficient in the eyes of the law it must accurately reflect the "significant" hazards found in your workplace.

RISK ASSESSMENT - CHANGING ELECTRIC LAMPS

ACTIVITY	PERSON AT RISK	SIGNIFICANT HAZARDS	RISK*			RISK CONTROL MEASURES	RESIDUAL RISK**		
			L	S	DR		L	S	DR
Gaining access to faulty light fitting	Staff	Use of the incorrect method for access to fitting may lead to injuries from falls	4	4	16	• Staff to select the most suitable method for accessing the light fitting. • Use of ladders or stepladders to be used only for short-duration work. • Standing on chairs, tables etc. to be forbidden. (Refer to Risk Assessment - Working at Height for ladder and stepladder use and further working at height control measures.)	3	2	6
Working on lighting fittings (general)	As above	Failure to isolate the power supply may lead to electric shock	3	4	12	• Lighting switch to be turned off and power supply to the light fitting to be isolated by removing fuses or turning off circuit breaker in the power distribution board.	2	1	2
Removing reflector, diffuser from fluorescent light fitting	As above	Incorrect removal may lead to reflector or diffuser falling and injuring others	3	3	9	• Staff to ensure other people in the vicinity are kept away from the work area. • Correct tools for removal to be used, e.g. correct type of screwdriver to remove any screws.	2	1	2
Removing filament lamps and shades	As above	Failure to allow filament lamp and shades to cool down may lead to burns to hands	4	4	16	• Filament lamps and shades to be allowed to cool down before attempted removal.	2	2	4
Removing or replacing fluorescent tubes	As above	Incorrect handling of tubes may lead to them shattering causing cuts from broken glass	3	3	9	• Fluorescent tubes to be handled carefully keeping them away from obstructions. • Tubes to be removed first from one end and then carefully lifted out from the other end.	2	1	2

RISK ASSESSMENT - CHANGING ELECTRIC LAMPS

ACTIVITY	PERSON AT RISK	SIGNIFICANT HAZARDS	RISK*			RISK CONTROL MEASURES	RESIDUAL RISK**		
			L	S	DR		L	S	DR
Replacing light bulbs	As above	Fitting wrong size of bulb may lead to over heating of fitting causing a fire	4	2	8	• Replacement filament bulbs to be the correct rating for the fitting or shade.	3	1	3

LIKELIHOOD (L) = Frequent (5) - Probable (4) - Occasional (3) - Improbable (2) - Remote (1)
SEVERITY (S) = Catastrophic (5) - Major (4) - Reportable (3) - Serious (2) - Minor (1)
Degree of Risk (DR) = LIKELIHOOD x SEVERITY
* Numbers used are for illustrative purposes only.
** Residual risk is the level of risk that remains after suitable and sufficient control measures are introduced.

Signed originator.. Job title..

Date completed... Date for revision..

Changing electric light fittings

Changing an electric light fitting must be done with care. There are several possible risks involved, including cuts from broken glass, burns from incorrect handling, plus the associated dangers of working at height and the possibility of finding asbestos.

Assess the risks

If these risks are left unmanaged, they could cause accidents and potentially put you on the wrong side of the law. To ensure that this doesn't happen, you should complete a risk assessment for your specific activities, which identifies all "significant" hazards and appropriate "reasonable" ways of reducing risks to an acceptable level.

Managing the risks

To help you identify the hazards associated with changing electric light fittings and the appropriate ways of controlling them, use our example **Risk Assessment - Changing Electric Light Fittings**. It covers the generic hazards associated with this type of activity and then suggests control measures to reduce risks to an acceptable level. Because carrying out this task invariably involves some work at height, we suggest you also refer to our **Risk Assessment - Working at Height**.

Tip. You should make sure that staff who carry out this activity are competent to do so by virtue of their training and experience.

You should ensure that your document only addresses "significant" hazards, i.e. any that could, and more importantly are likely to, cause an accident or injury.

Make your instructions clear

Don't include activities in your document that simply don't need to be there. Work to the principle that if there is any chance of your staff being unaware of the safe way of doing something, then you will need to make it clear in your document. Finally, always ensure that any control measures you identify and follow are decided upon the principle of "so far as is reasonably practicable".

Note. The list of potential hazards is not exhaustive. For your risk assessment to be considered suitable and sufficient in the eyes of the law it must accurately reflect the "significant" hazards found in your workplace.

RISK ASSESSMENT - CHANGING ELECTRIC LIGHT FITTINGS

ACTIVITY	PERSON AT RISK	SIGNIFICANT HAZARDS	RISK*			RISK CONTROL MEASURES	RESIDUAL RISK**		
			L	S	DR		L	S	DR
Gaining access to faulty light fitting	Staff	Use of the incorrect method for access to fitting may lead to injuries from falls	4	4	16	• Staff to select the most suitable method for accessing the light fitting. • Use of ladders or stepladders to be only for short duration work. • Standing on chairs, tables etc. to be forbidden. • (For further risk control measure, refer to Risk Assessment - Working at Height.)	3	2	6
Removing reflector, diffuser and tube from fluorescent light fitting	As above	Incorrect removal may lead to reflector or diffuser falling and injuring others	3	3	9	• Staff to ensure other people in the vicinity are kept away from the work area. • Only the correct tools to be used for removal, e.g. correct type of screwdriver to be used to remove screws.	2	1	2
As above	As above	Incorrect handling of tubes may lead to them shattering causing cuts from broken glass	3	3	9	• Fluorescent tubes to be handled carefully keeping them away from obstructions.	2	1	2
Removing filament lamps and shades	As above	Failure to allow filament lamp and shade to cool down may lead to burns to hands	4	4	16	• Filament lamps and shades to be allowed to cool down before attempted removal.	2	2	4
Removing faulty fittings from a tiled ceiling	As above	Failure to check for the presence of asbestos may lead to contamination	4	4	16	• Asbestos register to be checked before removal of fittings from tiled ceilings. • (If the ceiling tiles are found to contain asbestos refer to the Risk Assessment - Drilling Holes into Textured Coatings.)	3	2	6

RISK ASSESSMENT - CHANGING ELECTRIC LIGHT FITTINGS

ACTIVITY	PERSON AT RISK	SIGNIFICANT HAZARDS	RISK*			RISK CONTROL MEASURES	RESIDUAL RISK**		
			L	S	DR		L	S	DR
Removing lamps and fittings (general)	Staff	Failure to isolate the power supply may lead to electric shock	3	4	12	• Light switch to be turned off and power supply to the light fitting to be isolated by removing fuses or turning off circuit breaker in the power distribution board. • Power supply at the fitting to be tested for isolation before any work takes place.	2	1	2
Removing lamps and fittings (general)	As above	Undoing fixings may lead to overbalancing and falling from height	4	3	12	• Only the correct tools to be used to remove fixings, e.g. proper type and size of screwdriver etc. • A secure working position to be maintained.	3	1	3

LIKELIHOOD (L) = Frequent (5) - Probable (4) - Occasional (3) - Improbable (2) - Remote (1)
SEVERITY (S) = Catastrophic (5) - Major (4) - Reportable (3) - Serious (2) - Minor (1)
Degree of Risk (DR) = LIKELIHOOD x SEVERITY
* Numbers used are for illustrative purposes only.
** Residual risk is the level of risk that remains after suitable and sufficient control measures are introduced.

Signed originator.. Job title..

Date completed.. Date for revision...

Changing electric socket outlets

Changing an electric socket outlet needn't be dangerous; in fact, if managed properly, the residual risks are minimal. However, failure to ensure that risks are reduced to an acceptable level may result in an accident, and even loss of life.

Managing the risks

To help you identify the hazards associated with changing sockets and some appropriate ways of controlling them, use our example **Risk assessment - Changing Electric Socket Outlets**. It covers the generic hazards associated with this type of activity and suggests control measures to reduce risks to an acceptable level.

You should ensure that your document only addresses "significant" hazards, i.e. any that could, and more importantly are likely to, cause an accident or injury.

Make your instructions clear

Don't include activities in your document that simply don't need to be there. Work to the principle that if there is any chance of your staff being unaware of the safe way of doing something, then you will need to make it clear in your document. Finally, always ensure that any control measures you identify and follow only go so far "as is reasonably practicable".

Note. The list of potential hazards is not exhaustive. For your risk assessment to be considered suitable and sufficient in the eyes of the law it must accurately reflect the "significant" hazards found in your workplace.

RISK ASSESSMENT - CHANGING ELECTRIC SOCKET OUTLETS

ACTIVITY	PERSON AT RISK	SIGNIFICANT HAZARDS	RISK*			RISK CONTROL MEASURES	RESIDUAL RISK**		
			L	S	DR		L	S	DR
Work prior to removing faulty socket outlet, connection unit, cooker unit etc.	Staff	Failure to isolate the power supply may lead to electric shock	3	4	12	• Power supply to the socket outlet to be isolated by removing fuses or turning off circuit breaker in the power distribution board. • Power supply at the socket outlet to be tested for isolation before any work takes place.	2	1	2
Removing faulty outlet and associated wiring	As above	Using incorrect sized screwdriver may lead to it slipping causing hand/arm injury	3	2	6	• Only the correct size and type of screwdriver to be used. • Outlet to be removed carefully to expose wiring. • Live (red/brown) and neutral (blue/black) cables to be disconnected before the earth cable (green/yellow).	2	1	2
Refitting new outlet	As above	As above	3	2	6	• The correct size of screwdriver to be used. • Earth cable to be connected first, and then live and neutral.	2	1	2
As above	As above	Cables with damaged insulation may cause electric shock when the mains supply is turned on	3	3	9	• The condition of insulation on all cables to be checked for damage. • Damaged cables to be replaced where necessary before fitting new outlet.	2	1	2
Replacing a fused outlet	As above	Incorrect fuse size may lead to loss of protection under fault conditions	3	4	12	• Where the outlet is fitted with a fuse then the fuse must match the rating of the appliance that is connected to it.	2	2	4

RISK ASSESSMENT - CHANGING ELECTRIC SOCKET OUTLETS

ACTIVITY	PERSON AT RISK	SIGNIFICANT HAZARDS	RISK*			RISK CONTROL MEASURES	RESIDUAL RISK**		
			L	S	DR		L	S	DR
Checking final connections	Staff	If connections are of the wrong polarity, fuses or circuit breaker may fail to operate correctly	3	4	12	• Polarity checks to be made using a suitable instrument before connecting any appliance to the outlet.	2	2	4
Reconnecting mains supply	As above	Incorrect size of fuse or circuit breaker may lead to loss of protection under fault conditions	3	4	12	• A fuse or circuit breaker of the correct size to be fitted to give full circuit protection.	2	2	4

LIKELIHOOD (L) = Frequent (5) - Probable (4) - Occasional (3) - Improbable (2) - Remote (1)
SEVERITY (S) = Catastrophic (5) - Major (4) - Reportable (3) - Serious (2) - Minor (1)
Degree of Risk (DR) = LIKELIHOOD x SEVERITY
* Numbers used are for illustrative purposes only.
** Residual risk is the level of risk that remains after suitable and sufficient control measures are introduced.

Signed originator.. Job title..

Date completed.. Date for revision..

Cleaning in kitchens

Although cleaning is traditionally a low-risk activity, in a kitchen environment there are a number of risks present that must be managed to prevent accidents.

Cleaning safely

Risks left unmanaged could potentially put you on the wrong side of the law. To ensure that this doesn't happen, you should complete a risk assessment for cleaning in a kitchen, which identifies all "significant" hazards and identifies appropriate "reasonable" ways of reducing risks to an acceptable level.

Cleaning in these areas brings additional hazards and the risk of harm both to people carrying out the cleaning and others should be assessed. To ensure good hygiene levels, all kitchens where food and drink is prepared should be maintained to a high standard. This may mean cleaning using chemical substances in the vicinity of hot equipment such as cookers, toasters, grills, as well as cleaning work surfaces and floors etc.

Managing the risks

To help you identify the hazards associated with kitchen cleanliness and the appropriate ways of controlling them, use our example **Risk Assessment - Cleaning in Kitchens**. It covers the generic hazards associated with this type of activity and then suggests control measures to reduce risks to an acceptable level.

Note 1. If your staff use cleaning chemicals that have a hazard symbol on the container you will also need to carry out an assessment under the **Control of Substances Hazardous to Health Regulations 2002** (as amended 2004). It will be beneficial to substitute these substances for less hazardous ones.

Note 2. If you have a larger type kitchen, such as a commercial kitchen, which is equipped with a ducted grease extract system, then you will need to include the regular cleaning of this equipment in your fire risk assessment. We recommend that you utilise the services of a specialist contractor to carry out this work which may be a condition under your company insurance policies.

You should ensure that your document only addresses "significant" hazards, i.e. any that could, and more importantly are likely to, cause an accident or injury.

Make your instructions clear

Don't include activities in your document that simply don't need to be there. Work to the principle that if there is any chance of your staff being unaware of the safe way of doing something, then you will need to make it clear in your document. Finally, always ensure that any control measures you identify and follow only go so far "as is reasonably practicable".

Note. The list of potential hazards is not exhaustive. For your risk assessment to be considered suitable and sufficient in the eyes of the law it must accurately reflect the "significant" hazards found in your workplace.

RISK ASSESSMENT - CLEANING IN KITCHENS

ACTIVITY	PERSON AT RISK	SIGNIFICANT HAZARDS	RISK*			RISK CONTROL MEASURES	RESIDUAL RISK**		
			L	S	DR		L	S	DR
Wet cleaning of floors	Cleaning staff, others	Slips on wet floors may lead to personal injuries	3	4	12	• Cleaners to erect a signboard stating which floor areas are in the process of being cleaned. • A "two-mop" system of cleaning to be used, i.e. wet mop to remove dirt and grease, a second mop to clean up residual water. • Where possible, cleaning to take place out of normal kitchen working hours.	3	1	3
Cleaning of work surfaces using chemical cleaners	Cleaning staff	Regular use of chemical cleaners may lead to skin conditions	4	3	12	• Only non-caustic, low alkaline cleaning chemicals to be used. • Rubber gloves to be provided and worn by all cleaning staff. • Cleaning chemicals to only be used in accordance with the manufacturers' instructions.	2	2	4
Cleaning of greasy working surfaces etc. using steam cleaners	As above	Incorrect use of steam cleaners may lead to burns and scalds	3	3	9	• All cleaning staff to be instructed in machine use. • Rubber gloves to be provided and worn by all cleaning staff when using the machine. • Cleaning areas to be kept clear of other people while steam cleaning is undertaken.	2	1	2
Cleaning of cooking equipment	As above	Cleaning equipment that is still hot may lead to skin burns	4	2	8	• Cleaners to ensure that all cooking equipment is turned off and has been allowed to cool before cleaning.	2	1	2
Cleaning or changing of grease extract filters	As above	Falls from height when attempting to clean or change high level grease filters	4	3	12	• Cleaning staff to use suitable equipment to access high-level grease filters, e.g. podium steps or stepladders that allow three points of contact. • Filters requiring cleaning to be brought down to low level before cleaning.	3	2	6

RISK ASSESSMENT - CLEANING IN KITCHENS

ACTIVITY	PERSON AT RISK	SIGNIFICANT HAZARDS	RISK*			RISK CONTROL MEASURES	RESIDUAL RISK**		
			L	S	DR		L	S	DR
Cleaning of spillages	Cleaning and kitchen staff	Slips on wet or greasy floors may lead to broken bones, fractures etc.	4	3	12	• All spillages to be cleaned up as soon as possible. • Greasy surfaces to be treated to remove residual grease. • Warning notices to be placed over areas immediately following spillages until cleaning can take place.	3	2	6
Cleaning blocked sink drains	As above	Misuse of a chemical drain cleaner may lead to skin burns or eye damage	3	4	12	• Staff using a chemical drain cleaner to follow manufacturers' instructions at all times. • Staff to wear protective gloves and eye shields. • Reference to be made to any COSHH assessment for the substance being used. • If initial treatment fails to clear blockage professional assistance to be sought.	3	2	6

LIKELIHOOD (L) = Frequent (5) - Probable (4) - Occasional (3) - Improbable (2) - Remote (1)
SEVERITY (S) = Catastrophic (5) - Major (4) - Reportable (3) - Serious (2) - Minor (1)
Degree of Risk (DR) = LIKELIHOOD x SEVERITY
* Numbers used are for illustrative purposes only.
** Residual risk is the level of risk that remains after suitable and sufficient control measures are introduced.

Signed originator.. Job title..

Date completed.. Date for revision..

General building maintenance above ground level

Carrying out general building maintenance above ground level can present risks to staff, which left unmanaged could cause accidents and potentially put you on the wrong side of the law.

Managing the risks

To help you identify the hazards associated with general building maintenance above ground level and the appropriate ways of controlling them, use our example **Risk Assessment - General Building Maintenance Above Ground Level**. It covers the generic hazards associated with this type of activity and suggests control measures to reduce risks to an acceptable level.

Note. This risk assessment only deals with the general aspects of this type of work. You should refer to our **Working at Height** risk assessment for further information on access and working above ground level.

You should ensure that your document only addresses "significant" hazards, i.e. any that could, and more importantly are likely to, cause an accident or injury.

Make your instructions clear

Don't include activities in your document that simply don't need to be there. Work to the principle that if there is any chance of your staff being unaware of the safe way of doing something, then you will need to make it clear in your document. Finally, always ensure that any control measures you identify and follow are decided upon the principle of "so far as is reasonably practicable".

Note. The list of potential hazards is not exhaustive. However, for your risk assessment to be considered suitable and sufficient in the eyes of the law it must accurately reflect the "significant" hazards found when carrying out general building maintenance above ground level at your places of work.

RISK ASSESSMENT - GENERAL MAINTENANCE ABOVE GROUND LEVEL

ACTIVITY	PERSON AT RISK	SIGNIFICANT HAZARDS	RISK*			RISK CONTROL MEASURES	RESIDUAL RISK**		
			L	S	DR		L	S	DR
Access to above ground work areas	Staff	Selection of incorrect equipment for work above ground level may lead to falls resulting in serious injuries or death	3	5	15	• Staff supervisors to ensure that the work to be carried out is assessed and that the correct means of access equipment will be used. • Supervisors to determine and document a safe method of working prior to work starting. • Only staff who are competent to work above ground level.	3	2	6
Carrying out short-duration work above ground level (less than 30 minutes)	As above	Over reaching from the wrong type of access equipment may lead to falls	3	4	12	• Supervisors to ensure that where ladders are used for short-duration work that staff are competent to work safely from them and that they are erected properly and secured correctly. • Staff to ensure that all working positions from ladders and stepladders maintain three points of contact and that equipment is positioned at the correct height and erected in a position so that over reaching is prevented.	3	1	3
Carrying out longer duration work above ground level (over 30 minutes)	As above	Selection of incorrect equipment for work above ground level may lead to falls resulting in serious injuries or death	3	5	15	• Supervisors to ensure that ladders are not used for such work. • Scaffolding (either fixed or scaffolding towers) or a mobile elevated work platform (MEWP) to be used for longer duration work above ground level. • All scaffolding to be erected by competent staff.	3	2	6
Working using ladders	As above	Ladders rested against PVC gutters may twist, leading to falls resulting serious injuries	3	4	12	• Ladders not to be erected against PVC gutters. • Where necessary a purpose designed ladder stand-off device to be used.	3	1	3

RISK ASSESSMENT - GENERAL MAINTENANCE ABOVE GROUND LEVEL

ACTIVITY	PERSON AT RISK	SIGNIFICANT HAZARDS	RISK*			RISK CONTROL MEASURES	RESIDUAL RISK**		
			L	S	DR		L	S	DR
Handling of tools and equipment above ground level	Staff	Transporting tools and equipment to and from the ground to high level may result in such items falling causing personal injuries	3	3	9	• Hand tools to be taken above ground using a tool bag or container hoisted up using a line. • Staff at the lower level to wear head protection to prevent injuries from falling objects. • Where work is to be carried out from the working platform of a MEWP, tools and equipment to be loaded before the working platform is raised. • Waste from cleaning gutters etc. to be contained in a bucket and lowered using a line.	3	1	3
Working on roofs	As above	Working on roofs without the correct equipment may lead to falls off or through roofs resulting in serious injuries or death	3	5	15	• Staff to only work on sloping roofs from a purpose-designed roof ladder or from the platform of a MEWP. • Work on flat roofs to be from purpose-designed crawling boards after the roof has been assessed for the weight of man and boards. • Where designated walkways exist on roofs, staff to adhere to them. • Staff to not access fragile roofs until they have been assessed by a supervisor and a safe system of work devised.	3	2	6

LIKELIHOOD (L) = Frequent (5) - Probable (4) - Occasional (3) - Improbable (2) - Remote (1)
SEVERITY (S) = Catastrophic (5) - Major (4) - Reportable (3) - Serious (2) - Minor (1)
Degree of Risk (DR) = LIKELIHOOD x SEVERITY
* Numbers used are for illustrative purposes only. ** Residual risk is the level of risk that remains after suitable and sufficient control measures are introduced.

Signed originator.. Job title..

Date completed... Date for revision...

Holes in floors and excavations

Working adjacent to holes in floors or excavations could present risks to staff and others which, left unmanaged, could cause accidents resulting in serious personal injury.

Managing the risks

To help you identify the hazards associated with this type of activity and the appropriate ways of controlling them, use our example **Risk Assessment - Holes in Floors and Excavations**. It covers the generic hazards associated with this type of activity and suggests control measures to reduce risks to an acceptable level. You should ensure that your document only addresses "significant" hazards, i.e. any that could, and more importantly are likely to, cause an accident or injury.

With this type of activity the main hazard will be falling from height. The law does not define "height", as a slip, trip and fall from any height, regardless of how small, may lead to injuries being sustained.

Make your instructions clear

Don't include activities in your document that simply don't need to be there. Work to the principle that if there is any chance of your staff being unaware of the safe way of doing something, then you will need to make it clear in your document. Finally, always ensure that any control measures you identify and follow are decided upon the principle of "so far as is reasonably practicable".

Note. The list of potential hazards is not exhaustive. However, for your risk assessment to be considered suitable and sufficient in the eyes of the law it must accurately reflect the "significant" hazards associated with working near holes or excavations.

RISK ASSESSMENT - HOLES IN FLOORS AND EXCAVATIONS

ACTIVITY	PERSON AT RISK	SIGNIFICANT HAZARDS	RISK*			RISK CONTROL MEASURES	RESIDUAL RISK**		
			L	S	DR		L	S	DR
Working adjacent to holes in floors	Staff, other people	Falling into an unguarded hole may lead to physical injuries	3	5	15	• All holes in floors to be fitted with a substantial cover when not in use. • Barriers to be placed around all uncovered holes both during work activities or until a permanent cover is fitted. • Staff working around holes in floors to be supplied with fall arrest equipment. • Staff to be briefed on a safe system of work.	3	2	6
As above	As above	Failure to maintain the security of guards etc. may lead to falls into holes resulting in serious physical injuries	3	5	15	• All barriers around holes to be regularly checked to ensure that they are in place and that their condition is sound. • All coverings to holes to be regularly checked to ensure that they are in place and that their condition is sound.	3	2	6
As above	Staff	Failure to prevent staff from falling whilst working around holes in floors may lead to serious physical injuries	3	5	15	• Staff working in the close vicinity of holes in floors to be supplied with suitable fall arrest equipment. • Staff to be trained in the use of fall arrest equipment.	3	2	6
Work adjacent to excavations	As above	Failure to guard the edges of excavations may lead to falls resulting in serious physical injuries	3	5	15	• All excavations to be fitted with barriers to the edges for the full length of the excavation. • Temporary barriers to be interlocked to ensure continuity. • Staff to be briefed on a safe system of work.	3	2	6

RISK ASSESSMENT - HOLES IN FLOORS AND EXCAVATIONS

ACTIVITY	PERSON AT RISK	SIGNIFICANT HAZARDS	RISK*			RISK CONTROL MEASURES	RESIDUAL RISK**		
			L	S	DR		L	S	DR
Work adjacent to excavations	Staff	Failure to maintain the security of guards may lead to falls into holes resulting in serious physical injuries	3	5	15	• All barriers around excavations to be regularly checked to ensure that they are in place and that their condition is sound.	3	2	6

LIKELIHOOD (L) = Frequent (5) - Probable (4) - Occasional (3) - Improbable (2) - Remote (1)
SEVERITY (S) = Catastrophic (5) - Major (4) - Reportable (3) - Serious (2) - Minor (1)
Degree of Risk (DR) = LIKELIHOOD x SEVERITY
* Numbers used are for illustrative purposes only.
** Residual risk is the level of risk that remains after suitable and sufficient control measures are introduced.

Signed originator... Job title..

Date completed... Date for revision...

Homeworkers - general

Employees who regularly work from home should be treated the same way as other employees. Their work activities will need to be assessed and any hazards highlighted addressed so that the level of risk is reduced as much as possible. Failure to do so may lead to homeworkers being injured or suffering from ill-health.

Managing the risks

To help you to identify the hazards associated with working from home and the appropriate ways of controlling them, use our example **Risk Assessment - Homeworkers - General**. It covers the generic hazards associated with this type of activity and suggests control measures to reduce risks to an acceptable level. You should ensure that your document only addresses "significant" hazards, i.e. any that could, and more importantly are likely to, cause an accident or injury.

Make your instructions clear

Don't include activities in your document that simply don't need to be there. Work to the principle that if there is any chance of your staff being unaware of the safe way of doing something, then you will need to make it clear in your document. Finally, always ensure that any control measures you identify and follow are decided upon the principle of "so far as is reasonably practicable".

Note. The list of potential hazards is not exhaustive. However, for your risk assessment to be considered suitable and sufficient in the eyes of the law it must accurately reflect the "significant" hazards found when your staff work from home.

Note. This risk assessment only deals with the generic risks associated with homeworking. Your assessment should take into consideration the actual tasks that your homeworkers carry out on your behalf. It is recommended that these risk assessments are carried out in conjunction with the individual homeworker so that the requirements are fully understood.

RISK ASSESSMENT - HOMEWORKERS - GENERAL

ACTIVITY	PERSON AT RISK	SIGNIFICANT HAZARDS	RISK*			RISK CONTROL MEASURES	RESIDUAL RISK**		
			L	S	DR		L	S	DR
Getting around in general	Staff, others	Physical injuries resulting from slips, trips and falls caused by obstructions, training cables, worn floor coverings, poor layout of equipment etc. within work areas	3	3	9	• Work areas to be kept free from obstructions. • Trailing cables to be kept clear of walkways and secured. • Spillages to be cleaned up immediately. • Floor coverings to be kept in a safe condition. • Furniture and equipment to be arranged so that it does not cause an obstruction. • Lighting to be adequate.	3	1	3
Use of work equipment	As above	Physical injuries resulting from coming into contact with dangerous parts of work equipment may lead to entanglement or cutting injuries	3	3	9	• All work equipment (in particular shredders, laminators etc.) to be suitable for use and dangerous parts to be guarded. • All work equipment to be maintained in a serviceable condition. • Staff to be trained in the use of work equipment and to be informed of how to report faulty equipment. • Equipment not to be left in a manner that presents risks to others, e.g. children.	3	2	6
Electrical safety of work equipment when in use	Staff	Faulty electrical equipment may lead to fatal electrical shock	3	5	15	• All plugs and socket outlets to be maintained in good condition. • All electrical cables and equipment leads to be kept free from cuts or abrasions and to be regularly checked. • All portable appliances to be PAT tested and records of the testing to be held by the supervisor/manager. • Staff to be informed of how to report faulty electrical items of work equipment.	3	3	9
Manual handling	As above	Physical injuries caused by incorrect handling and lifting methods	3	4	12	• All manual handling to be kept to a minimum. • Staff to be trained in safe manual handling methods. • Staff to receive a separate manual handling risk assessment.	3	2	6

RISK ASSESSMENT - HOMEWORKERS - GENERAL

ACTIVITY	PERSON AT RISK	SIGNIFICANT HAZARDS	RISK*			RISK CONTROL MEASURES	RESIDUAL RISK**		
			L	S	DR		L	S	DR
Use of display screen equipment	Staff	Work-related upper limb disorders may be caused by incorrect layout and posture when using display screen equipment	3	4	12	• Staff to undertake a workstation assessment to cover equipment layout, use and posture. • Staff to be made aware of workstation posture, and of the need to take rest breaks etc., through training.	3	2	6
Working in the home environment	Staff, others	Risks from fires may cause serious injuries or loss of life	3	5	15	• Combustible materials to be kept away from heat sources. • Portable heaters to be located away from combustible materials. • Electrical sockets not to be overloaded. • Good housekeeping to be maintained and rubbish removed regularly. • Flammable substances to be kept in a locked cupboard etc.	3	2	6
As above	Staff	Staff working in isolation may suffer from stress-related illnesses	3	3	9	• Regular face-to-face contact to be maintained by manager/ supervisor. • Regular communication with on-site staff to be arranged.	3	1	3

LIKELIHOOD (L) = Frequent (5) - Probable (4) - Occasional (3) - Improbable (2) - Remote (1)
SEVERITY (S) = Catastrophic (5) - Major (4) - Reportable (3) - Serious (2) - Minor (1)
Degree of Risk (DR) = LIKELIHOOD x SEVERITY
* Numbers used are for illustrative purposes only. ** Residual risk is the level of risk that remains after suitable and sufficient control measures are introduced.

Signed originator.. Job title...

Date completed.. Date for revision..

Housekeeping

Untidy workplaces with floor coverings in a poor condition and piles of waste material left lying about etc. not only give a poor impression but are a major factor in the cause of many accidents at work.

Managing the risks

To help you identify the hazards and appropriate ways of controlling them, use our example **Risk Assessment - Housekeeping**. It deals with the most common generic hazards found in work environments and suggests control measures to reduce risks to an acceptable level.

You should ensure your document only addresses "significant" hazards, i.e. any that could and more importantly are likely to, cause an accident or injury.

Make your instructions clear

Work to the principle that if there is any chance of your staff being unaware of the safe ways of keeping the workplace free from housekeeping hazards, then you will need to make it clear on your document. Finally, always ensure any control measures you identify and follow only go so far "as is reasonably practicable".

Note. The list of potential hazards is not exhaustive, as you will know your workplace better than we do. However, for your risk assessment to be considered suitable and sufficient in the eyes of the law it must accurately reflect the "significant" hazards found with housekeeping standards in your workplace.

RISK ASSESSMENT - HOUSEKEEPING

ACTIVITY	PERSON AT RISK	SIGNIFICANT HAZARDS	RISK*			RISK CONTROL MEASURES	RESIDUAL RISK**		
			L	S	DR		L	S	DR
Moving about in general	Operative(s)	Risk of slips, trips and falls caused by poorly maintained floors, etc.	4	3	12	• Floors to be maintained in good condition. • Floor covering to be kept in good repair. • Floors not to be highly polished. • Stairways to be kept clear of obstacles and handrails provided.	3	1	3
As above	As above	Risk of slips, trips and falls caused by spilled liquids	4	3	12	• All spillages to be cleaned up immediately. • Follow manufacturers' recommendations for the cleaning up of oils, chemicals etc.	3	1	3
Storage of goods (low level)	As above	Incorrect storage of goods may lead to tripping hazards or blocked fire escape routes	5	5	25	• The storage of goods on floors to be kept to specific areas with adequate walkways in between. • Fire doors and escape routes to be kept free of obstacles. • All walkways, stairs etc. to be kept free of obstacles. • In warehouses, walking areas to be marked out.	3	2	6
Storage of goods (high level)	As above	Risk of falling or muscular injury from handling goods in high-level storage	4	3	12	• Use of correct means of access (podium steps etc.) to prevent falls. • Heavier items to be stored at lower level only. • Operatives to be given specific manual handling training.	3	1	3
Using filing cabinets	As above	Leaving drawers open can lead to operatives banging into them	4	2	8	• Staff to be instructed not to leave filing cabinet drawers open. • Supervisors to regularly check and remind staff of the hazards.	3	1	3

RISK ASSESSMENT - HOUSEKEEPING

ACTIVITY	PERSON AT RISK	SIGNIFICANT HAZARDS	RISK*			RISK CONTROL MEASURES	RESIDUAL RISK**		
			L	S	DR		L	S	DR
Incorrect storage in filing cabinets	Operative(s)	Top-heavy filing cabinets may tip over injuring staff	4	3	12	• Filing cabinets to be used such that the bottom drawers are used first. • Supervisors to carry out regular checks.	3	2	6
Removal of waste from work areas	As above	Excessive waste may lead to fire hazards	4	4	16	• Waste materials to be stored in bins and removed at the end of each working shift/day. • Supervisors to check work areas at the end of each shift/day.	3	2	6
The use of trailing cables	As above	Trailing cables may lead to slips, trips and falls	4	3	12	• All cables to be kept away from areas where staff walk. • Cable management systems to be used for cables to desks, island sites etc. • Cable protectors to be placed over temporary trailing cables where they cross aisles and walkways.	2	1	2
Storage of chemicals and flammable liquids	As above	Chemical substances and highly flammable liquids etc. may cause personal injury or fire	4	4	16	• All chemical substances to be kept locked away when not in use. • All highly flammable liquids etc. to be kept in a specially provided cabinet when not in use.	3	2	6

LIKELIHOOD (L) = Frequent (5) - Probable (4) - Occasional (3) - Improbable (2) - Remote (1)
SEVERITY (S) = Catastrophic (5) - Major (4) - Reportable (3) - Serious (2) - Minor (1)
Degree of Risk (DR) = LIKELIHOOD x SEVERITY
* Numbers used are for illustrative purposes only. ** Residual risk is the level of risk that remains after suitable and sufficient control measures are introduced

Signed originator.. Job title..

Date completed... Date for revision...

Mobile tower scaffolds

If tower scaffolds are incorrectly assembled, then this can lead to accidents involving serious personal injuries.

Managing the risks

To help you to identify the hazards associated with using tower scaffolds and the appropriate ways of controlling them, use our sample **Risk Assessment - Mobile Tower Scaffolds**. It covers the generic hazards associated with this type of activity and suggests control measures to reduce risks to an acceptable level. You should ensure your document only addresses "significant" hazards, i.e. any that could, and more importantly are likely to, cause an accident or injury.

Make your instructions clear

Don't include activities in your document that simply don't need to be there. Work to the principle that if there is any chance of your staff being unaware of the safe way of doing something, then you will need to make it clear in your document. Finally, always ensure that any control measures you identify and follow are decided upon the principle of "so far as is reasonably practicable". The list of potential hazards is not exhaustive. However, for your risk assessment to be considered suitable and sufficient in the eyes of the law it must accurately reflect the "significant" hazards found when assembling, moving or dismantling tower scaffolds at your place of work.

Note. This risk assessment only deals with the generic risks associated with tower scaffolds. You should follow the manufacturer's instructions at all times and such scaffolds should only be erected, dismantled and moved by competent staff.

RISK ASSESSMENT - MOBILE TOWER SCAFFOLDS

ACTIVITY	PERSON AT RISK	SIGNIFICANT HAZARDS	RISK*			RISK CONTROL MEASURES	RESIDUAL RISK**		
			L	S	DR		L	S	DR
Erecting a tower scaffold	Operative	Falls from height, electric shocks	4	4	16	• Tower to be erected as per the "through the trap" (3T) or advanced guard rail system as recommended by the HSE. • Tower scaffolds to be erected by trained personnel only, i.e. those who have been on a course approved by PASMA. • Operatives not to climb on the outside of the tower at any time. • Towers to only be erected on solid, secure standing. • Towers not to be erected underneath power lines. • Guard rails, edge protection and stabilisers to be used where necessary.	3	2	6
Working at height from a tower scaffold	As above	Falls from height	4	4	16	• Those using the tower to stay within the confines of the tower at all times. • The tower not to be overloaded with equipment. • No parts of the tower to be removed or adjusted whilst in use. • Equipment not to be hoisted up the side of the tower.	3	2	6
Moving a tower scaffold	As above	Toppling, crushing those below	4	4	16	• Path to be cleared of all debris before tower moved. • Ground to be checked for stability. • Scaffolds to be checked on a regular basis for stability etc. by trained personnel.	3	3	6

RISK ASSESSMENT - MOBILE TOWER SCAFFOLDS

ACTIVITY	PERSON AT RISK	SIGNIFICANT HAZARDS	RISK*			RISK CONTROL MEASURES	RESIDUAL RISK**		
			L	S	DR		L	S	DR
Dismantling a tower scaffold	As above	Falls from height, toppling, crushing those below	3	4	12	• Tower scaffolds to be dismantled, moved and re-erected by trained personnel only. • Tower to be dismantled as per the "through the trap" (3T) method or advanced guard rail system as recommended by the HSE.	3	2	6

LIKELIHOOD (L) = Frequent (5) - Probable (4) - Occasional (3) - Improbable (2) - Remote (1)
SEVERITY (S) = Catastrophic (5) - Major (4) - Reportable (3) - Serious (2) - Minor (1)
Degree of Risk (DR) = LIKELIHOOD x SEVERITY
* Numbers used are for illustrative purposes only. ** Residual risk is the level of risk that remains after suitable and sufficient control measures are introduced.

Signed originator.. Job title..

Date completed.. Date for revision...

Painting and decorating

Painting and decorating is not hazard-free. Care needs to be taken to prevent an accident connected with working at height from a ladder or work platform. Plus there are the added dangers of using flammable materials in the workplace.

These hazards could present risks to staff and others which, left unmanaged, may cause accidents and potentially put you on the wrong side of the law. To ensure that this doesn't happen, you should complete a risk assessment for painting and decorating activities, which identifies all "significant" hazards and appropriate "reasonable" ways of reducing risks to an acceptable level. You should ensure that your document only addresses "significant" hazards, i.e. any that could, and more importantly are likely to, cause an accident or injury.

Managing the risks

To help you identify the hazards associated with painting and decorating and the appropriate ways of controlling them, use our example **Risk Assessment - Painting and Decorating**. It covers the generic hazards associated with this type of activity and suggests control measures to reduce risks to an acceptable level. This should help you to manage the risks associated with this task.

Make your instructions clear

Don't include activities in your document that simply don't need to be there. Work to the principle that if there is any chance of your staff being unaware of the safe way of doing something, then you will need to make it clear in your document. Finally, always ensure that any control measures you identify and follow are decided upon the principle of "so far as is reasonably practicable". **Note.** The list of potential hazards is not exhaustive. However, for your risk assessment to be considered suitable and sufficient in the eyes of the law it must accurately reflect the "significant" hazards associated with the painting and decorating tasks that your staff will be carrying out.

RISK ASSESSMENT - PAINTING AND DECORATING

ACTIVITY	PERSON AT RISK	SIGNIFICANT HAZARDS	RISK*			RISK CONTROL MEASURES	RESIDUAL RISK**		
			L	S	DR		L	S	DR
Working at height using a ladder	Members of staff	Falls from a ladder due to unsafe working practices may lead to serious or fatal injuries	4	5	20	• Ladders to be used only for short duration work where no other means of access is feasible. • Ladders to be checked before use. • No over-reaching to be allowed when working from the ladder. Three points of contact to be maintained when working from a ladder. • Paint containers to be hung from the ladder using a proprietary device.	3	3	9
As above	As above	Erecting ladders where PVC sheeting is used as a dustsheet may lead to ladders slipping, causing falls resulting in serious injuries	4	5	20	• Ladders not to be erected on PVC dustsheets. Where the surface is to be protected against paint splashes, then a fabric ground sheet to be used. • All ladders to be secured to prevent slipping.	3	3	9
Working at height using stepladders	As above	Falls due to incorrect choice of stepladder or incorrect working technique	4	3	12	• Consideration to be given to the use of podium type stepladders. • Three points of contact to be maintained when working from a stepladder. • Stepladders to be checked before use. • Staff to ensure a handhold is always available.	3	2	6
Working at height from a tower scaffold	As above	Falls from unstable tower scaffolds may lead to serious injuries	4	4	16	Tower scaffolds to be erected by trained personnel only. Guardrails, edge protection and stabilisers to be used where necessary. Towers to be erected on firm stable surfaces only.	3	2	6

RISK ASSESSMENT - PAINTING AND DECORATING

ACTIVITY	PERSON AT RISK	SIGNIFICANT HAZARDS	RISK*			RISK CONTROL MEASURES	RESIDUAL RISK**		
			L	S	DR		L	S	DR
Sanding down woodwork etc. before painting	Members of staff	Inhalation of paint, wood/metal dusts etc. may result in respiratory illnesses	4	3	12	• All staff to wear respiratory protection when sanding down old painted surfaces, woodwork, metalwork etc. • All dusts to be dampened down before sweeping up.	3	2	6
Moving about in general	As above	Contaminated floors may lead to injuries from slipping, tripping and falling	5	4	20	• Floor surfaces to be kept in a good clean condition. • Spilled paint and liquids to be cleaned up immediately. • Work areas to be cordoned off to prevent access by other people.	3	2	6
Use of flammable materials such as paint thinners etc.	As above	Failure to use and store flammable materials may lead to a fire resulting in burns etc. and property damage	3	4	12	• Flammable liquids to be kept to a minimum on site and locked in a flameproof cabinet when not in use. • Naked flames, e.g. from blowlamps etc., to be kept away from the area where flammable liquids are being used/stored. • Staff to be made aware of fire prevention methods associated with their work.	3	2	6
As above	As above	Failure to dispose of rags and cleaning cloths used in conjunction with flammable liquids may lead to a fire resulting in burns etc. and property damage	3	4	12	• All rags and cleaning cloths used with flammable liquids to be placed in a flameproof, lidded container after use. • Containers to be kept away from naked flames. • All such rags and cleaning cloths etc. to be disposed of properly.	3	2	6

RISK ASSESSMENT - PAINTING AND DECORATING

ACTIVITY	PERSON AT RISK	SIGNIFICANT HAZARDS	RISK*			RISK CONTROL MEASURES	RESIDUAL RISK**		
			L	S	DR		L	S	DR
Use of paints and varnishes etc.	Members of staff	Some types of paint may give off hazardous fumes that may cause respiratory illnesses etc.	3	3	9	• Where possible, paints and varnishes etc. to be of a non-hazardous type. • Staff to be instructed to read the safety label on all paint, varnish etc. containers before use. • Where a substance is identified as hazardous, a COSHH assessment to be carried out and specific control measures introduced.	3	2	6
As above	As above	Paint splashes on the body may lead to skin irritation etc.	3	3	9	• Staff to wear the relevant personal protective equipment when carrying out painting tasks, including coveralls, gloves, eye shields etc. • All splashes on the skin to be treated immediately.	3	1	3
Use of cutting tools during wallpapering	As above	The incorrect choice of cutting tool may lead to hand injuries	3	2	6	• Staff to use decorator's scissors for cutting wallpaper. • The use of knives to be forbidden.	3	1	3

LIKELIHOOD (L) = Frequent (5) - Probable (4) - Occasional (3) - Improbable (2) - Remote (1)
SEVERITY (S) = Catastrophic (5) - Major (4) - Reportable (3) - Serious (2) - Minor (1)
Degree of Risk (DR) = LIKELIHOOD x SEVERITY
* Numbers used are for illustrative purposes only. ** Residual risk is the level of risk that remains after suitable and sufficient control measures are introduced.

Signed originator.. Job title..

Date completed.. Date for revision...

Safe removal and disposal of small amounts of asbestos-containing materials

If asbestos-containing materials (ACMs) are removed and handled incorrectly, this could lead to serious risks to health and possible prosecution.

Managing the risks

To help you to identify the hazards associated with the removal and disposal of ACMs and the appropriate ways of controlling them, use our example **Risk Assessment - Safe Removal and Disposal of Small Amounts of Asbestos-Containing Materials**. It covers the generic hazards associated with this type of activity and suggests control measures to reduce risks to an acceptable level. You should ensure that your document only addresses "significant" hazards, i.e. any that could, and more importantly are likely to, cause an accident or injury.

Make your instructions clear

Don't include activities in your document that simply don't need to be there. Work to the principle that if there is any chance of your staff being unaware of the safe way of doing something, then you will need to make it clear in your document. Finally, always ensure that any control measures you identify and follow are decided upon the principle of "so far as is reasonably practicable".

Note. The list of potential hazards is not exhaustive. However, for your risk assessment to be considered suitable and sufficient in the eyes of the law it must accurately reflect the "significant" hazards found when removing and disposing of small amounts of asbestos-containing materials.

Note. This risk assessment only deals with the removal and disposal of small amounts of asbestos-containing materials. Larger amounts should be removed and disposed of by a licensed asbestos removal contractor.

RISK ASSESSMENT - SAFE REMOVAL OF SMALL AMOUNTS OF ASBESTOS-CONTAINING MATERIALS

ACTIVITY	PERSON AT RISK	SIGNIFICANT HAZARDS	RISK*			RISK CONTROL MEASURES	RESIDUAL RISK**		
			L	S	DR		L	S	DR
Removal of asbestos-containing materials	Staff	Breaking up of asbestos-containing materials can lead to the inhalation of asbestos fibres which may result in serious respiratory diseases	4	4	16	• All work to be planned so that the release of asbestos fibres is minimised. • Asbestos-containing materials not to be broken up. • All staff to wear disposable overalls, gloves and a respirator suitable for protection against asbestos dust. • All work areas to be kept clear of other staff members. • Asbestos-containing materials to be left whole, e.g. boards not broken up.	3	2	6
As above	As above	Handling asbestos-containing materials can lead to the inhalation of asbestos fibres which may result in serious respiratory diseases	3	4	12	• Control measures as above. • Additional control measures include: all asbestos-containing materials to be dampened down before handling.	3	2	6
As above	As above	Cutting or sawing asbestos-containing materials can lead to the inhalation of asbestos fibres which may result in serious respiratory diseases	4	4	16	• Asbestos-containing materials not to be cut or sawn.	3	2	6

RISK ASSESSMENT - SAFE REMOVAL OF SMALL AMOUNTS OF ASBESTOS-CONTAINING MATERIALS

ACTIVITY	PERSON AT RISK	SIGNIFICANT HAZARDS	RISK*			RISK CONTROL MEASURES	RESIDUAL RISK**		
			L	S	DR		L	S	DR
Disposal of small amounts of asbestos-containing materials	Staff, others	Failure to dispose of asbestos-containing materials properly can lead to the inhalation of asbestos fibres which may result in serious respiratory diseases	4	4	16	• Small amounts of asbestos-containing materials such as pieces of insulation board, lagging or floor tiles etc. to be placed in heavy-duty polythene bags. Bags to then be sealed and placed inside a second bag. • The second bag to have its contents labelled as containing asbestos.	3	2	6
Cleaning of work area	Staff	Failure to clean the work area may lead to the inhalation of asbestos fibres which may result in serious respiratory diseases	3	4	12	• All work surfaces to be wiped down with a damp cloth. • Where dust is produced, this should be wetted before sweeping up. • Only vacuum cleaners specifically suited for asbestos work (H Type) to be used to clean up asbestos dust.	3	2	6
Disposal of contaminated clothing etc.	As above	Failure to dispose of contaminated clothing can lead to the inhalation of asbestos fibres which may result in serious respiratory diseases	4	4	16	• All contaminated disposable clothing to be disposed of as asbestos waste and treated as above. • Other clothing to be placed in a heavy-duty polythene bag and washed after work has finished. • Staff not to travel to home etc. wearing contaminated clothing.	3	2	6

RISK ASSESSMENT - SAFE REMOVAL OF SMALL AMOUNTS OF ASBESTOS-CONTAINING MATERIALS

ACTIVITY	PERSON AT RISK	SIGNIFICANT HAZARDS	RISK*			RISK CONTROL MEASURES	RESIDUAL RISK**		
			L	S	DR		L	S	DR
Final disposal of asbestos-containing materials	Staff	Failure to dispose of asbestos-containing materials may lead to prosecution under environmental legislation	3	3	9	• All double-bagged asbestos-containing materials to be disposed of at a waste disposal site licensed to take asbestos waste.	2	2	4

LIKELIHOOD (L) = Frequent (5) - Probable (4) - Occasional (3) - Improbable (2) - Remote (1)
SEVERITY (S) = Catastrophic (5) - Major (4) - Reportable (3) - Serious (2) - Minor (1)
Degree of Risk (DR) = LIKELIHOOD x SEVERITY
* Numbers used are for illustrative purposes only.
** Residual risk is the level of risk that remains after suitable and sufficient control measures are introduced.

Signed originator.. Job title..

Date completed.. Date for revision..

Slips, trips and falls

Slips, trips and falls are one of the most common causes of accidents in the workplace. So use our document to identify the hazards and appropriate control measures.

Workplace hazard

To prevent accidents of this type you should complete a risk assessment of your workplace, which identifies all "significant" hazards and appropriate "reasonable" ways of reducing risks to an acceptable level.

Managing the risks

To help you identify the hazards and appropriate ways of controlling them, use our example **Risk Assessment - Slips, Trips and Falls**. It covers the generic hazards found in most work environments that can lead to staff slipping, tripping or falling and suggests control measures to reduce risks to an acceptable level.

You should ensure that your document only addresses "significant" hazards, i.e. any that could, and more importantly are likely to, cause an accident or injury.

Keep it to the point

There is no point in including activities that simply don't need to be there. Work to the principle that if there is any chance of your staff being unaware of the safe way of keeping your workplace safe and preventing slips, trips and falls, then you will need to make it clear on your document. Finally, always ensure any control measures you identify and follow only go so far "as is reasonably practicable".

Note. The list of potential hazards is not exhaustive because you know your workplace better than we do. However, for your risk assessment to be considered suitable and sufficient in the eyes of the law it must accurately reflect the "significant" hazards found in your workplace.

RISK ASSESSMENT - SLIPS, TRIPS AND FALLS

ACTIVITY	PERSON AT RISK	SIGNIFICANT HAZARDS	RISK*			RISK CONTROL MEASURES	RESIDUAL RISK**		
			L	S	DR		L	S	DR
Getting about in general	Operative(s), visitors etc.	Contaminated floors can lead to injuries from slipping, tripping and falling	5	4	20	• Floor surfaces to be kept in a good, clean condition. • Spilled liquids to be cleaned up immediately. • Warning notices to be put out when floor cleaning is in operation. • Floors surfaces are kept free from grease, oil etc. • Floor surfaces not to be left highly polished.	3	2	6
As above	As above	Floor coverings in poor condition can cause tripping accidents leading to fall injuries	4	4	16	• Floor finishes to be kept in good condition (carpets etc.). • Areas to be closed off until hazards are dealt with. • Regular inspection of floor areas to be carried out.	3	1	3
As above	Operative(s)	Trailing cables etc. can cause tripping accidents leading to fall injuries	4	4	16	• All trailing cables to be secured away from walkways. • Additional power points to be installed, to remove the need for extension leads. • Temporary trailing cables to be covered to prevent a tripping hazard.	3	1	3
Getting about in kitchen areas	Catering staff	Floors contaminated by cooking oils and fats, water, spilled foodstuffs etc. can cause slipping and tripping injuries	4	3	12	• A good cleaning regime to be in place. • Regular removal of waste products. • Regular inspections to be carried out. • Staff to wear suitable footwear.	3	1	3

RISK ASSESSMENT - SLIPS, TRIPS AND FALLS

ACTIVITY	PERSON AT RISK	SIGNIFICANT HAZARDS	RISK*			RISK CONTROL MEASURES	RESIDUAL RISK**		
			L	S	DR		L	S	DR
Getting about in external areas	Operative(s), visitors etc.	Pedestrian walk areas in poor condition can lead to trips and falls injuries	4	4	16	• Surfaces in paved area must be level and in good condition. • Other surface finishes (tarmac, concrete etc.) to be kept in good condition. • Pedestrian walkways to be regularly inspected. • Temporary barriers to be used to segregate hazardous areas until remedial work can be done - check barriers regularly. • Areas that are covered in snow and ice to be segregated.	3	1	3
As above	As above	Poorly lit areas can lead to trips and falling injuries	4	2	8	• External lighting to be suitable, i.e. does not cause shadows and is bright enough. • All external lighting to be properly maintained.	3	1	3
Working outside in poor weather conditions	Operative(s)	Working outside during wet, frosty or icy conditions can lead to slip and fall injuries	4	4	16	• Operatives to wear suitable footwear. • Work to be postponed if weather conditions deteriorate. • Salt etc. to be used to thaw out frost or snow covered walking areas.	3	2	6

LIKELIHOOD (L) = Frequent (5) - Probable (4) - Occasional (3) - Improbable (2) - Remote (1)
SEVERITY (S) = Catastrophic (5) - Major (4) - Reportable (3) - Serious (2) - Minor (1)
Degree of Risk (DR) = LIKELIHOOD x SEVERITY
* Numbers used are for illustrative purposes only.
** Residual risk is the level of risk that remains after suitable and sufficient control measures are introduced.

Signed originator.. Job title..

Date completed.. Date for revision..

Slips, trips and falls in kitchens

Slips, trips and falls in kitchen areas may present risks to staff, which left unmanaged could cause accidents and potentially put you on the wrong side of the law.

Managing the risks

To help you identify the hazards associated with kitchen work that cause slips, trips and falls and the appropriate ways of controlling them, use our example **Risk Assessment - Slips, Trips and Falls in Kitchens**. It covers the generic hazards associated with this type of activity and suggests control measures to reduce risks to an acceptable level.

Note. You should ensure that your document only addresses "significant" hazards, i.e. any that could, and more importantly are likely to, cause an accident or injury.

Make your instructions clear

Don't include activities in your document that simply don't need to be there. Work to the principle that if there is any chance of your staff being unaware of the safe way of doing something, then you will need to make it clear in your document. Finally, always ensure that any control measures you identify and follow are decided upon the principle of "so far as is reasonably practicable".

Note. The list of potential hazards is not exhaustive. However, for your risk assessment to be considered suitable and sufficient in the eyes of the law it must accurately reflect the "significant" hazards associated with the causes of slips, trips and falls in your kitchen. You will need further risk assessments

RISK ASSESSMENT - SLIPS, TRIPS AND FALLS IN KITCHENS

ACTIVITY	PERSON AT RISK	SIGNIFICANT HAZARDS	RISK*			RISK CONTROL MEASURES	RESIDUAL RISK**		
			L	S	DR		L	S	DR
Moving about in general	Kitchen Staff	Contaminated floors may lead to slips, trips and falls causing physical injuries	4	4	16	• A regular floor-cleaning regime to be put in place. • Staff to be instructed to clean up spillages as they occur. • Floors to be regularly inspected by supervisors.	3	2	6
As above	As above	Failure to wear suitable footwear may increase the possibility of slips and falls leading to physical injuries	4	3	12	• Staff to be provided with suitable footwear with slip resistant soles. • Supervisors to check that footwear provided is being worn.	3	1	3
As above	As above	Poorly maintained floor surfaces may increase the likelihood of slips and falls leading to physical injuries	3	3	9	• Floor surfaces to be regularly inspected to ensure that they are maintained in a satisfactory condition. • Smooth surfaces to be treated with anti-slips strips or abrading. • Floors to be deep cleaned to remove grease etc. on a regular basis.	3	1	3
Floor cleaning using electrically operated cleaning machines	Cleaners	Trailing leads from cleaning machines may lead to tripping incidents causing physical injuries.	3	3	9	• Cleaning staff to be trained in the use of cleaning machinery. • Sufficient socket outlets to be provided to minimise the need for long flexes.	2	1	2

RISK ASSESSMENT - SLIPS, TRIPS AND FALLS IN KITCHENS

ACTIVITY	PERSON AT RISK	SIGNIFICANT HAZARDS	RISK*			RISK CONTROL MEASURES	RESIDUAL RISK**		
			L	S	DR		L	S	DR
Working in kitchen areas	Kitchen Staff	Poor environmental conditions may lead to staff slipping, tripping and falling causing physical injuries	4	3	12	• Lighting standards to be maintained to ensure good visibility of floor conditions etc. • Lighting to be such that the presence of shadows is eliminated.	3	2	6
As above	As above	Leaking equipment may lead to contaminated floors resulting in slip and falls causing physical injuries	4	4	16	• Equipment to be regularly checked for leakages and maintenance arrangements to be put in place. • Where necessary equipment to be fitted with drip trays that will be emptied regularly. • Areas around fryers etc. to be fitted with a bunding system to retain leaks and spillages.	3	2	6

LIKELIHOOD (L) = Frequent (5) - Probable (4) - Occasional (3) - Improbable (2) - Remote (1)
SEVERITY (S) = Catastrophic (5) - Major (4) - Reportable (3) - Serious (2) - Minor (1)
Degree of Risk (DR) = LIKELIHOOD x SEVERITY
* Numbers used are for illustrative purposes only.
** Residual risk is the level of risk that remains after suitable and sufficient control measures are introduced.

Signed originator.. Job title..

Date completed.. Date for revision...

Unblocking drains and pipes

Unblocking drains and pipes can be a hazardous activity for those carrying out such work. These risks will exist whether you are unblocking drains and pipes by hand rodding, using high-pressure water jetting or even pipework dismantling.

If these risks are left unmanaged, they could cause accidents and potentially put you on the wrong side of the law. To ensure that this doesn't happen you should complete a risk assessment for such activities, which identifies all "significant" hazards and appropriate "reasonable" ways of reducing risks to an acceptable level. You should ensure that your document only addresses "significant" hazards, i.e. any that could, and more importantly are likely to, cause an accident or injury.

Managing the risks

To help you identify the hazards associated with these activities and the appropriate ways of controlling them, use our example **Risk Assessment - Unblocking Drains and Pipes**. It covers the generic hazards associated with this type of activity and suggests control measures to reduce risks to an acceptable level. You can use this as a basis for conducting your own assessment.

Make your instructions clear

Don't include activities in your document that simply don't need to be there. Work to the principle that if there is any chance of your staff being unaware of the safe way of doing something, then you will need to make it clear in your document. Finally, always ensure that any control measures you identify and follow are decided upon the principle of "so far as is reasonably practicable".

Note. The list of potential hazards is not exhaustive. However, for your risk assessment to be considered suitable and sufficient in the eyes of the law it must accurately reflect the "significant" hazards found when carrying out this type

RISK ASSESSMENT - UNBLOCKING DRAINS AND PIPES

ACTIVITY	PERSON AT RISK	SIGNIFICANT HAZARDS	RISK*			RISK CONTROL MEASURES	RESIDUAL RISK**		
			L	S	DR		L	S	DR
Removing manhole covers	Staff	Incorrect lifting techniques may lead to muscular injuries	4	3	12	• Staff to be trained in the correct method of removal. • Ergonomic lifting devices to be used where possible (hydraulically operated). • Where keys are used they are to be long-handled to minimise back strain.	3	2	6
Contact with foul water/ sewage	As above	Infection; illness from water splashes; ingested water etc.	4	3	12	• All staff to wear suitable personal protective equipment - rubber gloves, disposable or waterproof coveralls, Wellington boots, eye and/or face protection, respirator etc. • Staff to ensure good personal hygiene, washing with hot water (particularly before eating or drinking). • Staff to ensure that equipment is cleaned after use. • Cuts and grazes etc. to be treated immediately by cleaning and covering with a waterproof plaster.	3	2	6
Rodding of drains to clear blockages	As above	Incorrect rodding technique may lead to muscular injuries	3	3	9	• Staff to be trained in the use of rodding equipment, particularly in how to deal with blockages in drains. • Staff to ensure correct rodding heads are used for particular types of blockages.	3	1	3
Use of high-pressure water jet equipment to clear drains	As above and people in vicinity	Tripping hazards from hoses; falls due to loss of balance when handling high-pressure hoses; slippery conditions underfoot due to water spillage	4	2	8	• Areas to be guarded to prevent access by others. • Staff to wear suitable footwear, e.g. Wellington boots. • Staff to only run out the minimum amount of hose from hose reel. • Staff to keep surface water to a minimum and clean up regularly.	3	1	3

RISK ASSESSMENT - UNBLOCKING DRAINS AND PIPES

ACTIVITY	PERSON AT RISK	SIGNIFICANT HAZARDS	RISK*			RISK CONTROL MEASURES	RESIDUAL RISK**		
			L	S	DR		L	S	DR
Use of drain cleaning fluids etc.	Staff	Skin contact with chemical cleaners may lead to burns, skin irritation etc. Fumes from some chemicals may lead to respiratory problems	4	2	8	• Chemical cleaners to only be used as a last resort when other unblocking methods have failed. • COSHH assessments to be carried out prior to use. • Areas to be kept well ventilated. • Staff to follow the manufacturer's instructions at all times for use, storage and disposal. • Staff to wear the appropriate PPE.	3	1	3
Cleaning blocked drains and pipes (general)	As above	Working around water etc. may lead to slips, trips and falls	4	2	8	• Staff to ensure that floor surface areas are kept clean and free from slipping and tripping hazards. • Staff to wear suitable footwear, such as Wellington boots.	3	1	3
As above	As above	Regular contact with foul water may lead to Weil's disease	3	3	9	• All staff to receive training regarding Weil's disease. • All staff to ensure that cuts and grazes are immediately cleaned and the wound covered up using a waterproof plaster.	3	1	3

LIKELIHOOD (L) = Frequent (5) - Probable (4) - Occasional (3) - Improbable (2) - Remote (1)
SEVERITY (S) = Catastrophic (5) - Major (4) - Reportable (3) - Serious (2) - Minor (1) Degree of Risk (DR) = LIKELIHOOD x SEVERITY
* Numbers used are for illustrative purposes only. ** Residual risk is the level of risk that remains after suitable and sufficient control measures are introduced.

Signed originator.. Job title...

Date completed... Date for revision...

Use of ladders and stepladders

Using ladders and stepladders in the workplace can be dangerous. Accidents may involve falling from height, resulting in serious injuries and even death.

Managing the risks

To help you identify the hazards associated with ladder and stepladder use and the appropriate ways of controlling them, use our example **Risk Assessment - Use of Ladders and Stepladders**. It covers the generic hazards associated with this type of activity and suggests control measures to reduce risks to an acceptable level. **Note.** This risk assessment only deals with the use of ladders and stepladders in the more common situations. You should be aware that working at height should be the exception not the rule, and a ladder or basic stepladder may not necessarily be the best option for working at height. Ladder use should be restricted to work of a short duration, i.e. lasting no longer than 30 minutes. You should ensure that your risk assessment addresses "significant" hazards, i.e. any that could, and more importantly are likely to, cause an accident or injury. On completion of your document if you cannot introduce the relevant risk control measures, then you should consider an alternative means of access, such as a mobile elevated work platform, portable scaffolding or podium steps etc.

Make your instructions clear

Don't include activities in your document that simply don't need to be there. Work to the principle that if there is any chance of your staff being unaware of the safe way of doing something, then you will need to make it clear in your document. Finally, always ensure that any control measures you identify and follow are decided upon the principle of "so far as is reasonably practicable".

Note. The list of potential hazards is not exhaustive. However, for your risk assessment to be considered suitable and sufficient in the eyes of the law it must accurately reflect the "significant" hazards found when using ladders or stepladders.

RISK ASSESSMENT - USE OF LADDERS AND STEPLADDERS

ACTIVITY	PERSON AT RISK	SIGNIFICANT HAZARDS	RISK*			RISK CONTROL MEASURES	RESIDUAL RISK**		
			L	S	DR		L	S	DR
Part 1 - Choice of equipment	User	Choosing the wrong type of access equipment (ladders, stepladders) may lead to user falling, resulting in either serious injury or death	3	5	15	• The work activity to be planned so that working at height will be avoided where possible. • Ladders to be chosen only where the work is of short duration, i.e. no longer than 30 minutes. • Ladders to be used only for light work. • Ladders to be used only when the work will allow for a handhold at all times. • Ladders to be used only where three points of contact can be maintained at the working position. • Ladders to be chosen only where the worksite presents no other alternative means of access. • Ladders only of the correct height and type for the work to be chosen. • Only stepladders that have a suitable working platform, leaning bar, handhold and which are of the correct height to be chosen.	3	2	6

RISK ASSESSMENT - USE OF LADDERS AND STEPLADDERS

ACTIVITY	PERSON AT RISK	SIGNIFICANT HAZARDS	RISK*			RISK CONTROL MEASURES	RESIDUAL RISK**		
			L	S	DR		L	S	DR
Part 2 - Checking ladders before use	User	Using a damaged ladder may cause it to fail resulting in serious injury or death	4	5	20	• All ladders to be inspected before each time of use. • Ladder stiles to be checked for bends, splits, cracks or other damage. • Ladder rungs to be checked for secureness, wear, clean treads and general damage. (Missing rungs will make the ladder unserviceable.) • Ladder feet to be inspected for wear and damage. • Wooden ladders to be checked for warp and splits in stiles, worn, damaged or missing rungs. • Ladders to be checked for a label indicating their last formal test date. • Ladders to be checked for a label stating Class 1 or EN 131 that indicates their suitability for use in a work situation.	3	3	9
Part 2 - Checking stepladders before use	User	Using a damaged stepladder may cause it to fail resulting in serious injury	4	4	16	• All stepladders to be inspected before each time of use. • Stepladders to be inspected to ensure that there are no obvious defects such as damaged or twisted stiles, steps or damage to the working platform. • Stepladders to be checked so that any restraining devices are in good condition. • Stepladders to be checked so that stepladder feet are in good condition. • Wooden stepladders to be inspected for warp, splits and general wear to the frame and steps/working platform.	3	2	6

RISK ASSESSMENT - USE OF LADDERS AND STEPLADDERS

ACTIVITY	PERSON AT RISK	SIGNIFICANT HAZARDS	RISK*			RISK CONTROL MEASURES	RESIDUAL RISK**		
			L	S	DR		L	S	DR
Part 3 – ladders Use of ladders against a wall or building etc.	User	Unsecured ladders may cause both the ladder and the user to fall, resulting in serious injury or death	3	5	15	• All ladders to be secured at the base and the top to prevent slipping. Footing will be undertaken if unable to secure the base. • Ladders to be erected so that they are one metre above the actual working height and the top three rungs will remain clear. • Ladders not to be used where the ground conditions are uneven or not firm. • Ladders not to be used where the floor surface is slippery.	3	2	6
As above	As above	Falls when climbing ladders may result in serious injury or death	3	5	15	• Users to ensure that they are wearing suitable footwear for climbing. • Tools and equipment not to be carried whilst climbing ladders but to be taken up using a line or a tool belt.	3	2	6
As above	As above	Falls may occur if the ladder is not erected at the correct angle	3	5	15	• All ladders to be erected so that the angle of erection is 75°, i.e. four units up for each unit out from the wall, building etc.	2	2	4
As above	As above	Ladders erected against plastic guttering may lead to the ladder slipping, resulting in serious injury or death	3	5	15	• Ladders not to be erected against plastic guttering. Where necessary, ladder stand-offs or spreader bars to be used.	3	2	6

RISK ASSESSMENT - USE OF LADDERS AND STEPLADDERS

ACTIVITY	PERSON AT RISK	SIGNIFICANT HAZARDS	RISK*			RISK CONTROL MEASURES	RESIDUAL RISK**		
			L	S	DR		L	S	DR
Part 3 – Contd	User	Ladders erected close to overhead power supplies may lead to the user receiving an electric shock resulting in serous burns or death	3	5	15	• Ladders not to be erected within six metres horizontally of any overhead power lines unless they have been made "dead" or have been protected with temporary insulation.	3	2	6
As above	As above	Ladders erected so that they obstruct walkways or vehicle routes may lead to a collision causing the user to fall, resulting in serious injury or death	3	5	15	• Ladders to be erected so that they do not obstruct vehicle or pedestrian traffic areas. • Where this is unavoidable, suitable barriers or a lookout to be used.	3	2	6
As above	As above	Users who are not competent in ladder use may fall, resulting in serious injury or death	3	5	15	• Only competent staff (competent by training and experience) to use ladders in the workplace.	2	2	4

RISK ASSESSMENT - USE OF LADDERS AND STEPLADDERS

ACTIVITY	PERSON AT RISK	SIGNIFICANT HAZARDS	RISK*			RISK CONTROL MEASURES	RESIDUAL RISK**		
			L	S	DR		L	S	DR
Part 3 – Use of stepladders - general	User	Stepladders erected on uneven ground may cause the ladder and user to fall, resulting in serious injury	3	4	12	• Stepladders only to be used on firm, even floor surfaces. • Where possible, stepladders to be tied-in.	3	2	6
As above	As above	Work that imposes a side loading, such as side-on drilling through solid materials, e.g. bricks or concrete, may cause a stepladder and the user to fall, resulting in serious injury	3	4	12	• Side loading to be avoided by ensuring the stepladder is facing the work activity. • Where side loading is unavoidable, then the stepladders should be tied-in to prevent overturning. Where this is not possible, an alternative means of access should be deployed.	3	2	6
As above	As above	Failure to erect stepladders so that they are fully open may lead to the ladder and the user falling, resulting in serious injury	3	4	12	• Stepladders always to be erected so that they are in the fully open position with all restraining devices in place.	3	2	6

RISK ASSESSMENT - USE OF LADDERS AND STEPLADDERS

ACTIVITY	PERSON AT RISK	SIGNIFICANT HAZARDS	RISK*			RISK CONTROL MEASURES	RESIDUAL RISK**		
			L	S	DR		L	S	DR
Part 3 - contd	User	Stepladders without a handhold may cause the user to overbalance and fall resulting in serious injury	3	4	12	• Only stepladders with a handhold to be used. • Users to maintain three points of contact at the working position.	3	2	6
As above	As above	Ladders erected so that they obstruct walkways or vehicle routes may lead to a collision causing the user to fall, resulting in serious injury	3	4	12	• Ladders to be erected so that they do not obstruct vehicle or pedestrian traffic areas. • Where this is unavoidable, suitable barriers or a lookout to be used.	3	2	6

LIKELIHOOD (L) = Frequent (5) - Probable (4) - Occasional (3) - Improbable (2) - Remote (1)
SEVERITY (S) = Catastrophic (5) - Major (4) - Reportable (3) - Serious (2) - Minor (1)
Degree of Risk (DR) = LIKELIHOOD x SEVERITY
* Numbers used are for illustrative purposes only.
** Residual risk is the level of risk that remains after suitable and sufficient control measures are introduced.

Signed originator.. Job title..

Date completed... Date for revision...

Violence against staff

Violence towards employees is a growing problem in the workplace and you have a duty to safeguard their personal safety in this regard.

Violence at work

There are particular risks and hazards arising from violence to employees both from other members of staff or the public which, if left unmanaged, could cause injury and potentially put you on the wrong side of the law. To ensure that this doesn't happen you should complete a risk assessment for your specific activities, which identifies all "significant" hazards and appropriate "reasonable" ways of reducing risks to an acceptable level.

Managing the risks

To help you identify the hazards associated with workplace violence use our example **Risk Assessment - Violence against Staff**. It covers the generic issues associated with incidents of this type which result in harassment (because of gender, race etc.), verbal abuse/threats and attempted or actual physical assault. The assessment provided is not exhaustive, but use it as a guide to help you complete an assessment for your own staff, which relates to the work they carry out. Further advice on risk assessments of this nature can be obtained from the HSE: http://www.hse.gov.uk/pubns/violindx.htm.

You should ensure that your document only addresses "significant" hazards, i.e. any that could, and more importantly are likely to, cause an accident or injury.

Make your instructions clear

Always ensure any control measures you identify and follow are decided upon the principle of "so far as is reasonably practicable" and that you brief your final assessment out to your staff.

Note. To accompany such an assessment you should ensure that your company has a robust policy in place which sets out how you would deal with incidents of violence as a result of your employees' activities.

RISK ASSESSMENT - VIOLENCE AGAINST STAFF

ACTIVITY	PERSON AT RISK	SIGNIFICANT HAZARDS	RISK*			RISK CONTROL MEASURES	RESIDUAL RISK**		
			L	S	DR		L	S	DR
Working in reception areas	Staff	Verbal or physical threats/abuse	4	4	16	• Reception areas to be at the front of the building and to be well lit. To be constructed so that protective screens are in position, counters to be at a suitable height and visitors to be prevented access to the staff area. • Receptionists to have access to a panic alarm to summon assistance. • Security staff to monitor access and egress to/from the building.	3	2	6
Face-to-face meetings with members of the public	As above	As above	4	4	16	• Interview rooms to be "open plan" so that other staff members are in the vicinity to offer assistance. • Staff carrying out interviews to have access to a panic alarm to summon assistance. • All staff to be given training in dealing with abusive situations. • Where such meetings take place off site then staff to be issued with personal panic alarms. • Records to be kept of all such incidents and client personal profiles referred to before repeat visits.	3	2	6
Lone working	As above	As above	3	4	12	• Staff to be given training in the company Lone Working Policy and procedures. • Staff to regularly contact headquarters with details of their whereabouts and any issues. • Staff to be issued with personal panic alarms.	3	2	6

RISK ASSESSMENT - VIOLENCE AGAINST STAFF

ACTIVITY	PERSON AT RISK	SIGNIFICANT HAZARDS	RISK*			RISK CONTROL MEASURES	RESIDUAL RISK**		
			L	S	DR		L	S	DR
Cash handling	Staff	Attempted robbery, possibly with violence, if cash is visible	4	5	20	• All tills to be emptied on a regular basis throughout the working day. Company to consider "cashless" transactions only. • Tills to be situated out of reach of visitors, customers etc. and self-locking after each transaction. • No cash to be left on the premises overnight. • Panic alarm to be situated adjacent to till areas to allow staff to summon assistance. • If cash is to be collected from remote locations, e.g. clients' premises, then arrangements to be in place for regular banking throughout the working period. • All staff who handle cash to receive adequate training.	3	2	6
Dealing with unwelcome visitors/ trespassers	As above	Threats and violence when questioning their presence on the premises	3	4	12	• Main entrance doors to be monitored by security staff. • CCTV surveillance monitoring to be in place. • All internal doors to be fitted with coded security locks.	2	1	2

LIKELIHOOD (L) = Frequent (5) - Probable (4) - Occasional (3) - Improbable (2) - Remote (1)
SEVERITY (S) = Catastrophic (5) - Major (4) - Reportable (3) - Serious (2) - Minor (1)
Degree of Risk (DR) = LIKELIHOOD x SEVERITY
* Numbers used are for illustrative purposes only. ** Residual risk is the level of risk that remains after suitable and sufficient control measures are introduced.

Signed originator.. Job title..

Date completed.. Date for revision..

Winter precautions

Winter weather brings with it hazardous conditions that can affect you, your staff and potentially your customers. Use our document to help you manage the risks.

Snow and ice

If these conditions are left unmanaged, it could lead to accidents and potentially put you on the wrong side of the law.

To ensure that this doesn't happen, you should complete a risk assessment for your specific activities, which identifies all "significant" hazards and appropriate "reasonable" ways of reducing risks to an acceptable level.

Managing the risks

To help you identify the hazards associated with winter weather and the appropriate ways of controlling the risks through forward planning, use our example **Risk Assessment - Winter Precautions**. It covers the generic hazards associated with poor weather conditions and suggests control measures to reduce risks to an acceptable level.

You should ensure that your document only addresses "significant" hazards, i.e. any that could, and more importantly are likely to, cause an accident or injury.

Make your instructions clear

Don't include activities in your document that simply don't need to be there. Work to the principle that if there is any chance of your staff being unaware of the safe way of doing something, then you will need to make it clear in your document. Finally, always ensure that any control measures you identify and follow only go so far "as is reasonably practicable".

Note. The list of potential hazards is not exhaustive. However, for your risk assessment to be considered suitable and sufficient in the eyes of the law it must accurately reflect the "significant" hazards found in your workplace.

RISK ASSESSMENT - WINTER PRECAUTIONS

ACTIVITY	PERSON AT RISK	SIGNIFICANT HAZARDS	RISK*			RISK CONTROL MEASURES	RESIDUAL RISK**		
			L	S	DR		L	S	DR
Access and egress for pedestrians to/from main work areas	All staff and visitors	Potential for injury if a slip and fall occurs due to ice or snow	4	4	16	• Stocks of salt or grit to always be available. • All external walkways to be gritted before staff and visitors arrive in the morning and after they have left at night. • Water absorbent mats to be placed in entrance areas to buildings. • All entrances to be kept free of snow or ice. • Warning notices to be placed on main pedestrian routes to warn of the danger of slippery conditions.	3	2	6
As above	As above	Access and egress during hours of darkness may lead to accidents from slipping or tripping over obstacles	4	3	12	• All external walkway lighting to be checked on a regular basis. • All faulty lights to be reported and repairs put in hand. • Where external lights are time switch operated the times to be adjusted to cater for the hours of darkness relative to staff attendance.	3	1	3
Working outside during extreme winter	Staff	Potential for frost bite or hypothermia	3	3	9	• All staff working outside to wear appropriate winter weather personal protective equipment (PPE). • In extreme conditions tasks to be reviewed and additional rest breaks to be taken. • All staff to be briefed of the need to change out of wet clothing. • Facilities to be provided for wet clothing to be changed or dried.	2	1	2

RISK ASSESSMENT - WINTER PRECAUTIONS

ACTIVITY	PERSON AT RISK	SIGNIFICANT HAZARDS	RISK*			RISK CONTROL MEASURES	RESIDUAL RISK**		
			L	S	DR		L	S	DR
Working indoors (general)	Staff	A low workplace temperature may lead to discomfort and cause ill-health	3	3	9	• Workplace heating to be such that the indoor temperature reaches a minimum of 16°C before work commences. • All central heating systems to be serviced and checked before the onset of winter. • In the event of heating failure temporary heating to be provided where practical and safe to do so.	2	1	2
As above	As above	Poorly maintained temporary heating may lead to fires with a risk to life	3	4	12	• All temporary gas heating to be serviced and checked before use. • All temporary electric heaters to be checked and tested before use. • All heaters to be securely fixed to prevent them toppling over.	3	2	6
As above	As above	Drying clothes on heaters may lead to fires with a risk to life	3	4	12	• All staff to be briefed on the risks of placing wet clothing over heaters. • Supervisors to carry out regular checks.	2	2	4

LIKELIHOOD (L) = Frequent (5) - Probable (4) - Occasional (3) - Improbable (2) - Remote (1)
SEVERITY (S) = Catastrophic (5) - Major (4) - Reportable (3) - Serious (2) - Minor (1)
Degree of Risk (DR) = LIKELIHOOD x SEVERITY
* Numbers used are for illustrative purposes only.
** Residual risk is the level of risk that remains after suitable and sufficient control measures are introduced.

Signed originator.. Job title..

Date completed... Date for revision...

Working at height

If carried out incorrectly or by using the wrong type of access equipment, working at height could cause accidents and potentially put you on the wrong side of the law.

Working at height safely

To ensure that this doesn't happen, you should complete a risk assessment for this activity which identifies all "significant" hazards and appropriate "reasonable" ways of reducing risks to an acceptable level. Wherever possible, you should try to avoid all work at height, but where this is not practical then you must carry out a risk assessment and plan the work accordingly.

Managing the risks

To help you identify the hazards and appropriate ways of controlling them, use our example **Risk Assessment - Working at Height**. It covers the generic hazards associated with working at height and suggests control measures to reduce risks to an acceptable level.

You should ensure that your document only addresses "significant" hazards, i.e. any that could and more importantly are likely to, cause an accident or injury.

Brief your staff

Work to the principle that if there is any chance of your staff being unaware of the safe way of working at height, then you will need to make it clear on your document. Finally, always ensure any control measures you identify and follow only go so far "as is reasonably practicable".

Note. The list of potential hazards is not exhaustive, as each time your staff work at height the conditions may be totally different. For your risk assessment to be considered suitable and sufficient in the eyes of the law it must accurately reflect the "significant" hazards found at the time the activity takes place in your workplace.

RISK ASSESSMENT - WORKING AT HEIGHT

ACTIVITY	PERSON AT RISK	SIGNIFICANT HAZARDS	RISK*			RISK CONTROL MEASURES	RESIDUAL RISK**		
			L	S	DR		L	S	DR
Working at height using a ladder	Operative	Falls from a ladder due to unsafe working practices may lead to serious or fatal injuries	4	5	20	• Ladders to be used only for short duration work when no other means of access is feasible. • Ladders to be checked before use. • No over-reaching when working from the ladder - get down and reposition it. • Three points of contact to be maintained when working from a ladder.	3	3	9
As above	As above	Working from an unstable ladder or a ladder erected at the wrong angle may lead to falls	4	5	20	• Ladders to be checked before use. • Ladders to be erected on a firm base and secured at the top. • Ladder angle to be one unit out at the foot to four units in height.	3	3	9
Working at height using stepladders	As above	Falls due to incorrect choice of stepladder or incorrect working technique	4	3	12	• Consideration to be given to the use of podium type stepladders. • Three points of contact to be maintained when working from a stepladder. • Stepladders to be checked before use. • A handhold must be available. • No over-reaching or exerting sideways pressure.	3	2	6
Working at height from a tower scaffold	As above	Falls from tower scaffolds due to instability can lead to serious injuries	4	4	16	• Tower scaffolds to be erected by trained personnel only. • Guard rails, edge protection and stabilisers to be used where necessary. • Towers to be erected on firm stable surface only.	3	2	6

RISK ASSESSMENT - WORKING AT HEIGHT

ACTIVITY	PERSON AT RISK	SIGNIFICANT HAZARDS	RISK*			RISK CONTROL MEASURES	RESIDUAL RISK**		
			L	S	DR		L	S	DR
Moving a tower scaffold	Operative	Erecting and reassembly of tower scaffolds may be carried out incorrectly leading to operatives falling	4	4	16	• Tower scaffolds to be dismantled, moved and re-erected by trained personnel only. • Scaffolds to be checked on a regular basis for stability etc. by trained personnel.	3	2	6
Working from a mobile elevated working platform (MEWP)	As above	Use of incorrect type of MEWP may lead to it overturning with possibly fatal consequences	4	5	20	• The right MEWP for the job to be selected (consider ground conditions, working height, the task including the range/ sensitivity of movement, the anticipated load, e.g. people and tools). • The MEWP must have a valid test certificate before use.	3	2	6
As above	As above	Incorrect working practices may lead to a fall with possibly fatal consequences	3	5	15	• Operators to be trained in the use of the MEWP. • Operators to use secondary protection, e.g. safety harnesses. • Operators to have task specific training, e.g. use of chainsaws etc.	3	2	6
Working on roofs or fragile surfaces	As above	Failure to take additional precautions when working on roofs or fragile surfaces may lead to operatives falling with possibly fatal consequences	4	5	20	• Suitable means of access to the work area to be provided. • Work on roofs to be assessed for the safest, most suitable means of access to the work area, e.g. consider using MEWPS etc. • If using roof ladders or planks etc., they must be adequately supported and accompanied by suitable guardrails and edge protection. • Operatives should NOT access fragile roofs without a safe system of access.	3	3	9

RISK ASSESSMENT - WORKING AT HEIGHT

ACTIVITY	PERSON AT RISK	SIGNIFICANT HAZARDS	RISK*			RISK CONTROL MEASURES	RESIDUAL RISK**		
			L	S	DR		L	S	DR
Use of lanyards and restraint systems	Operative(s)	Use of faulty systems may lead to them failing causing fall injuries	3	4	12	• All lanyards and safety restraint systems to be checked before use and regularly tested. • Operatives to be trained in their examination and use.	3	2	6
Use of a rescue plan for lanyards and fall arrest systems	As above	Failure to have a rescue plan in place may lead to injuries from an operated fall protect system	3	4	12	• A suitable rescue plan to be in place to release operatives restrained by a fall arrest system. • Operatives to receive training in the rescue system.	3	2	6

LIKELIHOOD (L) = Frequent (5) - Probable (4) - Occasional (3) - Improbable (2) - Remote (1)
SEVERITY (S) = Catastrophic (5) - Major (4) - Reportable (3) - Serious (2) - Minor (1)
Degree of Risk (DR) = LIKELIHOOD x SEVERITY
* Numbers used are for illustrative purposes only.
** Residual risk is the level of risk that remains after suitable and sufficient control measures are introduced.

Signed originator.. Job title..

Date completed.. Date for revision..

Working from home (office-based staff)

Carrying out office-based duties from home is becoming increasingly popular, but you still have a duty to ensure their safety.

The home office

The hazards are similar to those faced in an on-site office including manual handling and DSE issues (see our **Risk Assessment - Office**).

You should complete a risk assessment for office work carried out at home, which identifies all "significant" hazards and appropriate "reasonable" ways of reducing risks to an acceptable level.

Managing the risks

To help you identify the hazards associated with office work carried out by homeworkers and appropriate ways of controlling the risks, use our example **Risk Assessment - Homeworking (Office-based Staff)**. It covers the generic hazards associated with this type of activity and suggests control measures to reduce risks to an acceptable level.

You should ensure that your document only addresses "significant" hazards, i.e. any that could, and more importantly are likely to, cause an accident or injury.

Make your instructions clear

Don't include activities in your document that simply don't need to be there. Work to the principle that if there is any chance of your staff being unaware of the safe way of doing something, then you will need to make it clear in your document. Finally, always ensure that any control measures you identify and follow only go so far "as is reasonably practicable".

Note. The list of potential hazards is not exhaustive. However, for your risk assessment to be considered suitable and sufficient in the eyes of the law it must accurately reflect the "significant" hazards found in their workplace.

RISK ASSESSMENT - WORKING FROM HOME (OFFICE-BASED STAFF)

ACTIVITY	PERSON AT RISK	SIGNIFICANT HAZARDS	RISK*			RISK CONTROL MEASURES	RESIDUAL RISK**		
			L	S	DR		L	S	DR
Manual handling of office equipment	Homeworker	Physical injury caused by incorrect techniques when handling items such as desktop computers, printers etc. at home	4	3	12	• All homeworkers to be given training relevant to their work and a generic assessment to be carried out.	3	1	3
As above	As above	Insufficient workspace leading to poor lifting techniques	4	3	12	• Staff to be made aware of the correct handling techniques in the home environment and their personal lifting capabilities.	3	1	3
As above	As above	New and expectant mothers more susceptible to injury	4	4	16	• New and expectant mothers must notify their manager of their condition and have their work capabilities reviewed.	3	2	6
Use of display screen equipment (DSE)	As above	Work related upper limb disorders caused by inappropriate workstation layout	4	3	12	• All DSE users to be given a workstation self-assessment form to complete after basic DSE awareness training. • Information to be given to all DSE users on the importance of workstation layout, correct seating and taking rest breaks etc.	3	1	3
Working at home in general	Homeworker and others who may be present	Fire hazards resulting in serious injuries and property damage	3	5	15	• Homeworker to be made aware of the general principles of fire prevention including: good housekeeping practices, ensuring electrical equipment is well maintained, electrical sockets not to be overloaded and maintaining a means of escape in the event of fire.	3	2	6
As above	Homeworker	Working in isolation may lead to stress-related illnesses as a result of working long hours, work demand etc.	3	4	12	• Regular face-to-face contact to be maintained between homeworker and supervisor/manager to ensure work patterns and workloads are appropriate or to deal with any other concerns. • Homeworkers to be encouraged to take regular breaks. • Homeworkers to be made aware of the causes of work-related stress and their role in controlling such risks.	3	2	6

RISK ASSESSMENT - WORKING FROM HOME (OFFICE-BASED STAFF)

ACTIVITY	PERSON AT RISK	SIGNIFICANT HAZARDS	RISK*			RISK CONTROL MEASURES	RESIDUAL RISK**		
			L	S	DR		L	S	DR
Working with electrically operated equipment, e.g. PCs, printers, shredders etc.	Homeworker	Failure to maintain electrically operated equipment may lead to fires or electric shock causing burns or fatality	3	5	15	• Homeworkers to ensure that all cables and plugs fitted to equipment are regularly checked for damage. • An extension cable only to be used as a temporary measure until a permanent socket outlet is fitted. • If cables are unavoidably run across walkways then they are to be fitted with cable protection devices.	2	2	4
As above	Homeworker and others who may be present	Coming into contact with moving parts of equipment may lead to hands, hair etc. becoming entangled causing injuries	3	3	9	• All work equipment to be supplied suitable for its purpose. • The homeworker to ensure that no unauthorised persons use the equipment provided. • No investigation of faults or repairs to be carried out whilst equipment is still powered up.	2	2	4

LIKELIHOOD (L) = Frequent (5) - Probable (4) - Occasional (3) - Improbable (2) - Remote (1)
SEVERITY (S) = Catastrophic (5) - Major (4) - Reportable (3) - Serious (2) - Minor (1)
Degree of Risk (DR) = LIKELIHOOD x SEVERITY
* Numbers used are for illustrative purposes only. ** Residual risk is the level of risk that remains after suitable and sufficient control measures are introduced.

Signed originator.. Job title..

Date completed.. Date for revision..

Working from home (sewing and ironing)

Failure to ensure that the seemingly minor risks associated with sewing and ironing are reduced to an acceptable level may result in accidents.

Managing the risks

To help you identify the hazards associated with this type of homeworking and some appropriate ways of controlling them, use our example **Risk Assessment - Homeworking (Sewing and Ironing)**. It covers the generic hazards associated with this type of activity and then suggests control measures to reduce the risks to an acceptable level.

You should ensure that your document only addresses "significant" hazards, i.e. any that could, and more importantly are likely to, cause an accident or injury.

Make your instructions clear

Don't include activities in your document that simply don't need to be there. Work to the principle that if there is any chance of your staff being unaware of the safe way of doing something, then you will need to make it clear in your document. Finally, always ensure that any control measures you identify and follow only go so far "as is reasonably practicable".

Note. The list of potential hazards is not exhaustive. For your risk assessment to be considered suitable and sufficient in the eyes of the law it must accurately reflect the "significant" hazards found in your employee's place of work.

RISK ASSESSMENT - WORKING FROM HOME (SEWING AND IRONING)

ACTIVITY	PERSON AT RISK	SIGNIFICANT HAZARDS	RISK*			RISK CONTROL MEASURES	RESIDUAL RISK**		
			L	S	DR		L	S	DR
Hand sewing garments	Homeworker	Punctured fingers due to misuse of needles	4	1	4	• Staff to wear a thimble to give finger protection. • Staff to be made aware of the need for concentration on the task. • Basic first aid treatment to be made available.	2	1	2
Use of an electric sewing machine	As above	Fingers may be drawn under the needle if garment is not fed through properly	4	2	8	• Staff to be instructed on how to use the machine, including the method of feeding garments into the sewing area. • Industrial standard sewing machines to be provided for all staff.	3	1	3
As above	As above	Injuries to fingers when changing needles if machine is still switched on	4	2	8	• Staff to be instructed to switch off the machine before attempting to change needles. • Staff to be trained in the method of changing needles.	3	1	3
As above	As above	Danger of electric shock if cable or plug is damaged	3	4	12	• Cables and plugs to be checked by user for wear on a regular basis. Cables and plugs to be checked as part of the company electrical items testing procedure.	2	2	4
Use of scissors or thread cutters	As above	Cuts to fingers if misused or the wrong tool used	3	2	6	• Only purpose-designed scissors and thread cutters to be used. • Knives not be used to cut thread or to unpick garments.	2	1	2

RISK ASSESSMENT - WORKING FROM HOME (SEWING AND IRONING)

ACTIVITY	PERSON AT RISK	SIGNIFICANT HAZARDS	RISK*			RISK CONTROL MEASURES	RESIDUAL RISK**		
			L	S	DR		L	S	DR
Use of a steam iron	Hcmeworker	Contact with iron soleplate during use can cause burns to hands, arms	4	2	8	• All workers trained in the use of a steam iron. • Heatproof rest for irons to be provided with a purpose designed ironing board. • Only industrial types of iron to be used. • Homeworkers to be instructed to keep other people away from the work area. • First aid treatment for burns to be briefed to staff.	3	1	3
As above	As above	Danger of electric shock if cable or plug is damaged	3	4	12	• Cables and plugs to be checked by user for wear on a regular basis. Cables and plugs to be checked as part of the company electrical items testing procedure.	2	2	4
As above	As above	Filling water container while iron is switched on may cause electric shock	3	4	12	• Staff to be instructed to switch iron off and remove plug before filling water container.	2	2	4
Working at home (general)	As above	Excessive workload may cause stress-related illness	3	3	9	• Supervisors to check workloads on a regular basis. • Homeworker to maintain regular contact with supervisor and to report any issues.	3	1	3

LIKELIHOOD (L) = Frequent (5) - Probable (4) - Occasional (3) - Improbable (2) - Remote (1)
SEVERITY (S) = Catastrophic (5) - Major (4) - Reportable (3) - Serious (2) - Minor (1) Degree of Risk (DR) = LIKELIHOOD x SEVERITY
* Numbers used are for illustrative purposes only. ** Residual risk is the level of risk that remains after suitable and sufficient control measures are introduced.

Signed originator.......... .... Job title..

Date completed.. Date for revision..

Working in loading and unloading bays

Work in loading and unloading bays could, if carried out incorrectly, lead to accidents involving serious personal injuries.

Managing the risks

To help you to identify the hazards associated with work in loading and unloading bays and the appropriate ways of controlling them, use our example **Risk Assessment - Working in Loading and Unloading Bays**. It covers the generic hazards associated with this type of activity and suggests control measures to reduce risks to an acceptable level. You should ensure that your document only addresses "significant" hazards, i.e. any that could, and more importantly are likely to, cause an accident or injury.

Make your instructions clear

Don't include activities in your document that simply don't need to be there. Work to the principle that if there is any chance of your staff being unaware of the safe way of doing something, then you will need to make it clear in your document. Finally, always ensure that any control measures you identify and follow are decided upon the principle of "so far as is reasonably practicable".

Note. The list of potential hazards is not exhaustive. However, for your risk assessment to be considered suitable and sufficient in the eyes of the law it must accurately reflect the "significant" hazards found when working in loading and unloading bays under your control.

Note. This risk assessment only deals with the generic risks associated with the environmental aspects of such areas and not the actual loading and unloading process itself. As each work environment will differ, then you should include details of the specific hazards associated with your work environment and give details of the control measures to mitigate such hazards in order to reduce the risks to a minimum.

RISK ASSESSMENT - WORKING IN LOADING AND UNLOADING BAYS

ACTIVITY	PERSON AT RISK	SIGNIFICANT HAZARDS	RISK*			RISK CONTROL MEASURES	RESIDUAL RISK**		
			L	S	DR		L	S	DR
Manual handling of goods	Staff	Staff could suffer from back pain etc. if regularly lifting/carrying heavy or awkward objects	3	3	9	• Where possible, mechanical aids to be used for moving goods. • Staff to be trained in the correct manual handling techniques. • Staff to ask for assistance when moving heavy items beyond their physical capability.	3	2	6
Use of fork lift trucks	As above	Incorrect use of forklift trucks may lead to serious injuries to staff and others	3	5	15	• Only trained drivers to operate forklift trucks. • A system to be in place to segregate trucks from pedestrians during loading/unloading operations. • Access to loading and unloading areas to be restricted to staff only. • The use of a banksman to be considered when loading and unloading when other vehicles are in the area. • Warning signs to be located in areas where forklift trucks operate.	3	3	9
Movement of vehicles	As above, drivers etc.	Serious injuries could occur if staff and others are hit by a moving vehicle	3	5	15	• Floor and traffic routes to be suitable for the vehicles using them. • Traffic routes to be suitably and clearly marked. • Speed restrictions to be suitably marked. • Vehicle routes to be kept free of obstructions. • Reversing of vehicles to be kept to a minimum and only carried out using a banksman. • Loading and unloading areas used at night to be adequately lit. • Staff who work in loading and unloading areas to be issued with high visibility clothing which is to be worn at all times. • Pedestrians to be kept clear of loading and unloading areas.	3	3	9
Working in loading bays	Staff	Serious injuries could occur if staff fall from loading bays	3	4	12	• Loading bays to have at least one pedestrian exit, which is to be signed as such. • Loading bays to be fenced with secure guardrails. • Edges of loading bays to be clearly marked.	3	2	6

RISK ASSESSMENT - WORKING IN LOADING AND UNLOADING BAYS

ACTIVITY	PERSON AT RISK	SIGNIFICANT HAZARDS	RISK*			RISK CONTROL MEASURES	RESIDUAL RISK**		
			L	S	DR		L	S	DR
Parking vehicles in loading/ unloading areas	Drivers, other staff	People may be injured by a moving vehicle if it is incorrectly parked	3	5	15	• Parking areas in loading bays to be level, clearly marked, well lit and with designated walking areas for pedestrians. • Vehicles not to be left unless the parking brakes have been firmly applied, the engine has stopped, the key has been removed and any mounted equipment has been lowered to the ground and secured. • Where necessary, wheel chocks are to be fitted to prevent vehicles from rolling away.	3	3	9
Getting around in general	As above	Poor standards of housekeeping may lead to slips, trips and falls resulting in personal injuries	3	4	12	• All pedestrian areas to be kept free of obstructions. • Spilled loads or used packaging etc. to be cleaned up and disposed of. • External floor surfaces that show oil or grease leakages from vehicles etc. to be treated and cleaned up.	3	2	6

LIKELIHOOD (L) = Frequent (5) - Probable (4) - Occasional (3) - Improbable (2) - Remote (1)
SEVERITY (S) = Catastrophic (5) - Major (4) - Reportable (3) - Serious (2) - Minor (1)
Degree of Risk (DR) = LIKELIHOOD x SEVERITY
* Numbers used are for illustrative purposes only.
** Residual risk is the level of risk that remains after suitable and sufficient control measures are introduced.

Signed originator.. Job title..

Date completed... Date for revision..

Working on fragile roofs

If work on a fragile roof is not controlled it could easily lead to a fatality. So make use of our risk assessment document to help ensure your stay on the right side of the law.

Managing the risks

To help you identify the hazards associated with working on fragile roofs and the appropriate ways of controlling them, use our example **Risk Assessment - Working on Fragile Roofs**. It covers the generic hazards associated with this type of activity and suggests control measures to reduce risks to an acceptable level.

You should ensure that your document only addresses "significant" hazards, i.e. any that could, and more importantly are likely to, cause an accident or injury.

Make your instructions clear

Don't include activities in your document that simply don't need to be there. Work to the principle that if there is any chance of your staff being unaware of the safe way of doing something, then you will need to make it clear in your document. Finally, always ensure that any control measures you identify and follow only go so far "as is reasonably practicable".

Note. The list of potential hazards is not exhaustive. However, for your risk assessment to be considered suitable and sufficient in the eyes of the law it must accurately reflect the "significant" hazards found when your staff work on fragile roofs.

RISK ASSESSMENT - WORKING ON FRAGILE ROOFS

ACTIVITY	PERSON AT RISK	SIGNIFICANT HAZARDS	RISK*			RISK CONTROL MEASURES	RESIDUAL RISK**		
			L	S	DR		L	S	DR
Planning of the work	Staff	Failure to plan the work properly may lead to falls with fatal results	4	5	20	• All work at height to be planned and a suitable method of work statement prepared. • Planning to include consideration as to whether or not the work can be done by methods other than by accessing the roof. • Weather conditions to be taken into account before work commences.	3	3	9
Access to the roof	As above	Failure to use a safe method of access may lead to falls with fatal results	4	5	20	• The method of access to be properly planned. • A cherry picker or mobile elevating work platform (MEWP) to be the preferred choice for access. • Ladders to be used for short duration access only. • Ladders to be secured at the base and erected at an angle of four up and one out at the base and to be stood on solid ground. • Scaffolding towers to be used in preference to ladders where possible.	3	3	9
Work on the roof	As above	Failure to ensure the stability of the roof structure and its capability to support workers may lead to falls through fragile roofing materials	3	5	15	• All roofs to be inspected for stability before starting work. • Duckboards to be used over fragile roofs and other fragile surfaces to spread the weight. • Guardrails, boards or other barriers such as toe boards to be erected to prevent anyone from falling off the edge of work platforms or roofs, or through holes or openings in the work platform floor.	3	2	6
Work on the roof using hand/ power tools	Staff and other people in the vicinity	Failure to secure tools or equipment may lead to objects falling and causing injuries	3	4	12	• Pedestrians to be kept away from the work area by installing suitable barriers. • All tools and equipment to be raised using safety lines. • All work platforms to be close boarded and be fitted with toe boards.	2	3	6
Using cherry pickers or MEWPs	Staff	Incorrect choice of access equipment may lead to it overturning etc. causing accidents and equipment damage	3	4	12	• The most suitable type of access equipment for the work to be used, i.e. consider reach, safe working load and suitability for the means of access. See manufacturer's or hirer's guidance. • All operators to be trained and competent to use the equipment provided. • Ground areas to be checked for level and stability.	2	3	6

RISK ASSESSMENT - WORKING ON FRAGILE ROOFS

ACTIVITY	PERSON AT RISK	SIGNIFICANT HAZARDS	RISK*			RISK CONTROL MEASURES	RESIDUAL RISK**		
			L	S	DR		L	S	DR
Work on roofs	As above	Lack of training may lead to accidents with serious injuries	4	5	20	• All staff that are required to work on fragile roofs to have received adequate training and to be competent to do so. • Supervisors to monitor work standards.	3	3	9
Supervision of work	Staff	Lack of adequate supervision may lead to work being carried out in a dangerous manner	3	5	15	• All work at height on fragile roofs to be adequately supervised. • Supervisors to be competent and experienced in this type of work. • Supervisors to monitor the work and update all risk assessments if the hazards change.	3	2	6
Work on fragile roofs (general)	As above	Failure to wear the correct type of personal protective equipment (PPE) may lead to injuries being sustained	4	3	12	• All staff to be issued with the correct type of PPE for the work in hand. • Faulty or worn items to be replaced in accordance with the company PPE procedure.	3	2	6
As above	As above	Failure of fall arrest equipment may lead to accidents resulting in serious injuries	4	5	20	• All fall arrest equipment to be regularly checked in accordance with company procedure. • All fall arrest equipment to be checked by the user before use for any signs of wear. • Faulty items to be replaced in accordance with company policy.	3	3	9

LIKELIHOOD (L) = Frequent (5) - Probable (4) - Occasional (3) - Improbable (2) - Remote (1)
SEVERITY (S) = Catastrophic (5) - Major (4) - Reportable (3) - Serious (2) - Minor (1)
Degree of Risk (DR) = LIKELIHOOD x SEVERITY
* Numbers used are for illustrative purposes only. ** Residual risk is the level of risk that remains after suitable and sufficient control measures are introduced.

Signed originator.. Job title...

Date completed.. Date for revision..

Workplace winter precautions

All employers are under a duty to keep their premises safe for the people that use them, whether their own staff or customers and visitors. The winter months can bring heavy rain, ice or snow that could, if not managed properly, result in hazardous conditions that may lead to trips, slips and falls.

Managing the risks

To help you to identify the hazards associated with the management of business premises during the winter and the appropriate ways of controlling them, use our example **Risk Assessment - Workplace Winter Precautions**. It covers the generic hazards associated with winter weather and suggests control measures to reduce risks to an acceptable level. You should ensure that your document only addresses "significant" hazards, i.e. any that could, and more importantly are likely to, cause an accident or injury.

Make your instructions clear

Don't include activities in your document that simply don't need to be there. Work to the principle that if there is any chance of an accident occurring because of the weather conditions then you will need to make it clear in your document. Finally, always ensure that any control measures you identify and follow are decided upon the principle of "so far as is reasonably practicable".

Note. The list of potential hazards is not exhaustive. However, for your risk assessment to be considered suitable and sufficient in the eyes of the law it must accurately reflect the "significant" hazards in your workplace during the winter months.

Note. This risk assessment deals with the generic risks associated with winter weather. The hazards are not exhaustive and your assessment should refer to the situation in your work environment.

RISK ASSESSMENT - WORKPLACE WINTER PRECAUTIONS

ACTIVITY	PERSON AT RISK	SIGNIFICANT HAZARDS	RISK*			RISK CONTROL MEASURES	RESIDUAL RISK**		
			L	S	DR		L	S	DR
Getting around premises - external roads and footpaths	Staff, other people	Slips, trips and falls may occur if walkways are left covered in snow or ice leading to physical injuries	3	4	12	• All main footpaths on the premises to be cleared of snow. • A staff member to be nominated to clear snow etc. an hour before normal business opening times. • A staff member to be nominated to apply grit or salt to areas likely to ice over an hour before normal business opening times. • Supplies of grit etc. to be made available prior to the onset of winter. • Signs to be displayed warning of the risk of icy conditions.	3	2	6
Accessing car parks	As above	Slips, trips and falls may occur if car parks are left covered in snow or ice resulting in physical injuries	3	4	12	• Where practical, car parks to be kept clear of snow. • Where this is impractical, then car parks to be kept cordoned off or locked to prevent access. Warning signs to be displayed stating the car park is out of use. • A staff member to be nominated to clear snow etc. from car park access pathways an hour before normal business opening times.	3	2	6
Restricting access to premises	As above	Failure to identify no-go areas may lead to slips, trips and falls resulting in physical injuries	3	4	12	• Areas where ground conditions are hazardous to be cordoned off. • Signposts to be displayed showing access routes.	3	2	6
Use of fire doors	As above	Failure to be able to open fire doors because of snow build-up may lead to people unable to exit the building in the event of a fire	3	5	15	• Fire doors to be checked for opening in the event of a snowfall by a nominated member of staff or a fire warden. • Final fire escape doors that open outwards from the building to have snow removed so that it doesn't restrict doors from opening.	3	2	6

RISK ASSESSMENT - WORKPLACE WINTER PRECAUTIONS

ACTIVITY	PERSON AT RISK	SIGNIFICANT HAZARDS	RISK*			RISK CONTROL MEASURES	RESIDUAL RISK**		
			L	S	DR		L	S	DR
Use of external fire escape routes	Staff, other people	Failure to keep external fire escape routes free from snow or ice may lead to slips, trips and falls when used to exit the building	3	5	15	• A staff member to be nominated to clear snow etc. from fire escape routes. • A staff member to be nominated to apply grit or salt to all fire escape routes.	3	2	6
Use of internal entrance areas	As above	Failure to keep internal entrance floor areas dry may lead to slips, trips and falls resulting in physical injuries	3	4	12	• All internal entrance areas to be regularly monitored for wet surfaces. • Door mats to be provided at all entrance doorways. • Facilities to be made available for the regular mopping of entrance floor areas in wet weather.	3	3	9

LIKELIHOOD (L) = Frequent (5) - Probable (4) - Occasional (3) - Improbable (2) - Remote (1)
SEVERITY (S) = Catastrophic (5) - Major (4) - Reportable (3) - Serious (2) - Minor (1)
Degree of Risk (DR) = LIKELIHOOD x SEVERITY
* Numbers used are for illustrative purposes only.
** Residual risk is the level of risk that remains after suitable and sufficient control measures are introduced.

Signed originator.. Job title...

Date completed.. Date for revision...

Section 2

Location-based risk assessments

Call centres

Work undertaken in call centres may present risks to staff, which left unmanaged could cause accidents or result in ill-health and potentially put you on the wrong side of the law. So use our document to identify the hazards and some appropriate control measures.

Managing the risks

To help you identify the hazards associated with the call centre environment and the appropriate ways of controlling them, use our example **Risk Assessment - Call Centres**. It covers the generic hazards associated with this type of activity and suggests control measures to reduce risks to an acceptable level.

Note. All call centres will be different and you should ensure that your document only addresses your "significant" hazards, i.e. any that could, and more importantly are likely to, cause an accident or injury in your workplace.

Make your instructions clear

Don't include activities in your document that simply don't need to be there. Work to the principle that if there is any chance of your staff being unaware of the safe way of doing something, then you will need to make it clear in your document. Finally, always ensure that any control measures you identify and follow only go so far "as is reasonably practicable".

Note. The list of potential hazards is not exhaustive. However, for your risk assessment to be considered suitable and sufficient in the eyes of the law it must accurately reflect the hazards presented in your call centre.

RISK ASSESSMENT - CALL CENTRES

ACTIVITY	PERSON AT RISK	SIGNIFICANT HAZARDS	RISK*			RISK CONTROL MEASURES	RESIDUAL RISK**		
			L	S	DR		L	S	DR
Working with display screen equipment	Call centre staff	Poor workstation layout and sitting for long periods may lead to postural problems causing back or arm pain	4	3	12	• Suitably designed workstations with the correct type of seating to be provided and assessed. • Staff to receive training in setting up their workstation. • Work to be planned so that staff can take regular breaks away from screen activity.	3	1	3
As above	As above	Excessive glare on display screens may cause headaches and eyestrain	4	2	8	• Windows to be fitted with blinds to reduce glare. • Display screens to be positioned to reduce glare. • Suitable lighting to be provided. • Eyesight tests to be given to staff who request it and spectacles suitable for DSE work to be provided.	3	1	3
Moving around in general	As above	Poor housekeeping may create hazards causing slips, trips and falls leading to injuries	4	3	12	• The standards of housekeeping to be monitored by supervisors. • All trailing cables to be kept to a minimum and away from walk areas. • All spillages to be cleaned up immediately. • All areas to be well lit.	3	1	3
Working in the call centre	As above	Staff may suffer burns, smoke inhalation etc. in the event of a fire	3	5	15	• A fire risk assessment to be carried out for the building to reduce the risk of fire. • All staff to be trained for action to be taken in the event of a fire. • Fire alarms to be tested weekly and fire drills held at six-monthly intervals.	3	2	6

RISK ASSESSMENT - CALL CENTRES

ACTIVITY	PERSON AT RISK	SIGNIFICANT HAZARDS	RISK*			RISK CONTROL MEASURES	RESIDUAL RISK**		
			L	S	DR		L	S	DR
Manual handling of equipment etc.	Call centre staff	Incorrect manual handling procedures may lead to physical injuries	3	3	9	• Only the IT maintenance staff, trained in manual handling, to move electrical equipment such as DSE screens, etc. • Trolleys to be used to move boxes of paper etc. • Boxes of paper to be broken down into individual packs to lessen the weight when carried to printers etc. • Storage of heavy items to be at a lower level in cupboards, shelving etc.	3	1	3
Call centre work	As above	Lack of job control and/ or verbal abuse from customers etc. may lead to stress	3	3	9	• Realistic call targets to be set on an individual basis. • Staff to receive training for their work. • A policy to exist setting out how abusive calls are to be dealt with. • Staff to be encouraged to discuss performance issues with their supervisor.	3	1	3
As above	As above	Staff may suffer from hearing damage if exposed to long periods of excessive noise or sudden and loud sounds when using telephones	3	3	9	• All headsets to be fitted with a volume control. • Staff to have a choice of either single or two earpiece headsets. • Staff to be trained to report cases of acoustic shock to their supervisor.	3	1	3
As above	As above	Staff may experience ear infections from dirty earpieces	3	2	6	• Staff to be trained to clean and disinfect their earpieces on a regular basis. • Cleaning materials to be provided.	3	1	3

RISK ASSESSMENT - CALL CENTRES

ACTIVITY	PERSON AT RISK	SIGNIFICANT HAZARDS	RISK*			RISK CONTROL MEASURES	RESIDUAL RISK**		
			L	S	DR		L	S	DR
Call centre work	Call centre staff	Call centre staff may suffer from voice problems including voice loss etc.	3	2	6	• Staff to be trained to use their microphones correctly. • Call centre work to be planned to give call handlers time away from customer contact work. • Staff to be encouraged to take regular drinks.	3	1	3
Using electrical equipment	As above	Staff may suffer electrical shocks resulting in burns etc. from faulty electrical equipment	3	4	12	• All portable electrical appliances to be regularly tested. • Staff to be trained to report faulty items to their supervisor. • Regular visual inspections of cables, plug tops etc. to be carried out by users and faulty items placed out of use and reported.	3	2	6

LIKELIHOOD (L) = Frequent (5) - Probable (4) - Occasional (3) - Improbable (2) - Remote (1)
SEVERITY (S) = Catastrophic (5) - Major (4) - Reportable (3) - Serious (2) - Minor (1)
Degree of Risk (DR) = LIKELIHOOD x SEVERITY
* Numbers used are for illustrative purposes only.
** Residual risk is the level of risk that remains after suitable and sufficient control measures are introduced.

Signed originator.. Job title...

Date completed.. Date for revision..

Construction sites (access for visitors)

Construction sites can be dangerous so all visitors should receive induction training and wear the appropriate PPE. Use our document to make life easier.

Managing the risks

To help you identify the hazards associated with site access and the appropriate ways of controlling them, use our example **Risk Assessment - Construction Sites (Access for Visitors)**. It covers the generic hazards associated with this type of activity and suggests control measures to reduce risks to an acceptable level.

You should ensure that your document only addresses "significant" hazards, i.e. any that could, and more importantly are likely to, cause an accident or injury to visitors.

Note. This risk assessment only deals with the more common hazards associated with construction sites. Your site may well have specific hazards we haven't covered so do ensure that your document reflects your particular situation.

Make your instructions clear

Don't include activities in your document that simply don't need to be there. Work to the principle that if there is any chance of visitors being unaware of the safe methods of access, then you will need to make it clear in your document. Finally, always ensure that any control measures you identify and follow only go so far "as is reasonably practicable".

Note. The list of potential hazards is not exhaustive. However, for your risk assessment to be considered suitable and sufficient in the eyes of the law it must accurately reflect the "significant" hazards found on your construction site.

RISK ASSESSMENT - CONSTRUCTION SITES (ACCESS FOR VISITORS)

ACTIVITY	PERSON AT RISK	SIGNIFICANT HAZARDS	RISK*			RISK CONTROL MEASURES	RESIDUAL RISK**		
			L	S	DR		L	S	DR
Entering the site	Visitors	Visitors may encounter hazards by not entering the site at the main entrance	4	3	12	• Main site entrance to be signed as the entrance for all visitors, including delivery drivers etc. • Where possible, the perimeter of the site to be fenced off to prevent unauthorised access.	3	2	6
As above	As above	Visitors entering the site unaccounted for may lead to them becoming exposed to hazardous operations resulting in accidents and injuries	3	3	9	• All visitors to the site to be logged in and out at the main entrance and issued with a visitors' identity card/badge. • Visitors found on site without an identity card/badge to be challenged and ordered off site.	3	1	3
As above	As above	Failure to make visitors aware of on-site hazards may lead to accidents resulting in injuries	4	3	12	• All visitors to site to receive an induction training session. • All known site hazards to be highlighted in the induction.	3	2	6
As above	As above	Failure of visitors to wear the appropriate personal protective equipment (PPE) to leave them susceptible to accidents and injuries	4	3	12	• Visitors to be expected to wear the relevant PPE and not to be allowed on site without it. • PPE requirements to be discussed as part of the induction training.	3	2	6

RISK ASSESSMENT - CONSTRUCTION SITES (ACCESS FOR VISITORS)

ACTIVITY	PERSON AT RISK	SIGNIFICANT HAZARDS	RISK*			RISK CONTROL MEASURES	RESIDUAL RISK**		
			L	S	DR		L	S	DR
Vehicle parking	Visitors	Failure to park vehicles in the designated place may lead to conflict with site work, resulting in accidents and personal injuries	3	3	9	• All parking areas for vehicles to be signposted. • Vehicles only to be allowed on site with permission from the site supervisor. • Loading and unloading on site to be agreed with the site supervisor before commencement. • All traffic routes on site to be clearly marked. • Site speed limits to be clearly marked.	3	1	3
Attendance on site	As above	Failure to observe site fire precautions may lead to serious injuries in the event of a fire	3	4	12	• Site fire precautions and action to be taken in the event of a fire to be explained as part of the site induction training. • All enclosed buildings to be designated "no smoking".	3	2	6

LIKELIHOOD (L) = Frequent (5) - Probable (4) - Occasional (3) - Improbable (2) - Remote (1)
SEVERITY (S) = Catastrophic (5) - Major (4) - Reportable (3) - Serious (2) - Minor (1)
Degree of Risk (DR) = LIKELIHOOD x SEVERITY
* Numbers used are for illustrative purposes only.
** Residual risk is the level of risk that remains after suitable and sufficient control measures are introduced.

Signed originator.. Job title..

Date completed.. Date for revision...

Swimming pools - general

Swimming pools are accessed by members of the public. Therefore, if the risks are not managed properly, it could lead to accidents involving serious personal injuries and drowning.

Managing the risks

To help you to identify the hazards associated with swimming pool management and the appropriate ways of controlling them, use our example **Risk Assessment - Swimming Pools - General**. It covers the generic hazards associated with activities in this environment and suggests control measures to reduce risks to an acceptable level. You should ensure that your document only addresses "significant" hazards, i.e. any that could, and more importantly are likely to, cause an accident or injury.

Make your instructions clear

Don't include activities in your document that simply don't need to be there. Work to the principle that if there is any chance of your staff being unaware of the safe way of doing something, then you will need to make it clear in your document. Finally, always ensure that any control measures you identify and follow are decided upon the principle of "so far as is reasonably practicable".

Note. The list of potential hazards is not exhaustive. However, for your risk assessment to be considered suitable and sufficient in the eyes of the law it must accurately reflect the "significant" hazards found in your swimming pool environment.

Note. This risk assessment only deals with the generic risks associated with the general use of swimming pools. It does not cover the water treatment or water hygiene aspects of swimming pool management, which should be the subject of a separate risk assessment. Neither does it deal with issues arising from pool design, which should be discussed with the installation contractors.

Note. The Health and Safety Executive publication **HSG179 Managing Health and Safety in Swimming Pools** can be used to assist you in preparing your risk assessment and contains valuable information relating to swimming pool design.

RISK ASSESSMENT - SWIMMING POOLS - GENERAL

ACTIVITY	PERSON AT RISK	SIGNIFICANT HAZARDS	RISK*			RISK CONTROL MEASURES	RESIDUAL RISK**		
			L	S	DR		L	S	DR
Normal swimming pool management	Staff, others	Failure to acquaint staff with the normal operating plan for the pool may lead to accidents, including drowning	3	5	15	• A normal operating plan (NOP) to be prepared for the pool and this is to be communicated to all staff. • NOP to follow the guidelines given in the HSE publication HSG179 Managing Health and Safety in Swimming Pools. • All staff to be trained in the requirements of the NOP as it relates to the roles they carry out.	3	3	9
As above	As above	Failure to acquaint staff with the emergency action plan for the pool may lead to accidents, including drowning	3	5	15	• An emergency action plan (EAP) to be prepared for the pool and this is to be communicated to all staff. • The EAP to follow the guidelines given in the HSE publication HSG179 Managing Health and Safety in Swimming Pools. • All relevant staff to be trained in the actions to be taken in an emergency in accordance with the EAP.	3	3	9
Display of safety signage	As above	Failure to provide relevant safety signage may lead to accidents, including drowning	3	5	15	• Swimming pools to have adequate safety signage to warn of dangers, to prohibit certain activities and to indicate safe conditions accordingly. • All signage to be provided in accordance with BS5499:2002 Part 11 Water Safety Signs. • All signs to be situated where they can be easily read by pool users. • Supervisory staff to ensure that signage conditions are observed by pool users and others.	3	3	9
Provision of life guards	Pool users	Failure to provide adequate lifeguard cover may lead to accidents, including drowning	3	5	15	• An adequate number of lifeguards to be on duty in accordance with the pool size, the numbers of people using the pool and the activities taking place (see the HSE publication HSG179 Managing Health and Safety in Swimming Pools for guidelines). • Lifeguards to be trained in water safety and life saving techniques.	3	3	9

RISK ASSESSMENT - SWIMMING POOLS - GENERAL

ACTIVITY	PERSON AT RISK	SIGNIFICANT HAZARDS	RISK*			RISK CONTROL MEASURES	RESIDUAL RISK**		
			L	S	DR		L	S	DR
Access to plant rooms	Staff, others	Failure to restrict access to plant rooms may lead to accidents involving machinery etc.	3	4	12	• All plant rooms to be kept locked when not in use. • Only authorised staff to enter plant rooms.	3	2	6
Access to chemical storage areas	As above	Failure to restrict access to chemical storage areas may lead to contact with hazardous materials resulting in ill-health conditions	3	4	12	• All chemical storage areas to be kept locked when not in use. • Only authorised staff to enter chemical storage areas.	3	2	6
Use of life saving equipment	As above	Failure to provide or maintain life saving equipment may lead to loss of life from drowning	3	5	15	• Life saving equipment to be provided that meets the needs of the pool and visitors. • Life saving equipment to be regularly checked to ensure it is in a serviceable condition. • Staff to be trained in the use of life saving equipment.	3	3	9
Provision of first aid staff and equipment	Pool users	Failure to provide adequate first aid staff and equipment may lead to health deterioration and injured pool users	3	5	15	• First aid staff to be provided to meet the requirements of pool attendances. • First aid staff to be fully trained. • A first aid box to be provided and any specialised equipment to be stored in the same area but away from the poolside. • All first aid equipment to be regularly checked to ensure it remains in good condition. • Mechanical resuscitation equipment to be used only by trained paramedics or medical staff.	3	3	9

RISK ASSESSMENT - SWIMMING POOLS - GENERAL

ACTIVITY	PERSON AT RISK	SIGNIFICANT HAZARDS	RISK*			RISK CONTROL MEASURES	RESIDUAL RISK**		
			L	S	DR		L	S	DR
Placement of water depth signs	Users	Bathers may enter or progress into water of unsafe depth (for them) if they cannot see or read depth markings, causing them to get into difficulties, which may lead to drowning	3	5	15	• Water depth signs to be provided that are clearly visible to bathers, both on the pool surrounds and in the water. • "No Diving" signs to be displayed so as to clearly indicate where diving is prohibited because of the water depth.	3	3	9
Use of the pool	As above	Excessive suction at outlets may cause entrapment injury and drowning	3	5	15	• The level of suction at each outlet to be regularly checked. • Outlets to pumps to be sufficiently spaced apart to prevent a body being drawn or trapped by two suction outlets	3	3	9

LIKELIHOOD (L) = Frequent (5) - Probable (4) - Occasional (3) - Improbable (2) - Remote (1)
SEVERITY (S) = Catastrophic (5) - Major (4) - Reportable (3) - Serious (2) - Minor (1)
Degree of Risk (DR) = LIKELIHOOD x SEVERITY
* Numbers used are for illustrative purposes only.
** Residual risk is the level of risk that remains after suitable and sufficient control measures are introduced.

Signed originator.. Job title..

Date completed.. Date for revision..

Warehouses (general access for visitors)

Warehouses can present risks to visitors who may be unaware of the dangers from work activities within this environment. So use our document to highlight what can happen and what can be done to minimise the risks.

Unknown dangers

Left unmanaged, such risks may cause accidents and potentially put you on the wrong side of the law. To ensure that this doesn't happen, you should complete a risk assessment for visitors, which identifies all "significant" hazards and appropriate "reasonable" ways of reducing risks to an acceptable level.

Managing the risks

To help you identify the hazards that the visitor may encounter and the appropriate ways of controlling them, use our example **Risk Assessment - Warehouses (General Access for Visitors)**. It covers the generic hazards that the visitor may be presented with and suggests control measures to reduce risks to an acceptable level.

You should ensure that your document only addresses "significant" hazards, i.e. any that could, and more importantly are likely to, cause an accident or injury.

Make your instructions clear

Don't include activities in your document that simply don't need to be there. Work to the principle that if there is any chance of visitors being unaware of the safe way to access this area, then you will need to make it clear in your document. Finally, always ensure that any control measures you identify and follow only go so far "as is reasonably practicable".

Note. The list of potential hazards is not exhaustive. However, for your risk assessment to be considered suitable and sufficient in the eyes of the law it must accurately reflect the "significant" hazards found in your warehouse.

RISK ASSESSMENT - WAREHOUSES (GENERAL ACCESS FOR VISITORS)

ACTIVITY	PERSON AT RISK	SIGNIFICANT HAZARDS	RISK*			RISK CONTROL MEASURES	RESIDUAL RISK**		
			L	S	DR		L	S	DR
Moving about in general	Visitors	Visitors may walk into areas where forklift trucks are moving and be involved in a vehicle accident	4	3	12	• All visitors to be escorted during their time in the warehouse. • Visitors to be instructed to keep to pedestrian areas. • Visitors to wear a high-visibility waistcoat or jacket when in the warehouse. • All warehouse transport, e.g. forklift trucks, to be fitted with warning lights and reversing alarms to warn pedestrians of their presence.	3	2	6
As above	As above	Visitors may be subjected to slips, trips and falls resulting in physical injuries	3	4	12	• All warehouse floors to be kept free from contamination likely to cause slipping accidents. • All warehouse floors to be kept free from obstructions likely to cause tripping accidents.	3	1	3
As above	As above	Visitors may suffer from head injuries caused by falling objects from high-level storage	3	4	12	• Visitors to be kept away from high-level storage areas if there is a risk of falling goods. • Visitors to be supplied with a safety helmet for use whilst they are in the warehouse.	2	1	2
As above	As above	Visitors may come into contact with machinery, e.g. conveyor systems, which may cause physical injuries	3	4	12	• All visitors to be instructed to keep clear of machinery whilst it is in use. • Machine operators to ensure that all machine guards are in place and that visitors are kept away from the machines.	2	1	2

RISK ASSESSMENT - WAREHOUSES (GENERAL ACCESS FOR VISITORS)

ACTIVITY	PERSON AT RISK	SIGNIFICANT HAZARDS	RISK*			RISK CONTROL MEASURES	RESIDUAL RISK**		
			L	S	DR		L	S	DR
Moving about in general	Visitors	Visitors may walk into areas where forklift trucks are moving and be involved in a vehicle accident	4	3	12	• All visitors to be escorted during their time in the warehouse. • Visitors to be instructed to keep to pedestrian areas. • Visitors to wear a high-visibility waistcoat or jacket when in the warehouse. • All warehouse transport, e.g. forklift trucks, to be fitted with warning lights and reversing alarms to warn pedestrians of their presence.	3	2	6
As above	As above	Visitors may be subjected to slips, trips and falls resulting in physical injuries	3	4	12	• All warehouse floors to be kept free from contamination likely to cause slipping accidents. • All warehouse floors to be kept free from obstructions likely to cause tripping accidents.	3	1	3
As above	As above	Visitors may suffer from head injuries caused by falling objects from high-level storage	3	4	12	• Visitors to be kept away from high-level storage areas if there is a risk of falling goods. • Visitors to be supplied with a safety helmet for use whilst they are in the warehouse.	2	1	2
As above	As above	Visitors may come into contact with machinery, e.g. conveyor systems, which may cause physical injuries	3	4	12	• All visitors to be instructed to keep clear of machinery whilst it is in use. • Machine operators to ensure that all machine guards are in place and that visitors are kept away from the machines.	2	1	2

Working in confined spaces

Working in confined spaces can be extremely hazardous and may present particular risks to staff, including the potentially life-threatening build-up of toxic fumes and dusts.

Residual risk

If these risks are left unmanaged, they could cause accidents and potentially put you on the wrong side of the law. To ensure that this doesn't happen, you should complete a risk assessment for such work, which identifies all "significant" hazards and appropriate "reasonable" ways of reducing risks to an acceptable level.

Note. The Confined Spaces Regulations 1997 state that you must first decide whether or not the work could be carried out without entering a confined space. Even if you decide to carry out the work remotely you will still need to carry out a risk assessment to deal with any residual risk.

Managing the risks

To help you identify the hazards associated with confined space working and the appropriate ways of controlling them, use our example **Risk Assessment - Working in Confined Spaces**. It covers the generic hazards associated with this type of activity and suggests control measures to reduce risks to an acceptable level.

You should ensure that your document only addresses "significant" hazards, i.e. any that could and, more importantly, are likely to cause an accident or injury.

Note. This risk assessment only deals with the general hazards associated with confined space working. It will be up to you to examine the specific hazards associated with your work area and to develop your own risk assessment based on your findings. Where possible you should try to eliminate such work and consider ways of carrying out the tasks remotely.

Make your instructions clear

Don't include activities in your document that simply don't need to be there. Work to the principle that if there is any chance of your staff being unaware of the safe way of doing something, then you will need to make it clear in your document. Finally, always ensure that any control measures you identify and follow only go so far "as is reasonably practicable".

Note. The list of potential hazards is not exhaustive. However, for your risk assessment to be considered suitable and sufficient in the eyes of the law it must accurately reflect the "significant" hazards found in your workplace.

RISK ASSESSMENT - WORKING IN CONFINED SPACES

ACTIVITY	PERSON AT RISK	SIGNIFICANT HAZARDS	RISK*			RISK CONTROL MEASURES	RESIDUAL RISK**		
			L	S	DR		L	S	DR
Reviewing work in confined spaces	Manager	Failure to review confined space work may place staff at risk	4	4	16	• All work in confined spaces to be reviewed before work commences. • All confined space work to be avoided where the work can be done externally.	2	2	4
Planning confined space work	As above	Failure to plan the work properly may place staff at risk	4	4	16	• All work in confined spaces to be planned and a safe system of work prepared. • All confined space work to be controlled by a permit-to-work system under the control of a competent manager. • All staff involved in confined space work to be suitably trained to carry out their tasks. • An emergency plan to be prepared before work commences.	3	2	6
Provision of tools and equipment for confined space work	Manager and staff	Failure to provide the correct type of work equipment and personal protective equipment (PPE) may lead to injuries or loss of life when working in confined spaces	3	5	15	• All tools to be suitable for the type of work to be carried out. • All equipment to be regularly maintained in good working order and marked accordingly. • A register to be maintained of all such equipment stating test dates etc.	3	2	6
Entry into confined spaces	Staff	Openings that are restricted may cause difficulties with normal movement or emergency evacuation	4	4	16	• Access and egress openings to be of a suitable size to allow physical movement. • No access or egress openings to be smaller than 700mm square. • Where self-contained breathing apparatus is worn then openings to be large enough to allow a worker (with the apparatus worn properly) to pass through.	2	2	4

RISK ASSESSMENT - WORKING IN CONFINED SPACES

ACTIVITY	PERSON AT RISK	SIGNIFICANT HAZARDS	RISK*			RISK CONTROL MEASURES	RESIDUAL RISK**		
			L	S	DR		L	S	DR
Working in confined spaces	Staff	Poor ventilation may cause a build up of contaminants causing danger from poor air quality, flammable gases or dusts etc.	4	5	20	• Requirement for ventilation to be assessed before work starts. • Suitable ventilation systems to be provided for confined space work. • Regular checks on air condition to be carried out. • Toxic monitoring to take place to ensure good air quality.	3	3	9
As above	As above	The presence of an explosive atmosphere may lead to fire and/or an explosion with fatal results	4	5	20	• The confined space to be tested for explosive atmosphere before work starts. • Ongoing testing to take place by the use of monitors that measure both the upper and lower explosive limits throughout the work process. • Combustible gas detectors to be fitted with an audible alarm to give warning of evacuation.	3	3	9
As above	As above	Oxygen deficiency or enrichment could result in a slowing down of pulse rate, disorientation, unconsciousness or loss of life	4	5	20	• An oxygen detection monitor to be used to monitor the air in the confined space. • Staff to ensure that the breathing air contains between 19.5%-21.4% oxygen. • Staff to be trained in understanding the difference between the effects of air deficiency and enrichment.	3	3	9

RISK ASSESSMENT - WORKING IN CONFINED SPACES

ACTIVITY	PERSON AT RISK	SIGNIFICANT HAZARDS	RISK*			RISK CONTROL MEASURES	RESIDUAL RISK**		
			L	S	DR		L	S	DR
Working in confined spaces	Staff	Failure to test for toxic gases or vapour may cause euphoria/ disorientating effect, drowsiness, headaches, weakness, injury, disability or loss of life	4	5	20	• Specific testers to be used for specific toxic gases, e.g. Hydrogen Sulphide, Carbon Dioxide etc. monitoring. • Where necessary, sludge or residue deposits to be disturbed during monitoring. • When toxic gases are discovered, then evacuation to take place and the area purged and retested before re-entry.	3	3	9
As above	As above	Failure to observe the build up of fumes and dusts etc. may cause explosion, disability, injury, burns, irritation, death etc.	4	5	20	• Staff to be trained to recognise the visual conditions and to evacuate if such conditions arise. • Monitoring equipment, specific for each fume, dust, mist, fog to be used to monitor the workspace.	3	3	9

LIKELIHOOD (L) = Frequent (5) - Probable (4) - Occasional (3) - Improbable (2) - Remote (1)
SEVERITY (S) = Catastrophic (5) - Major (4) - Reportable (3) - Serious (2) - Minor (1)
Degree of Risk (DR) = LIKELIHOOD x SEVERITY
* Numbers used are for illustrative purposes only.
** Residual risk is the level of risk that remains after suitable and sufficient control measures are introduced.

Signed originator.. Job title..

Date completed... Date for revision...

Working in domestic premises

Working in domestic premises may be more hazardous than you think. Use our risk assessment document to help ensure you've got everything covered.

Managing the risks

To help you identify the hazards associated with this type of activity and the appropriate ways of controlling them, use our example **Risk Assessment - Working in Domestic Premises**. It covers the generic hazards associated with this type of activity and suggests control measures to reduce risks to an acceptable level.

Make your instructions clear

Don't include activities in your document that simply don't need to be there. Work to the principle that if there is any chance of your staff being unaware of the safe way of doing something, then you will need to make it clear in your document. Finally, always ensure that any control measures you identify and follow only go so far "as is reasonably practicable".

Note. The list of potential hazards is not exhaustive. However, for your risk assessment to be considered suitable and sufficient in the eyes of the law it must accurately reflect the "significant" hazards found with the activities your staff undertake in domestic premises. You may also wish to refer to our other risk assessments, **Violence to Staff** and **Lone Working**.

RISK ASSESSMENT - WORKING IN DOMESTIC PREMISES

ACTIVITY	PERSON AT RISK	SIGNIFICANT HAZARDS	RISK*			RISK CONTROL MEASURES	RESIDUAL RISK**		
			L	S	DR		L	S	DR
Working at height in domestic premises	Staff	Staff may use client's stepladders etc. that are in a poor condition leading to falls and physical injuries	4	3	12	• Staff to be instructed not to use client's access equipment. • Staff to be provided with suitable access equipment for working at height.	3	1	3
Using electrical tools and equipment in domestic premises	As above	Staff using electrical power tools may be subject to electric shock causing burns or death if the client's electrical installation is in a poor condition	3	5	15	• All electrical power tools to either be battery operated or double insulated. • Staff not to use the client's electrical power tools. • Staff to use a residual current circuit breaker (RCCB) plugged into the client's electrical socket before plugging in power tools.	3	2	6
Visiting domestic premises	As above	Staff may encounter a violent client leading to personal attack and physical injuries	3	4	12	• Staff to check the client's history where doubts exist for personal safety. • Where clients have a history of violent behaviour, staff to visit in pairs. • All cases of personal attack to be reported to the police. • All staff to be issued with a personal attack alarm. • Staff to be trained to recognise, avoid or defuse potentially dangerous situations.	3	2	6

RISK ASSESSMENT - WORKING IN DOMESTIC PREMISES

ACTIVITY	PERSON AT RISK	SIGNIFICANT HAZARDS	RISK*			RISK CONTROL MEASURES	RESIDUAL RISK**		
			L	S	DR		L	S	DR
Visiting domestic premises	Staff	Staff visiting domestic premises where the client has an infectious disease may lead to ill-health	3	3	9	• Staff to only visit domestic premises by appointment. • A checklist to be used to identify any risks to staff from illness or infectious diseases. • Where there is a risk of ill-health to staff then visits should not take place.	3	1	3
Carrying out hot work in domestic premises	As above	Failure to consider the risks from hot works, such as soldering etc., may lead to fires	3	4	12	• Only trained staff to carry out hot work. • All necessary fire precautions to be observed. • Staff to inspect the workplace on completion of work to ensure that no signs of ignition are present.	3	1	3
Carrying out electrical work in domestic premises	Staff and client	Failure to carry out electrical work safely may lead to electric shock	3	3	9	• Only trained staff to carry out electrical work. • All electrical work to be tested on completion. • All work to be carried out to the latest edition of the IEE wiring regulations.	3	1	3

LIKELIHOOD (L) = Frequent (5) - Probable (4) - Occasional (3) - Improbable (2) - Remote (1)
SEVERITY (S) = Catastrophic (5) - Major (4) - Reportable (3) - Serious (2) - Minor (1)
Degree of Risk (DR) = LIKELIHOOD x SEVERITY
* Numbers used are for illustrative purposes only. ** Residual risk is the level of risk that remains after suitable and sufficient control measures are introduced.

Signed originator... Job title..

Date completed.. Date for revision..

Working in garages and workshops

Work undertaken in garages and workshops often involves working in a restricted area around inspection pits and on floor surfaces with the potential for oil and grease spillages.

Oils and greases

These and other risks to staff and others, left unmanaged, could cause accidents and potentially put you on the wrong side of the law. To ensure that this doesn't happen, you should complete a risk assessment for such work which, identifies all "significant" hazards and appropriate "reasonable" ways of reducing risks to an acceptable level.

You should ensure that your document only addresses "significant" hazards, i.e. any that could, and more importantly are likely to, cause an accident or injury.

Managing the risks

To help you identify the hazards associated with garage and workshop activities and the appropriate ways of controlling them, use our example **Risk Assessment - Working in Garages and Workshops**. It covers the generic hazards associated with this type of activity and suggests control measures to reduce risks to an acceptable level.

Make your instructions clear

Don't include activities in your document that simply don't need to be there. Work to the principle that if there is any chance of your staff being unaware of the safe way of doing something, then you will need to make it clear in your document. Finally, always ensure that any control measures you identify and follow are decided upon the principle of "so far as is reasonably practicable".

Note. The list of potential hazards is not exhaustive. However, not all garages and workshops are the same as all will have different equipment and work activities. For your risk assessment to be considered suitable and sufficient in the eyes of the law it must accurately reflect the "significant" hazards found in your garage/workshop environment.

Note. You should also refer to our other risk assessments such as our **Risk Assessment - Use of Hand Tools** for additional information on risks that may occur when working in this environment.

RISK ASSESSMENT - WORKING IN GARAGES AND WORKSHOPS

ACTIVITY	PERSON AT RISK	SIGNIFICANT HAZARDS	RISK*			RISK CONTROL MEASURES	RESIDUAL RISK**		
			L	S	DR		L	S	DR
Manual handling of heavy or bulky items such as vehicle parts, welding kits and oil drums etc.	Staff	Manually handling and lifting heavy or bulky items may lead to back injuries	4	4	16	• Engine hoists to be provided and used when removing or replacing engines in vehicles. • A scissor table to be provided and used when lowering or replacing gearboxes in vehicles. • A tyre/wheel trolley to be used when removing or fitting large commercial vehicle wheels. • Transportation of gas cylinders to be carried out using a purposely-designed trolley. • Transportation of oil drums to be carried out using a drum trolley.	3	2	6
Moving around in garages and workshops	As above	Moving around in garages and workshops if the floor surface is contaminated with oils or greases may lead to physical injuries from slips and falls	4	4	16	• Floors to have a non-slip finish and be kept free from damage. • Oil and grease containers to be kept on drip trays to prevent spillage. • Facilities to exist to clean up spillages. • Staff to wear suitable footwear to prevent slipping on floor surfaces.	3	2	6
Working on or near vehicle inspection pits	As above	Failure to ensure inspection pits are covered when not in use may lead to staff falling into them causing physical injuries	3	4	12	• All inspection pits to have covers fitted when not in use. • Inspection pits in use to be fitted with guards to prevent others from falling into them. • Only garage/workshop staff to be allowed into the area where an inspection pit is in use.	3	2	6

RISK ASSESSMENT - WORKING IN GARAGES AND WORKSHOPS

ACTIVITY	PERSON AT RISK	SIGNIFICANT HAZARDS	RISK*			RISK CONTROL MEASURES	RESIDUAL RISK**		
			L	S	DR		L	S	DR
Raising of vehicles from the floor	Staff	Poorly maintained lifting equipment may fail causing physical injuries to staff	4	4	16	• All lifting equipment such as vehicle hoists, jacks and axle stands etc. to be maintained in good condition. • All staff to be instructed to place faulty items out of use and to mark them accordingly. • All vehicles being lifted using jacks to be suitably chocked and axle stands to be used to support the vehicle weight.	3	2	6
Working on vehicle fuel tanks	As above	Failure to remove fuel from a tank before hot work such as welding and brazing may lead to fires and explosion causing severe burns and loss of life	4	5	20	• A proprietary fuel retriever/adaptor to be used when draining petrol from tanks and lines. • Where possible, hot work on fuel tanks to be avoided and cold cutting/repair techniques or tank replacement to be considered. • If hot work is to be carried out on fuel tank, then the tanks are to be emptied, cleaned and made inert.	3	3	9
Spraying using Isocyanate (2 pack) paints	As above	Exposure to Isocyanate paints may cause asthma or worsen existing conditions	4	3	12	• Staff to wear air-fed breathing apparatus when spraying Isocyanate paints. • All painting to take place in a ventilated spraying booth. • Mist clearance times for spray booths to be marked on the entrance doors. • Spray booths to be kept at a slightly negative pressure to prevent mist leakage. • Staff who spray with Isocyanates to receive regular health surveillance and urine checks.	3	2	6

RISK ASSESSMENT - WORKING IN GARAGES AND WORKSHOPS

ACTIVITY	PERSON AT RISK	SIGNIFICANT HAZARDS	RISK*			RISK CONTROL MEASURES	RESIDUAL RISK**		
			L	S	DR		L	S	DR
Working where vehicle engines are running	Staff	Staff working where vehicle engines are running may suffer from the effects of noxious exhaust fumes causing ill-health	4	4	16	• Before vehicle engines are run in the garage/workshop an exhaust scavenger system to be fitted to the vehicle exhaust pipe. • All garage/workshop areas to be kept well ventilated. • Vehicle engines to be run for no longer than is necessary.	3	2	6
Welding	As above	Failure to remove welding fumes may lead to chest irritation, breathing difficulties and ill-health	3	3	9	• All welding work to be carried out using local ventilation. • Only trained staff to carry out welding operations.	3	1	3
Vehicle body repair	As above	The use of body repair filler may lead to inhalation of harmful fumes	4	3	12	• Less hazardous filler to be used where possible. • Bodywork repair to be carried out in a well-ventilated area. • Staff to wear respiratory protection during the work.	3	1	3

LIKELIHOOD (L) = Frequent (5) - Probable (4) - Occasional (3) - Improbable (2) - Remote (1)
SEVERITY (S) = Catastrophic (5) - Major (4) - Reportable (3) - Serious (2) - Minor (1)
Degree of Risk (DR) = LIKELIHOOD x SEVERITY
* Numbers used are for illustrative purposes only. ** Residual risk is the level of risk that remains after suitable and sufficient control measures are introduced.

Signed originator.. Job title..

Date completed.. Date for revision..

Working in laboratories

Working in laboratories carries specific risks, usually involving hazardous chemicals. Make use of our risk assessment document to help keep you on the straight and narrow.

Managing the risks

To help you identify the hazards associated with such work and the appropriate ways of controlling them, use our example **Risk Assessment - Working in Laboratories**. It covers the generic hazards associated with activities in this type of environment and suggests control measures to reduce risks to an acceptable level.

Make your instructions clear

Don't include activities in your document that simply don't need to be there. Work to the principle that if there is any chance of your staff being unaware of the safe way of doing something, then you will need to make it clear in your document. Finally, always ensure that any control measures you identify and follow only go so far "as is reasonably practicable".

Note 1. The list of potential hazards we have included is not exhaustive. However, for your risk assessment to be considered suitable and sufficient in the eyes of the law it must accurately reflect the "significant" hazards found with the activities that take place in your laboratory environment.

Note 2. Where chemical substances are used you may need to carry out additional risk assessments as defined by the **Control of Substances Hazardous to Health Regulations 2002 (as amended)**.

RISK ASSESSMENT - WORKING IN LABORATORIES

ACTIVITY	PERSON AT RISK	SIGNIFICANT HAZARDS	RISK*			RISK CONTROL MEASURES	RESIDUAL RISK**		
			L	S	DR		L	S	DR
Carrying out laboratory work (general)	Staff	Untrained staff may place themselves (and others) at risk of injury or ill-health through exposure to hazardous substances etc.	4	4	16	• Only fully trained (or staff undertaking training whilst under supervision) to carry out work in the laboratory. • All staff to undertake induction training before commencing work in the laboratory.	3	2	6
Use of chemical substances	Staff and others	The incorrect use, storage or disposal of chemical substances may lead to ill-health	4	5	20	• All hazardous chemical substances to have a separate risk assessment as stated under the **Control of Substances Hazardous to Health Regulations 2002** (as amended). • Material Hazard Data Sheets to be obtained from manufacturers/suppliers of all hazardous chemical substances. • All chemical substances to be stored in accordance with the manufacturer's instructions. • All chemical substances and containers to be disposed of in accordance with the manufacturer's/supplier's instructions.	3	3	9
Housekeeping in laboratories	Staff	Failure to keep floors etc. clean may lead to slips and trips causing physical injuries	3	3	9	• All laboratory floors to be kept clean. • Spill kits to be provided and all spillages to be dealt with immediately. • All work surfaces to be cleaned at the end of the working shift.	2	2	4

RISK ASSESSMENT - WORKING IN LABORATORIES

ACTIVITY	PERSON AT RISK	SIGNIFICANT HAZARDS	RISK*			RISK CONTROL MEASURES	RESIDUAL RISK**		
			L	S	DR		L	S	DR
Carrying out laboratory work (general)	Staff	Failure to wear the correct personal protective equipment (PPE) may lead to physical injuries and ill-health	4	4	16	• All staff to wear eye protection when there is a risk of eye injuries. • All staff to wear hand protection where there is a risk of hand injuries. • All staff to wear respiratory protection where there is a risk of inhaling hazardous fumes etc. • All staff to wear laboratory coats at all times. • All staff to wear any other protective items provided to prevent bodily contact with hazardous substances.	3	2	6
Eating and drinking	As above	Eating and drinking in the laboratory environment may lead to ill-health or poisoning	3	5	15	• Food and drink to be prohibited in all laboratory areas. • Staff to be instructed to undertake good hygiene practices i.e. washing etc. before eating and drinking.	2	2	4
Using flammable liquids	As above	Failure to observe safe working practices with flammable liquids may lead to fires causing burns or loss of life	3	5	15	• Flammable liquids to be stored in a fire resistant spark proof enclosure with spillage containment. • The total volume of flammable liquids to be kept below 50 litres. • All staff to be trained in the appropriate action to take in the event of a fire.	2	3	6
Build up of waste materials	As above	Failure to remove waste may lead to a hazardous environment with the increased likelihood of fires	3	4	12	• All waste materials to be stored in the appropriate containers. • All waste to be removed at the end of each working day/shift. • Flammable waste to be stored in a flameproof container.	2	2	4

RISK ASSESSMENT - WORKING IN LABORATORIES

ACTIVITY	PERSON AT RISK	SIGNIFICANT HAZARDS	RISK*			RISK CONTROL MEASURES	RESIDUAL RISK**		
			L	S	DR		L	S	DR
Carrying out laboratory work (general)	Staff	Failure to maintain fume cupboards and exhaust ventilation may lead to staff being overcome by hazardous fumes etc.	4	4	16	• All staff to be instructed on the proper use of fume cupboards and exhaust ventilation systems. • All fume cupboards to be subject to a six-monthly and annual inspection and records to be kept. • All ventilation systems to be subject to an annual inspection and records kept. • Only trained staff to carry out activities where the use of a fume cupboard or exhaust ventilation is required.	2	2	4

LIKELIHOOD (L) = Frequent (5) - Probable (4) - Occasional (3) - Improbable (2) - Remote (1)
SEVERITY (S) = Catastrophic (5) - Major (4) - Reportable (3) - Serious (2) - Minor (1)
Degree of Risk (DR) = LIKELIHOOD x SEVERITY
* Numbers used are for illustrative purposes only.
** Residual risk is the level of risk that remains after suitable and sufficient control measures are introduced.

Signed originator.. Job title..

Date completed... Date for revision...

Working in LPG storage areas

Anyone working in LPG storage areas must be extremely careful in how canisters are handled and ensure that they are kept away from naked flames.

Managing the risks

To help you identify the hazards associated with working in this environment and the appropriate ways of controlling them, use our example **Risk Assessment - Working in LPG Storage Areas**. It covers the generic hazards associated with this type of activity and suggests control measures to reduce risks to an acceptable level.

Make your instructions clear

Don't include activities in your document that simply don't need to be there. Work to the principle that if there is any chance of your staff being unaware of the safe way of doing something, then you will need to make it clear in your document. Finally, always ensure that any control measures you identify and follow only go so far "as is reasonably practicable".

Note. The list of potential hazards is not exhaustive. However, for your risk assessment to be considered suitable and sufficient in the eyes of the law it must accurately reflect the "significant" hazards found in the LPG storage areas on your premises.

RISK ASSESSMENT - WORKING IN LPG STORAGE AREAS

ACTIVITY	PERSON AT RISK	SIGNIFICANT HAZARDS	RISK*			RISK CONTROL MEASURES	RESIDUAL RISK**		
			L	S	DR		L	S	DR
Working on LPG storage installations	Staff	Failure to observe safety procedures may lead to gas leaks causing fires or an explosion	3	5	15	• Only trained and competent staff to work on LPG installations. • All staff to be trained on the action to take in an emergency. • No modifications to the installation to be undertaken that will affect its integrity.	2	3	6
As above	As above	Smoking or the presence of naked flames in LPG storage areas may lead to fires or explosion if there is a gas leak	3	5	15	• All LPG storage areas to be designated and signed as "No Smoking". • All LPG storage areas to be designated and signed "No Naked Flames". • Supervisors to monitor LPG areas to ensure all rules are being observed.	2	3	6
As above	As above	Failure to secure LPG cylinders in storage areas may lead to them falling and causing a gas leak and an explosive atmosphere	3	5	15	• All LPG cylinders in storage areas to be secured to prevent falling. • All LPG cylinders to be stored upright with their valves uppermost.	2	3	6
As above	As above	Failure to take the necessary action in the event of an emergency may lead to injury etc.	4	4	16	• An emergency plan to be prepared for LPG storage areas. • All staff to be trained in emergency procedures.	2	2	4

RISK ASSESSMENT - WORKING IN LPG STORAGE AREAS

ACTIVITY	PERSON AT RISK	SIGNIFICANT HAZARDS	RISK*			RISK CONTROL MEASURES	RESIDUAL RISK**		
			L	S	DR		L	S	DR
Use of LPG cylinders	Staff	The use of cylinders with damaged regulators or hoses may lead to gas leaks resulting in an explosive atmosphere	4	4	16	• All regulators and hoses to be inspected for damage before use. • Regulators not to be used for any other gas than that for which it is labelled. • Regulators to be tightened by hand only using the correct size spanner. • Hoses to be suitable for the working pressure required.	2	2	4
Moving LPG cylinders	As above	Failure to handle cylinders properly may lead to strains, sprains and foot injuries	3	3	9	• All staff to be trained in manual handling techniques. • LPG cylinders to be moved using a purposely-designed trolley. • Staff to wear PPE when handling cylinders.	2	2	4

LIKELIHOOD (L) = Frequent (5) - Probable (4) - Occasional (3) - Improbable (2) - Remote (1)
SEVERITY (S) = Catastrophic (5) - Major (4) - Reportable (3) - Serious (2) - Minor (1)
Degree of Risk (DR) = LIKELIHOOD x SEVERITY
* Numbers used are for illustrative purposes only.
** Residual risk is the level of risk that remains after suitable and sufficient control measures are introduced.

Signed originator.. Job title..

Date completed.. Date for revision..

Working in manholes

Manholes may contain anything from asphyxiating gases to contaminated water. Use our risk assessment document to help avoid accidents, injuries and ill-health.

Managing the risks

To help you identify the hazards associated with work in manholes and the appropriate ways of controlling them, use our example **Risk Assessment - Working in Manholes**. It covers the generic hazards associated with this type of activity and suggests control measures to reduce risks to an acceptable level.

Make your instructions clear

Don't include activities in your document that simply don't need to be there. Work to the principle that if there is any chance of your staff being unaware of the safe way of doing something, then you will need to make it clear in your document. Finally, always ensure that any control measures you identify and follow only go so far "as is reasonably practicable".

Note. The list of potential hazards is not exhaustive. However, for your risk assessment to be considered suitable and sufficient in the eyes of the law it must accurately reflect the "significant" hazards found while working in manholes. You may also wish to refer to our **Risk Assessment - Working in Confined Spaces**.

RISK ASSESSMENT - WORKING IN MANHOLES

ACTIVITY	PERSON AT RISK	SIGNIFICANT HAZARDS	RISK*			RISK CONTROL MEASURES	RESIDUAL RISK**		
			L	S	DR		L	S	DR
Lifting manhole covers	Staff	Failure to lift manhole covers correctly may lead to back injuries	4	3	12	• All manhole covers to be lifted with the correct type and size lifting equipment. • All staff who lift manhole covers to be trained in the manual handling and lifting technique. • Heavy cast steel covers etc. to be lifted with a hydraulic lifting device.	3	2	6
Access into manholes	As above	Manholes may contain flammable or asphyxiating gases which could give rise to explosion or staff having breathing difficulties	3	4	12	• All staff to be trained in manhole access methods. • All staff to carry out testing for flammable gases before the complete removal of the manhole cover. • On removal of the manhole, cover tests to be carried out at low level for asphyxiating gases. • A permit-to-work system to be in place for manhole work.	3	2	6
As above	As above	Slips and falls causing physical injuries may occur when climbing into or out of manholes	3	3	9	• All staff to inspect manhole steps before they are used. • All staff to wear appropriate protective footwear. • In deep manholes staff to wear a secured harness and be attached to a winch line.	2	1	2
Working in manholes	As above	Manholes may contain contaminated water which could result in Weil's disease	4	3	12	• All residual water to be pumped out of manholes prior to work starting. • All staff to maintain good hygiene practices before consuming food or drink. • All cuts and grazes to be covered with waterproof dressings.	2	2	4

RISK ASSESSMENT - WORKING IN MANHOLES

ACTIVITY	PERSON AT RISK	SIGNIFICANT HAZARDS	RISK*			RISK CONTROL MEASURES	RESIDUAL RISK**		
			L	S	DR		L	S	DR
Working in manholes	Staff	Staff may be overcome by asphyxiating gases during work in manholes	3	4	12	• All staff to be trained to take action if a staff member is overcome by asphyxiating gases. • Staff working in manholes which have a history of gas to use gas monitors fitted with alarms during the working period. • Where necessary, staff to be fitted with breathing apparatus.	3	2	6
As above	As above	Working in manholes adjacent to roadways may lead to a build up of vehicle exhaust fumes causing ill-health	4	3	12	• All roadside manholes to be suitably ventilated before and during work. • Mechanical ventilation to be provided where a build up of exhaust fumes is likely. • Petrol or diesel engine-driven equipment to not be used in manholes.	3	2	6

LIKELIHOOD (L) = Frequent (5) - Probable (4) - Occasional (3) - Improbable (2) - Remote (1)
SEVERITY (S) = Catastrophic (5) - Major (4) - Reportable (3) - Serious (2) - Minor (1)
Degree of Risk (DR) = LIKELIHOOD x SEVERITY
* Numbers used are for illustrative purposes only.
** Residual risk is the level of risk that remains after suitable and sufficient control measures are introduced.

Signed originator.. Job title..

Date completed... Date for revision...

Working in plant and equipment rooms

Working in plant and equipment rooms presents risks to staff as they may contain heavy, noisy and dangerous machinery. So use our document to highlight the risks and some options to manage them.

Managing the risks

To help you identify the hazards associated with work in these areas and the appropriate ways of controlling them, use our example **Risk Assessment - Working in Plant and Equipment Rooms**. It covers the generic risks associated with work in this type of location and suggests control measures to reduce such risks to an acceptable level.

You should ensure that your document only addresses "significant" hazards, i.e. any that could, and more importantly are likely to, cause an accident or injury.

Note. This risk assessment only deals with the generic risks associated with some of the more common locations of plant and equipment. You will need to prepare an assessment that deals with the particular type of plant or equipment room your staff will be working in.

Make your instructions clear

Don't include activities in your document that simply don't need to be there. Work to the principle that if there is any chance of your staff being unaware of the safe way of doing something, then you will need to make it clear in your document. Finally, always ensure that any control measures you identify and follow only go so far "as is reasonably practicable".

Note. The list of potential hazards is not exhaustive. However, for your risk assessment to be considered suitable and sufficient in the eyes of the law it must accurately reflect the "significant" hazards found in the individual plant or equipment location.

RISK ASSESSMENT - WORKING IN PLANT AND EQUIPMENT ROOMS

ACTIVITY	PERSON AT RISK	SIGNIFICANT HAZARDS	RISK*			RISK CONTROL MEASURES	RESIDUAL RISK**		
			L	S	DR		L	S	DR
Working in lift motor rooms at high level	Staff	Access to lift motor rooms may involve work at height where falls may lead to serious injuries	3	4	12	• Access to lift motor rooms to be assessed before attempts are made to enter. • Where access is via a fixed ladder its condition to be assessed before use. • Staff to wear suitable footwear when climbing.	3	2	6
Movement of tools and equipment into high-level equipment rooms	As above	Lifting of tools and equipment whilst climbing fixed or ordinary ladders may lead to staff or objects causing physical injuries	4	3	12	• No tools or equipment to be carried by staff when climbing ladders to gain access to high-level equipment rooms. • All tools and equipment to be taken up using ropes/lines etc.	3	1	3
Working in noisy equipment rooms	As above	Where plant or equipment is in operation noise levels may be excessive and cause hearing damage	3	3	9	• All plant and equipment to be isolated before work is undertaken in these areas. • For short-term work staff to wear ear protection at all times.	3	1	3
Working in plant or equipment rooms (general)	As above	Work near revolving machinery may lead to entanglement and personal injuries	4	3	12	• Staff to ensure that all machinery guards are in place. • Staff to not work on machinery whilst it is in motion. • Staff to follow the designated permit-to-work and safe system of work at all times.	2	2	4

RISK ASSESSMENT - WORKING IN PLANT AND EQUIPMENT ROOMS

ACTIVITY	PERSON AT RISK	SIGNIFICANT HAZARDS	RISK*			RISK CONTROL MEASURES	RESIDUAL RISK**		
			L	S	DR		L	S	DR
Working in cold rooms	Staff	Staff working in refrigeration (cold) rooms may be susceptible to physical risk if they become trapped	3	4	12	• All work in cold rooms to be carried out under a permit-to-work system. • All cold rooms to have their alarm systems and emergency exits checked before work commences. • All staff to wear the appropriate personal protective equipment (PPE).	2	3	6
Entry into electric sub-stations etc.	As above	Failure to observe safety precautions may lead to electric shock causing burns or loss of life	3	5	15	• A permit-to-work system to be in place for all sub-station work. • Where possible all power supplies to be isolated. • Only trained competent staff, adequately supervised, to work in electric substations.	3	3	9

LIKELIHOOD (L) = Frequent (5) - Probable (4) - Occasional (3) - Improbable (2) - Remote (1)
SEVERITY (S) = Catastrophic (5) - Major (4) - Reportable (3) - Serious (2) - Minor (1)
Degree of Risk (DR) = LIKELIHOOD x SEVERITY
* Numbers used are for illustrative purposes only.
** Residual risk is the level of risk that remains after suitable and sufficient control measures are introduced.

Signed originator.. Job title..

Date completed... Date for revision...

Working in roof spaces

Working in roof spaces presents particular risks to staff as it combines working at height with the restrictions of a confined area. Particular care should be taken when carrying out hot work in these spaces.

Risk of fall

If these risks are left unmanaged it may cause an accident and potentially put you on the wrong side of the law.

To ensure that this doesn't happen, you should complete a risk assessment for all such work, which identifies all "significant" hazards and appropriate "reasonable" ways of reducing risks to an acceptable level.

Managing the risks

To help you identify the hazards associated with roof space work and the appropriate ways of controlling them, use our example **Risk Assessment - Working in Roof Spaces**. It covers the generic hazards associated with this type of activity and suggests control measures to reduce risks to an acceptable level.

You should ensure that your document only addresses "significant" hazards, i.e. any that could and, more importantly, are likely to cause an accident or injury.

Note. You should also refer to our **Risk Assessment - Working at height** that detail the risks and control measures that may affect the access to and egress from a roof space.

Make your instructions clear

Don't include activities in your document that simply don't need to be there. Work to the principle that if there is any chance of your staff being unaware of the safe way of doing something, then you will need to make it clear in your document. Finally, always ensure that any control measures you identify and follow only go so far "as is reasonably practicable".

Note. The list of potential hazards is not exhaustive. However, for your risk assessment to be considered suitable and sufficient in the eyes of the law it must accurately reflect the "significant" hazards found with your particular activity.

RISK ASSESSMENT - WORKING IN ROOF SPACES

ACTIVITY	PERSON AT RISK	SIGNIFICANT HAZARDS	RISK*			RISK CONTROL MEASURES	RESIDUAL RISK**		
			L	S	DR		L	S	DR
Gaining access to roof spaces	Staff	Risk of falls leading to broken limbs etc. if the correct method of access is not used	4	4	16	• All roof spaces to be assessed as to the most suitable method of access. • Fixed ladders to be examined before use. • All other forms of access equipment, e.g. ladders or stepladders, to be fit for purpose and staff to be trained in their use.	3	2	6
Working in roof spaces	As above	Risks of falls through the roof leading to physical injuries if support methods across roof joists are not used	4	3	12	• If roof spaces are not "boarded out" then crawling boards, planks etc. to be used to support the weight of staff. • Staff to not walk across roof spaces by standing on roof joists. • Staff to be trained in the methods of moving about in roof spaces.	3	2	6
As above	As above	Lack of adequate lighting may lead to slips or falls leading to physical injuries	4	3	12	• Temporary lighting to be provided before work commences if no permanent lighting exists. • All light bulbs to be encased to prevent injuries from broken glass. • All trailing cables to be kept clear of work area.	3	1	3
Carrying out hot work in roof spaces	As above	Failure to observe fire precautions may lead to a building fire and injuries from smoke inhalation, burns or loss of life	4	4	16	• Staff to ensure that flammable material is kept away from sources of heat such as blowtorches etc. • Staff to ensure that they inspect the work area for signs of combustion before leaving the roof space.	3	2	6

RISK ASSESSMENT - WORKING IN ROOF SPACES

ACTIVITY	PERSON AT RISK	SIGNIFICANT HAZARDS	RISK*			RISK CONTROL MEASURES	RESIDUAL RISK**		
			L	S	DR		L	S	DR
Work in areas with fibreglass insulation	Staff	Failure to wear personal protective equipment (PPE) may lead to skin or eye irritation etc.	4	2	8	• All staff working where fibreglass insulation exists to wear disposable coveralls, eye protection and a dust mask. • Staff to wash hands, forearms and face on completion of work.	2	1	2
Using power tools on roof spaces	As above	Use of trailing power cables may lead to trips resulting in physical injuries or electric shocks	3	3	9	• Trailing cables, e.g. extension leads, to be kept clear of walkways. • Electrical supply for all extension leas to be obtained via a RCCB (residual current circuit breaker) in order to prevent electric shocks.	2	1	2
Handling equipment into and out of roof spaces	Other people	Failure to keep other people clear of the work area may lead to accidents from falling equipment	3	3	9	• Entrance to work area to be fitted with guards to prevent access by others. • Work area to be adequately signed indicating no access for other people.	2	1	2

LIKELIHOOD (L) = Frequent (5) - Probable (4) - Occasional (3) - Improbable (2) - Remote (1)
SEVERITY (S) = Catastrophic (5) - Major (4) - Reportable (3) - Serious (2) - Minor (1)
Degree of Risk (DR) = LIKELIHOOD x SEVERITY
* Numbers used are for illustrative purposes only. ** Residual risk is the level of risk that remains after suitable and sufficient control measures are introduced.

Signed originator... Job title...

Date completed... Date for revision...

Notes

NOTES

Notes

Notes